EFFECTIVE ADULT LITERACY PROGRAMS:

A Practitioner's Guide

Renee S. Lerche

for

THE NETWORK, INC.

CAMBRIDGE
THE ADULT EDUCATION COMPANY
New York • Toronto

ISBN 0-8428-2219-4
9 8 7 6 5 4 3 2 1

ACKNOWLEDGEMENTS

This guide incorporates the work, values, and thoughts of many people who have committed themselves to addressing the literacy problems of many Americans. I am deeply indebted to the people who helped bring it to fruition. Barbara A. Marchilonis, National Adult Literacy Project Manager at the NETWORK, Inc., was instrumental in conceptualizing and carrying out the Promising Practices Search which forms the basis of our practice recommendations. I am grateful for the long hours she committed to sorting out the logistical details of this complex endeavor that was the field study and for her work in preparing the government documents that described our findings. David P. Crandall, Executive Director of The NETWORK, Inc. who also served as National Director of NALP, offered us his abilities as negotiator, evaluator, and creative thinker. I thank him for his good counsel and insightfulness which were supplied liberally throughout the Project. Julianne C. Turner and Jurg Jenzer, Research Associates of The NETWORK, spent many hours and miles of travel to bring home the rich and useful data that permitted the writing of this book. Their analysis of what they saw in the field was critical to understanding what contributes to effective literacy practice. Finally, but certainly not least, Janice S. Johnson, NALP Administrative Assistant, provided consistent and caring support to all of us at the NETWORK involved with this project. I deeply appreciate her commitment to the educationally disadvantaged adults who are and should be the recipients of effective literacy services.

I would also like to thank our collaborators at Far West Laboratory for Educational Development, William G. Spady, Margaret Robinson, Donna Bellarado, Janet McGrail, and John Thomas. And, our Senior Policy Advisors and Experts who offered sound advice and review of our study plans: Judith Alamprese, Gordon Berlin, Jeanne S. Chall, S. Alan Cohen, Marva Nettles Collins, Helen B. Crouch, Priscilla Douglas, Thomas M. Duffy, David Harman, Carmen St. John Hunter, Donald McCune, Ruth Nickse, Herman Niebuhr, Jr., Patricia Rickard, Richard L. Stiles, Thomas G. Sticht, Rosalyn E. Stoker, Antonia Stone, Robert Taggart, Peter Waite, Nina Wallerstein, and Jane Zinner. Of course, our Washington based Project Team led by our National Institute of Education (NIE) Project Officer Michael Brunner, and Diane Welch Vines, Director of the National Adult Literacy Initiative, and Paul Delker, Director, Division of Adult Education Services; all were extremely helpful in framing our work and keeping us on target.

This work, however, could not have been undertaken or completed without the assistance of my Senior Editor, Brian Schenk and the support of my friend and publisher, Benita Somerfield. To Brian, I would like to extend my deepest appreciation for his patience, his commitment to the field, and for ensuring that this book represents a comprehensive and useful guide to effective literacy practice. He was much more than an editor; he was a colleague whose ideas were influential in determining our recommendations for program design, implementation, and operations. Similarly, Benita Somerfield was more than publisher, she was an advocate for quality literacy practice, a colleague, supportive friend, and counselor. I thank her for her gentle nudging when the work became frustrating.

I want to also thank Dr. Jeanne Chall who taught me that one has to have the courage to speak the truth as one sees it, no matter how controversial that may be. I was honored to have her support on this project.

Finally, I owe my greatest debt of gratitude to the many literacy programs that allowed us to include them in our study. I thank them for allowing me the opportunity to report on their success.

CONTENTS

LIST OF EXHIBITS

SECTION I
General Introduction

Chapter 1
Author's Introduction

Although there is much controversy over the statistics, it is estimated that twenty-three million Americans are illiterate—they may lack even basic reading skills and therefore cannot understand job advertisements, labels on consumer products, or voter information. Another twenty-three million are functionally illiterate—they have reading problems serious enough to interfere with their ability to handle the minimal demands of daily living competently. Minorities particularly suffer from the problems engendered by functional illiteracy. Forty-four percent of Black teenagers are considered functionally illiterate, and fifty-six percent of Hispanic teenagers are functionally illiterate in English.

Yet only two to four percent of the population in need is currently served by literacy programs. And many of those enrolled in programs "stop out" of them, never persisting long enough to gain the skills necessary to compete in an increasingly complex and technologically oriented society. Now, more than ever before, successful competition depends upon certain minimal proficiencies in reading, writing, computation, and problem solving, and this fact holds implications for how we define the mission of adult literacy initiatives.

Illiteracy is typically defined as the inability to read, write, and comprehend short, simple sentences. However, the possession of such basic literacy skills is no longer an adequate measure of an individual's ability to function competently as an informed citizen, worker, and community and family member. We think that a more acceptable definition of literacy/functional competence also focuses on the applications of skills in an adult's daily life on the job, in the home, and in the community. Functional illiteracy, then, is perhaps best defined as the inability to read, write, or compute well enough to accomplish the kinds of basic and pervasive tasks necessary for everyday adult living.

To the individual involved, the social and psychological costs of functional illiteracy can be debilitating. One former adult illiterate captured her experience in the following words: "I always felt bad. . . . I felt so ashamed . . . less of a person. It's a scary feeling, really. You just feel so backward, so out of place a lot of times" (Lerche, 1983).

The costs of functional illiteracy to the national economy are enormous. Forty percent of adults with annual incomes under $5,000 are functionally illiterate. Yearly costs in welfare programs and unemployment compensation are estimated at six billion dollars. Further, it is estimated that functional illiterates constitute sixty percent of the prison population and eighty-five percent of the youngsters who appear in juvenile courts.

Calling attention to the "illiteracy problem" in a statement before the U.S. House

1

of Representatives Subcommittee on Postsecondary Education, former Secretary of Education Terrell Bell commented:

> One effect of illiteracy is the disproportionate percentages of functional illiterates on the public welfare rolls and in our criminal institutions. Although people go on welfare for a wide variety of reasons, across the board, for men and women, for Blacks and whites, and for all age groups, a primary common denominator is the level of schooling attained. (quoted in Bush, 1983)

Almost all educators say the number of people who lack basic functional literacy skills continues to increase. Reports from the National Assessment of Educational Progress and the American Library Association suggest that functional illiteracy may be growing among the young. Indeed, many young people fail to acquire the skills necessary for living in an information-saturated technological society while in school—including some who manage to graduate from high school as well as those who drop out—and these young adults fall further and further behind as technology and information increase.

Obviously, there are substantial costs associated with adult illiteracy. Chief among them are costs to our country's economic growth and development, the vitality of our democracy, and the human dignity of all our citizens. When we consider all the data, what becomes absolutely clear is that the cost of doing nothing far outweighs the money and resources currently expended to address the problem.

Functional illiteracy is the problem. However, adult education and literacy programs, as they currently exist, are only part of the solution. Adult basic education and literacy programs generally have not had the resources and organization to meet the needs of the vast numbers of unskilled adults. Despite the publicity that has recently surrounded the issue, few efforts have focused on coordinated, systematic, and programmatic solutions to the literacy problems faced by so many Americans. More importantly, there have been serious constraints on the few attempts to promote a sharing of existing resources and information on effective programmatic or instructional practices or to increase programs' capacities to serve educationally disadvantaged adults. As one Ford Foundation study concluded, adult illiterates are a "vastly underserved" population.

President Reagan's and former Secretary of Education Bell's Initiative on Adult Literacy has brought renewed national attention to the need to expand and revitalize literacy training and development. The National Adult Literacy Project was designed to help meet this call by:

- improving service through the spread of the best information available on literacy practice and instruction
- promoting cooperation and collaboration between public and private sectors to offer literacy instruction to the many adults who need and desire it

To accomplish this mission, one critical task was to conduct a nationwide Promising Practices Search. Although our search was designed to be comprehensive and broad-based, it was not to scientifically prove the effectiveness of existing programs or to yield an exhaustive directory. Rather, our primary concern was to collect and report data in a way that would provide literacy educators with the most current, state-of-the-art information on literacy practice. Moreover, we wanted to offer guidance on how to use this information to initiate, modify, and improve program design and operation.

Reflection on our fieldwork and survey results has provided us with a unique perspective on the state of adult literacy education in the United States. We saw the dedication and commitment of literacy educators, but we also observed the severe obstacles they encounter as they work to make their programs successful.

Chief among those obstacles are the constraints imposed upon programs by limited financial and human resources. Many program directors (particularly those who run community-based programs) reported that much of their time and energy is expended on soliciting funds and resources, and even so, they have barely managed to maintain a minimal level of support for their programs. This "marginality" of literacy programs has serious consequences for program effectiveness. It not only has an impact on the number and kind of staff members the program can employ and train (not to mention the impact on the morale of the staff), but it also severely inhibits the program's ability to design systems and plan for future population needs and services. It also reduces the program's capacity to purchase the technology—computer hardware and software—that could enhance program management and the delivery of instruction.

In addition to financial resource constraints, programs often face problems with "legitimizing" what they are doing and what they need to accomplish their objectives. Especially for programs that employ largely part-time staff (who are usually not certified as adult education teachers), there is the problem of getting these literacy practitioners to see themselves as "legitimate" professional educators whose students do not necessarily benefit from the techniques used in early childhood, secondary, or higher education. Difficulties in securing the support necessary to develop and validate effective *adult* programs and instructional practice has contributed to the need to address this legitimacy issue. More professional development opportunities for staff and volunteers and greater technical assistance to help programs implement innovations and make improvements in practice are often suggested as the means necessary to generate the view of adult literacy practitioners as trained educators in a unique field of specialty.

Although the problems faced by literacy programs and their staffs often seem monumental, our search showed us that much is being done by dedicated professionals, volunteers, and community members. We are encouraged by the many promising practices we have been able to describe. Further, we are encouraged that even the most difficult-to-reach populations are being served by some segment of what seems to have evolved as a natural service delivery system. For example, we observed the following general characteristics of the programs we studied:

- Community-based organizations—a term applied to organizations located in neighborhoods and controlled by neighborhood boards—tend to reach out to those individuals in the community with the lowest levels of skills. These programs serve older students (generally thirty years of age and older) who have been away from any form of schooling for many years. Many of these participants do not read at all or have the most minimal of reading skills.

- Public adult basic education programs—those primarily supported by federal and state monies and generally operated out of local school districts—serve those adults with some minimal skills but who are still in need of adult basic education.
- Public adult basic education programs as well as programs within post-secondary and correctional institutions are those that serve adults who seek secondary adult education, high school equivalency, or alternative diploma programs.
- Military and employment and training programs usually serve those individuals who, although they lack some basic skills, are generally performing at a moderately skilled level.

What all of this implies is that each segment of the current service delivery system plays an essential part in reaching and serving the many constituencies of educationally disadvantaged adults.

In order to strengthen the capacity of providers to reach more people more effectively, it is critical that we identify what practices work, for whom they work, and under what conditions they work. Thus, we began our Promising Practices Search by focusing attention on the parts and components of programs. We did not attempt to locate model programs that we could recommend for wholesale adoption, but we did accept the challenge of uncovering the structures that weave the identified promising practices into a coherent and integrated system of literacy instruction and program management. Indeed, our central finding is that programs with a commitment to systematically planning, implementing, and evaluating the components of their programs as integrated parts of the whole educational enterprise—those that create a coherent system of adult literacy instruction tied to the goals of the agency and its community—appear to be the ones that are the most successful.

The text before you reports and expands upon the findings of the National Adult Literacy Project's Promising Practices Search. It offers not only information on the current practice of literacy training and development but also the guidance to refine that practice.

Because many millions of Americans continue to suffer the consequences and costs of illiteracy, we must continue to call attention to the means of marshaling our resources for the systematic delivery of quality adult education services to those in need of these services. We believe *Effective Adult Literacy Programs: A Practitioner's Guide* reflects that commitment.

References

Bush, B. "Why We Can't Afford Illiteracy and What We Can Do about It." *Foundation News,* Volume 24, Number 1, pages 18–21, 1983.

Lerche, R. S. "Competency Assessment: A Model for Matching Adult Learners to a High School Completion Program." Ed.D. Thesis, Harvard University, School of Education, 1983.

Renee S. Lerche
Andover, MA
August 1985

Chapter 2
Overview of NALP Study

In an original planning document, the National Adult Literacy Project (NALP) set three major tasks for itself:

- provide information on effective instructional techniques and materials to a wide array of public and private adult literacy programs
- conduct short-term research and development projects to identify important knowledge gaps about effective adult literacy instruction that will contribute to the improvement of materials and practices currently in use
- conduct a data-gathering effort to collect the best information on the nature and extent of illiteracy and report that information to practitioners and to the public

The memorandum went on to declare: "All project activities will be aimed at maximizing the practical effectiveness of literacy training efforts and at supporting practitioners' efforts to provide services to educationally disadvantaged adults."

To ensure that any information or technical assistance that NALP staff might provide would be firmly grounded in the reality of actual practice, the researchers chose to use practitioners in the field (rather than university-based theoreticians) as their primary source of information about promising practices. However, recognizing that programs operating out of different institutional bases would face differing design and implementation constraints and opportunities, the NALP study undertook to identify and solicit information from programs in the following six categories: (1) state and local public adult education programs, (2) community-based programs, (3) programs operating within correctional institutions, (4) programs within the military, (5) programs operating within postsecondary education institutions, and (6) employment and training programs.

The NALP staff then went on to identify eight components of program operation about which practitioners would need information: (1) recruitment; (2) orientation; (3) counseling; (4) diagnostic testing; (5) assessment of student skill achievement; (6) instructional methods, materials, and management systems; (7) student follow-up systems; and (8) program evaluation. In addition, NALP staff compiled data on program management, including staff development and evaluation.

To identify programs with exemplary practices in any or all of these eight components that might serve as models and to obtain detailed information from these programs, the NALP study proceeded in three stages:

- *Nomination of programs*—Members of the NALP senior policy group,

7

directors of adult education in state departments of education, experts within the U.S. Department of Education, members of the Coalition for Literacy, and other acknowledged literacy experts were asked to nominate those programs that, in their opinion, exemplified "promising practices" in the field of adult literacy education. By March 1984, a total of 335 programs had been nominated, representing the following sections:

state/local public education programs   130
community-based programs   93
correctional institution programs   15
military programs   15
postsecondary education programs   32
employment and training programs   50

- *Survey of nominated programs through questionnaire*—The questionnaire shown in Exhibit 2.1 was mailed to all 335 nominated programs. Of these, 225 programs completed and returned the questionnaire by the July 1984 cutoff date; these programs are listed in Section IV.

- *Field site visits*—After an analysis of the survey questionnaires, some thirty-eight programs were chosen for site visits, during which data provided on the survey questionnaire would be explored in further detail. Interviews were conducted during the site visits with the program director, teachers, counselors, and students. Interviewers used the guidelines shown in Exhibit 2.2 as the basis for gathering desired information, though interviewees often volunteered information far beyond the scope of the questions shown in the guidelines. A list of the programs that volunteered information during site visits is given at the end of the chapter.

The 225 programs that responded to the national survey were from forty-three states, the District of Columbia, Puerto Rico, and the Virgin Islands, and included one program in Canada. An analysis of the survey questionnaires shows the following data:

- 45% of the surveyed programs are located in the eastern United States.
- 45% of the surveyed programs operate in an urban environment.
- 33% of the surveyed programs are state or local public education programs.
- 29% of the surveyed programs are community-based programs.
- 42% of the surveyed programs reported having students thirty years of age or older. (This is an aggregate figure; in fact, community-based programs in the main reported older average student age, while employment and training programs indicated they served primarily younger adults.)
- 53% of the surveyed programs reported that, on the average, their students read at the fourth to seventh grade level at program entry.
- 23% of the surveyed programs reported that they serve only those students who read below the third grade level.
- 50% of the programs that reported serving only nonreaders are community-based programs.
- 86% of the surveyed programs reported they offer basic skills education.

- 68% of the surveyed programs reported that they offer English as a second language.
- 62% of the surveyed programs reported that they offer adult secondary education or GED preparation.

Although programs were asked to supply demographic data and information on such aspects of program operation as sources of funding, hours of operation, use of credentialed instructors, average cost per learner, and estimated dropout rate, the size of the sample and the wide variations in reported data (and in some cases, the absence of data) make a computation of statistical averages relatively meaningless. For example, given the fact that the programs surveyed reported a range in the number of students served from 9 (for Minnesota Mutual Life Insurance Company's ESL program) to 70,500 (for South Carolina's statewide adult education program), a statistical average would not represent a national average against which programs could measure their relative effectiveness. Such information was useful chiefly in helping the researchers maintain a balanced perspective in making recommendations about practices found in specific programs that might contribute to the improvement of the field in general. It was also useful in selecting programs for site visits that would represent a number of different viewpoints.

Section II of this text represents a synthesis of the information obtained from the survey questionnaires and the site visits that we believe fulfills the goals cited at the opening of this chapter. Although we have made specific recommendations, we have also provided descriptions of the range of practices we found in the field so that individual practitioners can determine for themselves which practices would be effective for them. Section III goes beyond our original goals to describe aspects of program management that practitioners must confront and to suggest what general conclusions can be drawn from the NALP study.

EXHIBIT 2.1 National Adult Literacy Project Survey Questionnaire

---

Name of person or persons
filling out this survey _____

Title _____

Name of Program _____

Address _____

_____

Phone _____

1. a. What best describes your program? Check those that apply.

     _____ English as a Second Language
     _____ Basic Skills Education
     _____ GED Preparation
     _____ Alternative High School Credentialing Program
     _____ Vocational
     _____ Job Training
     _____ Other. Please describe. _____

     _____

     _____

    b. How do you describe your program site? Check one.

     _____ rural
     _____ urban
     _____ suburban

    c. When does your program operate?

     _____ number of months of the year
     _____ number of days per week
     _____ number of hours per day
     _____ other commitments: _____

     _____

     _____

    d. If information is available, how much does it cost per learner to operate your

    program? _____

e. What is your funding source? Check appropriate sources.

_____ local
_____ state
_____ federal
_____ private
_____ other. Please describe. _____

_____

_____

f. Average age of learners enrolled in your program: _____

g. Sex: Number of Males _____   Number of Females _____

h. How many grades in school has the average learner completed before entering the program? _____

i. What is the average learner's reading grade level upon entering the program?

_____ 0–3
_____ 4–7
_____ 8–12
_____ Other. Please describe. _____

_____

_____

j. How many learners do you serve each year? _____

k. How many learners complete your program per year? _____

2. a. What are some important qualities instructors need to have to be effective in your program? _____

   b. Are your instructors "credentialed"? _____

   c. Do you provide training for your instructors?
      What kind? _____ pre-service _____ in-service _____ both

      Describe: _____

      _____

   d. Do you believe this training is necessary for the success of your program?

      _____

      _____

3. Learner dropout rates are a serious problem for many adult literacy programs.

   a. Is this a problem for your program? _____
      Estimate your dropout rate. _____ %

   b. What ways, if any, have you developed to keep students in your program?

      _____

      Has it solved the problem? _____

4. a. Some important features of adult literacy programs are listed below. Your program may have some or all of these features. First, place an X by those features that are a part of your program.

X's	Rank Order		X's	Rank Order	
____	____	recruiting	____	____	instructional materials
____	____	orientation	____	____	measures of learner
____	____	counseling			progress
____	____	learner diagnostic	____	____	learner follow-up
		testing	____	____	program evaluation
____	____	teaching methods			

Second, look at your X's and decide how you would rank order them. Show which features are important to your program's success. Place a 1 in the rank order column by the most important feature, a 2 by the next important feature, and so on.

b. Please provide some details below about those features you marked with an X.

Recruiting ⎯⎯⎯⎯⎯⎯⎯⎯⎯⎯⎯⎯⎯⎯⎯⎯⎯⎯⎯⎯

⎯⎯⎯⎯⎯⎯⎯⎯⎯⎯⎯⎯⎯⎯⎯⎯⎯⎯⎯⎯⎯⎯⎯⎯⎯⎯

⎯⎯⎯⎯⎯⎯⎯⎯⎯⎯⎯⎯⎯⎯⎯⎯⎯⎯⎯⎯⎯⎯⎯⎯⎯⎯

Orientation ⎯⎯⎯⎯⎯⎯⎯⎯⎯⎯⎯⎯⎯⎯⎯⎯⎯⎯⎯⎯

⎯⎯⎯⎯⎯⎯⎯⎯⎯⎯⎯⎯⎯⎯⎯⎯⎯⎯⎯⎯⎯⎯⎯⎯⎯⎯

⎯⎯⎯⎯⎯⎯⎯⎯⎯⎯⎯⎯⎯⎯⎯⎯⎯⎯⎯⎯⎯⎯⎯⎯⎯⎯

Counseling ⎯⎯⎯⎯⎯⎯⎯⎯⎯⎯⎯⎯⎯⎯⎯⎯⎯⎯⎯⎯⎯

⎯⎯⎯⎯⎯⎯⎯⎯⎯⎯⎯⎯⎯⎯⎯⎯⎯⎯⎯⎯⎯⎯⎯⎯⎯⎯

⎯⎯⎯⎯⎯⎯⎯⎯⎯⎯⎯⎯⎯⎯⎯⎯⎯⎯⎯⎯⎯⎯⎯⎯⎯⎯

Diagnostic testing (name and test[s] used) ⎯⎯⎯⎯⎯⎯⎯⎯

⎯⎯⎯⎯⎯⎯⎯⎯⎯⎯⎯⎯⎯⎯⎯⎯⎯⎯⎯⎯⎯⎯⎯⎯⎯⎯

⎯⎯⎯⎯⎯⎯⎯⎯⎯⎯⎯⎯⎯⎯⎯⎯⎯⎯⎯⎯⎯⎯⎯⎯⎯⎯

Teaching methods ⎯⎯⎯⎯⎯⎯⎯⎯⎯⎯⎯⎯⎯⎯⎯⎯⎯⎯

⎯⎯⎯⎯⎯⎯⎯⎯⎯⎯⎯⎯⎯⎯⎯⎯⎯⎯⎯⎯⎯⎯⎯⎯⎯⎯

⎯⎯⎯⎯⎯⎯⎯⎯⎯⎯⎯⎯⎯⎯⎯⎯⎯⎯⎯⎯⎯⎯⎯⎯⎯⎯

Instructional materials ⎯⎯⎯⎯⎯⎯⎯⎯⎯⎯⎯⎯⎯⎯⎯⎯⎯

⎯⎯⎯⎯⎯⎯⎯⎯⎯⎯⎯⎯⎯⎯⎯⎯⎯⎯⎯⎯⎯⎯⎯⎯⎯⎯

Measures of learner progress ⎯⎯⎯⎯⎯⎯⎯⎯⎯⎯⎯⎯⎯⎯

⎯⎯⎯⎯⎯⎯⎯⎯⎯⎯⎯⎯⎯⎯⎯⎯⎯⎯⎯⎯⎯⎯⎯⎯⎯⎯

Learner follow-up _____

_____

_____

Program evaluation _____

_____

_____

5. How do you know your program works? Please be specific:

_____

_____

_____

PROGRAM MATERIALS CHECKLIST

1. Does your program use:

_____ teacher-made materials
_____ commercial materials
_____ both

a. If you checked teacher-made materials, please describe.

_____

_____

How are teacher-made materials used? Give a few examples of how teacher-made materials are used with learners.

_____

_____

b. If you checked commercial materials, please list what materials you use.

_____

_____

How do you use commercial materials? For example, do you use them in sequential order or do you use only certain parts of commercial materials?

_____

_____

c. If you checked <u>both</u> kinds of materials, please describe how they are used together? Give some examples of how they are used with learners.

_____

_____

2. Check the following program materials that you are willing to share with us.

_____ your program brochure/description
_____ copies of teacher-made materials
_____ copies of teacher-made tests
_____ list of commercial tests used (diagnosis and/or assessment)
_____ newspaper or magazine articles written about your program
_____ newsletters published by your program
_____ copies of student recordkeeping forms
_____ program effectiveness data
_____ learner test scores
_____ copies of program evaluation instruments
_____ copies of completed program evaluations

Please enclose the checklist with the checked materials above in the envelope provided along with the information survey and return them to us as soon as possible. <u>Thank you</u>.

**EXHIBIT 2.2 National Adult Literacy Project Site Visit
Interview Guide**

INTERVIEW GUIDE
Program Director

PART I—PROGRAM MANAGEMENT
(approximately one-hour interview)

1. I'd like to know more about how this program actually came about. (Program's historical development, were there any major changes, philosophy change, how many years has the program been in operation?)

   Probes: If there were many directors, how have these changes affected the program? (positively, negatively)

2. I'd like to know more about how your program is managed.

   A. First, I'd like to ask you some questions about your staff. How many staff are employed?

   Probes: • Full-time?

   • Part-time?

   • Volunteer?

   • How do you integrate part-time and volunteer teachers into your program? (orientation, meetings, in-service, decision making)

   • Does your program have established procedures (personnel policies) for:
   —hiring
   —firing
   —job descriptions, job evaluations

   • Are these procedures followed?
   Give some examples.

   Which procedures are not followed?
   How is that? Give some examples?

B. Now, I'd like to ask you some questions about recordkeeping:

Probes: • How do you keep track of your learners?

—What kinds of details do you record?

—What kinds of recordkeeping methods do you use? (e.g., computer, paper file, other?)

—What information do you collect and keep?

—Are standardized forms used for intake, learner progress, drop out, exit, and follow-up information?

—How do you know someone completed the program? (What is on file—transcript, other?)

—What credentials, if any, do the learners take away with them if they complete the program? (e.g., certificate, other?)

C. Let's focus on decision making. I'm also interested in how your program makes decisions.

• How are decisions made in general? Give some examples.

Probes: • Do teachers/students participate in any program decisions— which ones? How do they participate?

• Who really has the most influence over the program and what happens in it?

D. Now, some questions about management and how your program relates to other agencies. Do you think the way the program is managed helps the instructional part of your program be more successful? Why/why not? Give some examples.

• Could you describe for me what support services you provide for your learners?

Probes: • Child care, counseling—personal and/or job counseling?

• Do you have the need to refer your learners to other agencies for services? If so, which ones?

• How do you describe your relationships with these agencies? (positive/negative) Ask for examples.

• Do you collaborate in any special way with other agencies?

• What difference has this program made to the community?

E. I'd like to complete this first set of questions with some general questions:

- What would you say are the major strengths of your program? What would you say are the weaknesses of your program?

- What stands out in your mind as a key feature of your program that helps learners stay in the program? And that helps learners succeed?

- Are there any obstacles you face now in your program? What are they? And how do you circumvent them?

- In an effort to approach the ideal, which you identified earlier, how do you feel your program could be improved?

- Please describe what kind of staff is needed to run a program like yours.

STOP

End of Part I.

Take ½ hour break to record impressions, thoughts, notes. Get ready for Part II (review the questions).

INTERVIEW GUIDE
Program Director

PART II—PRACTICE PROFILE

(approximately one-hour interview)

Now, I'd like to focus on the eight program components mentioned earlier. (Refer to the sheet with the components again.) I know you've already given me a brief description of what you are doing in each of these from the survey, but now I'd like to be able to create with you a practice profile on your program. To do this, I have to understand what your program really looks like, especially if I were to describe it to someone else who might want to know what they should do to adopt your program. This might seem hard at first, but I think it will be a very useful piece of information to you as well as to others who might be interested in adopting a program like yours. Under each component I'll repeat what was written about the component from the program survey. Please correct any misinterpretation I might make; clarify or add any information you think would be helpful.

A. Recruitment

Let's begin with <u>recruitment</u>. On the survey, you said: _____

_____

_____

<u>Identify the ideal</u>. Say: If your project was adopted for use in another place, would there be any other forms of recruitment that you think would be even better?

<u>Identify the unacceptable</u>. Say: Likewise, would they need to use as many kinds of recruitment as you do? Would less be okay? How much less?

Ideal Variation(s)	Acceptable Variation(s)	Unacceptable Variation(s)

B. Orientation and Counseling

On the survey, you said: _____

_____

_____

<u>Identify the ideal</u>. Say: If your project was adopted for use in another place, would there be any other forms of orientation and counseling that you think would be even better?

<u>Identify the unacceptable</u>. Say: Likewise, would they need to use as many kinds of orientation and counseling as you do? Would less be okay? How much less?

a. What is the method (e.g., individual, group)?

b. What are the qualifications of the people doing the orientation/counseling?

c.   Are there any options presented to the learner? If so, what are they?

d.   Are student goals discussed and do they affect placement?

e.   Who makes the placement decisions?

Ideal Variation(s)	Acceptable Variation(s)	Unacceptable Variation(s)

C.   Diagnostic Testing

On the survey, you said: _____

_____

_____

Identify the ideal. Say: If your project was adopted for use in another place, would there be any other forms of diagnostic testing that you think would be even better?

Identify the unacceptable. Say: Likewise, would they need to use as many kinds of diagnostic testing as you do? Would less be okay? How much less?

a.   Describe your diagnostic process. How many times are learners tested? (e.g., once, twice, etc.)

b.   Who conducts the testing? What are their qualifications?

c.   Who evaluates the test results and makes decisions about the learner?

d.   Are there any other diagnostic instruments you use in addition to the ones you listed on the survey?

e.   What tests have you developed? What skills do they test?

f.   How are test results recorded and evaluated?

g. In what form is feedback given to learners? (e.g., during counseling session, etc.)

h. What role does diagnostic testing play in determining placement?

i. Are tests the only means of determining placement? (e.g., student goals, standardized criteria, expert judgment)

Ideal Variation(s)	Acceptable Variation(s)	Unacceptable Variation(s)

D. Instructional Methods

On the survey, you said: _____

_____

_____

Identify the ideal. Say: If your project was adopted for use in another place, would there be any other forms of instructional methods that you think would be even better?

Identify the unacceptable. Say: Likewise, would they need to use as many kinds of instructional methods as you do? Would less be okay? How much less?

a. What is the structure of instruction? (e.g., individual, small group [1–6], medium group [6–15], large group)

b. What specific reading methods do you use?

c. What is the mode of instruction? (e.g., teacher-led class, field study project, home-based learning, computers, self-paced instruction [learning packets], films, listening/language labs, cable TV.)

d. Describe the instruction site. (e.g., designated room for instruction; is the space quiet, open, accessible to the handicapped, etc.)

Ideal Variation(s)	Acceptable Variation(s)	Unacceptable Variation(s)

E. Instructional Materials

On the survey, you said: _____

_____

_____

Identify the ideal. Say: If your project was adopted for use in another place, would there be any other forms of instructional materials that you think would be even better?

Identify the unacceptable. Say: Likewise, would they need to use as many kinds of instructional materials as you do? Would less be okay? How much less?

a. Who chooses materials?

b. What process do you use to select materials?

c. Is there a core curriculum?

d. How does the core curriculum relate to your unique philosophy of learning?

e. GED — life skills

f. Teacher-made

g. Texts

- life skills materials
- adult-relevant materials

h. Computer software

i. Commercial kits

- content (e.g., life skills, etc.)

Ideal Variation(s)	Acceptable Variation(s)	Unacceptable Variation(s)

Assessment

On the survey, you said: _____

_____

_____

Identify the ideal. Say: If your project was adopted for use in another place, would there be any other forms of assessment that you think would be even better?

Identify the unacceptable. Say: Likewise, would they need to use as many kinds of assessment as you do? Would less be okay? How much less?

a. How is success defined? Is it learner-defined? Is it program-defined?

b. How is learner progress measured during the instructional process?

- tests
- who administers tests?

c. How is learner progress measured at the end of the program?

- tests
- who administers tests?

Ideal Variation(s)	Acceptable Variation(s)	Unacceptable Variation(s)

F. Learner Follow-up

On the survey, you said: _____

_____

_____

Identify the ideal. Say: If your project was adopted for use in another place, would there be any other forms of learner follow-up that you think would be even better?

Identify the unacceptable. Say: Likewise, would they need to use as many kinds of learner follow-up as you do? Would less be okay? How much less?

a. What learners are followed up?

b. How long are they followed?

c. How is the learner follow-up conducted?

d. How is the learner follow-up data stored?

e. Is the follow-up data actively used?

f. If it is used, how is it used? (e.g., is it used for refining and changing the program?)

Ideal Variation(s)	Acceptable Variation(s)	Unacceptable Variation(s)

H. Program Evaluation

On the survey, you said: _____

_____

_____

Identify the ideal. Say: If your project was adopted for use in another place, would there be any other forms of program evaluation that you think would be even better?

Identify the unacceptable. Say: Likewise, would they need to use as many kinds of program evaluations as you do? Would less be okay? How much less?

a. Who conducts the program evaluation?

b. Who developed the program evaluation?

c. What and who is evaluated? How do you do it?

d. What procedures do you follow in evaluation?

- format (checklist, narrative, etc.)
- formal? informal?
- in-house document? state document?
- frequency?

e. What does the evaluation look like in its final form (do they have an example)?

f. Does the program's budget allocate funds for a program evaluation?

g. How does the program use the evaluation results?

- is it used in any kind of program decision making?

Ideal Variation(s)	Acceptable Variation(s)	Unacceptable Variation(s)

INTERVIEW GUIDE

Program Director

PART III—FOLLOW-UP FOR DAY 2
(approximately one-hour interview)

1. After having reviewed information from Day 1, prepare key questions and probes to complete needed information, clarify vague answers, elicit more information, etc.

2. (Hand the director the sheet with the eight components.) On your survey, you rated _____ as the most important component in your program. How did you mean that? Please explain.

   Probes: • Is it the one you think you do best?

   • If not, select the one you do best. Give examples, stories, anecdotes.

   • Are there other important program components or elements (besides these eight) that we missed?

3. I'd like to complete this final interview with some general questions:

   • What would you say are the major strengths of your program? What would you say are the weaknesses of your program?

   • What makes your program unique?

   • How do you see your program as being different from other programs?

   • What stands out in your mind as a key feature of your program that helps learners stay in the program? And that helps learners succeed?

- Are there any obstacles you face now in your program? What are they? And how do you circumvent them?

- In an effort to approach the ideal, which you identified earlier, how do you feel your program could be improved?

- Please describe what kind of staff is needed to run a program like yours.

INTERVIEW GUIDE
Teacher/Tutor

1. Can you tell me about your work in the program?

   Probes:
   a. How long have you been with the program?

   b. Have you always taught the same subject matter in the program?

   c. Have you taught in different parts of the program?

   d. What's it like to work here?

   e. Please describe what kind of teacher works best in your program—to maximize learner achievement?

2. Can you describe in some detail how your program accomplishes:

   a. Learner diagnostic testing

   b. Instructional methods

   c. If I were in your classroom during one of your classes, what would I see happening? What would be going on? Please describe what one of your classes is like.

   d. What event or series of activities that you can remember really sparked the most learning in your classroom?

   e. Instructional materials

   f. What role does the learner play in the development of your own (teacher-made) material? Do you use learner-generated ideas and material? If so, explain how. Do you match your materials with the learners' requests?

   g. Assessment of learner skills

   h. What do you want your students to be able to do differently when they leave the program? What do you want them to be able to do now that they weren't able to do when they entered?

    i.   Follow-up of learners

    j.   Program evaluation

    k.   Are you satisfied with the way in which your program accomplishes each of these components?

        What would you change? Be specific. (Review the list again.)

    l.   Most programs have things about them they'd like to change or problems they'd like to solve. Give me some examples. Can you name some problems your program is trying to solve?

    m.   What difference has this program made to the community?

3.   Let's talk briefly about program management.

    a.   What do you think about the way your program is managed? How are decisions made?

    b.   Do you or students share in program decisions?

        If yes, describe.
        If no, would you want to?

4.   (Hand the teacher the sheet with the eight components.) On the survey we sent to your director, _____ was rated the most important component of your program. How do you feel about this?

    a.   Is it the one you think you do best?

        • If not, select the one you do best. Give examples, stories, anecdotes.

        • Are there other important program components or elements (besides these eight) that we missed?

    b.   What makes your program unique?

        • How do you see your program as being different from other programs?

        • What, if any, could be described as the weaknesses of your program?

        • As I leave today, tell me what you and your program do best. (List strengths.)

INTERVIEW GUIDE

Counselor

1.   I'd like to learn more about your role in the program. Tell me about what you do here.

Probes: • How long have you been with the program?

• Ask about their job description.

• Are you able to do all the things your job requires?

• What are some of the rewards/frustrations in your job?

• If I were with you when you were counseling a student, what would I see happening? What would be going on? Please describe what one of your sessions is like.

• How do you counsel the different types of learners in your program?

2. Open discussion. Tell me about:

—Learner diagnostic testing
—Assessment of learner skills
—Follow-up of learners
—Program evaluation
—What stands out in your mind as critical (or essential) to helping learners stay and succeed in your program?

3. How are decisions made about the program? the students? etc.

4. How would you rate the way the program operates? Do you think it has any relationship to the program's success? In what ways?

• What kind of effect has this program had on the community?

5. Most programs have things about them they'd like to change or problems they'd like to solve. Can you name some problems your program is trying to solve?

• What would you say are the basic strengths of your program?

• What are some of the things regarding learner orientation and counseling you think can be improved in your program?

6. (Hand the counselor the sheet with the eight components.) On the survey your director filled out for us (he/she) rated _____ as the most important component in your program. How do you feel about this?

• Is it the one you think you do best?

• If not, select the one you do best. Give examples, stories, anecdotes.

• Are there other important program components or elements (besides these eight) that we missed?

• What makes your program unique?

- How do you see your program as being different from other programs?
- What, if any, could be described as the weaknesses of your program?
- As I leave today, tell me what you and your program do best. (List strengths.)

INTERVIEW GUIDE
Learners

1. (Warm-up Conversation) Where are you from? Have you lived here all your life? Do you have a family? etc.

2. How did you decide to come to this program?

   Probes: • How long have you been in the program?

   • How did you hear about program (recruitment)?

3. How did you find out what classes would be like and what courses you would be taking?

4. Are there counselors available to work with students? How have you used the counselors here?

5. Were you tested at the beginning to find out what you were going to learn?

   • How did you feel about the testing?

   • Was it helpful?

6. Did you get to plan what you wanted to learn? What do you want to learn? Are you working toward what you want to learn? (Ask for examples, description.)

7. How do you feel about the progress you are making in the program? How can you tell you are making progress? How does your teacher let you know how you are doing?

8. How useful are the books you are using?

9. Would you mind telling me an important experience you had in this program that really stands out in your mind?

10. What are some of the things you don't like about the program?

11. What are some of the things you really like about the program?

12. If you could change anything about the program, what would you make different?

13. I've heard that most students stay in this program for a while. Why do you think most students keep coming?

14. Can you give me an example of something you've done in class that was really interesting to you?

15. What can you do now that you couldn't do when you entered the program?

REFLECTIVE REMARKS

Directions: Include on this sheet any remarks you have which may pertain to any categories listed below. Use the questions under each category as prompts for reflections about interviews. Code reflective remarks using the numbers of the categories below.

1. Reflections on Analysis. What are you learning? What themes are emerging? What patterns are present? Do you see connections between pieces of data?

2. Reflections on Method.
   a. Ideas about the effectiveness (ineffectiveness) of the study's design; comments on procedures employed in study.
   b. Comments on rapport with subjects—include ideas about how to deal with problems.
   c. Record decisions about possible changes in methodology.

3. Reflections on ethical dilemmas and conflicts. Comments on conflicts between your values and responsibilities to your subjects.

4. Reflections on the observer's frame of mind. Notes about your opinions, beliefs, attitudes and prejudices which may color your perceptions at the site. Also, comments on how these assumptions were confirmed or disconfirmed. (It is a good idea to record all preconceptions before going in field.)

5. Points of Clarification. Notes to clear up points which may have been confusing; corrections of informational errors (e.g., you confused the names of two teachers).

DOCUMENT SUMMARY FORM

Site _____

Document number _____

Date rec'd or picked up: _____

Name or description of document:

Event or contact, if any, with which document is associated:

Date: _____

Significance or importance of document:

Brief summary of contents:

IF DOCUMENT IS CENTRAL OR CRUCIAL TO A PARTICULAR CONTACT (e.g., a meeting agenda, newspaper clipping discussed in an interview, etc.) MAKE A COPY AND INCLUDE WITH WRITE-UP.

EXHIBIT 2.3 Programs Interviewed in Site Visits

The following list of programs that were interviewed in the NALP study site visits is grouped by type of program, and programs are listed alphabetically by state and by city within state under the group headings. A full citation of address and telephone number can be found in the program profile section of Section IV.

State and Local Public Adult Education Programs

Sequoia District Adult School
Redwood City, CA
Cuba Miller, Assistant Director

Franklin County Adult Basic Education, Tutorial Program
Farmington, ME
Claude Vachon, Director

Portland Adult Community Education (PACE)
Portland, ME
Kathleen Lee, Coordinator, Adult Basic Education

Lowell Adult Education Program
Lowell, MA
Frederick Assad Abisi, Director of Adult Education

Somerville Center for Adult Learning Experience (SCALE)
Somerville, MA
Ruth E. Derfler, GED/ADP Lead Teacher

Community-Based Programs

Refugee Link Program
Tempe, AZ
Nancy Meyers, Coordinator

Los Angeles County Library Literacy Programs
Language Learning Centers
Downey, CA
Connie Phillips, Literacy Project Coordinator

Push Literacy Action Now, Inc. (PLAN, Inc.)
Washington, DC
Michael Fox, Executive Director

Alternative Schools Network
Chicago, IL
Jack Wuest, Director

Literacy Volunteers of Chicago
Chicago, IL
George Hagenauer, Director

Lafayette Adult Reading Academy
Lafayette, IN
JoAnn Vorst, Director

Directions in Adult Learning (DIAL)
Hanscom Air Force Base, MA
Pamela Cornell Buchek, Director

Bank Street Basic Skills Academy
New York, NY
Virginia Kwarta, Acting Director

Literacy Volunteers of New York City, Inc.
New York, NY
Karen Griswold, Associate Director

Lutheran Settlement House Women's Program
Philadelphia, PA
Katherine Reilly, Director

Programs Within Correctional Institutions

Nebraska Center for Women
Adult Basic Education
York, NE
Janice Axdahl, Education/Vocation Coordinator

Sing Sing Correctional Facility
Literacy Volunteers
Ossining, NY
Christine Mattia, Supervisor of Volunteer Tutors

State Correctional Institution at Camp Hill
Correctional Education Program
Camp Hill, PA
Calvin W. Williams, Director of Education

South Dakota State Penitentiary
Calvin Coolidge High School
Sioux Falls, SD
Lloyd E. Stivers, Principal

Programs Within the Military

Academic Remedial Training (ART)
Recruit Training Command
San Diego, CA
MRCS(SW) D. W. Richie

Job-Oriented Basic Skills (JOBS) School
Service School Command
San Diego, CA
Master Chief Petty Officer R. L. Ferris, Director

Basic Skills Education Program
Army Education Division
Fort Bragg, NC
Rebecca C. Wilson, Supervisory Education Specialist

Navy Functional Skills Program
Philadelphia Naval Base
Philadelphia, PA
Virginia Gibbons, Site Coordinator, Teacher, and Director

American Preparatory Institute
Central Texas College
Killeen, TX
Dr. Betty Lacey, Dean of Academic Programs

Programs Within Postsecondary Education Institutions

San Diego Community College
Continuing Education Centers
San Diego, CA
Autumn Keltner, ABE/ESL Coordinator

Southeast Community College
Adult Guided Studies
Lincoln, NE
Curtis D. Sederburg, Coordinator, Adult Academic Studies Division

Caldwell Community College and Technical Institute
Lenoir, NC
Martha E. Hollar, ABE Director

Portland Community College
Volunteer Tutoring Program
Portland, OR
Susan Bach, Coordinator of Educational Services

Edmonds Community College
Developmental Education
Lynnwood, WA
Greg Golden, Director of Learning Resources

Employment and Training Programs

Vocational Education Special Projects
San Mateo County Office of Education
Redwood City, CA
Joe Cooney, Director

Jobs for Youth–Boston, Inc.
Boston, MA
David J. Rosen, Director of Educational Services

Clerk Typist Training Program
Prudential Insurance Company of America
Newark Private Industry Council, Inc.
Newark, NJ
Josephine B. Janifer, Director

SECTION II

Components of

Effective Programs

Within the seven chapters of this section, we will describe the eight components for which programs must design specific operational plans: (1) recruitment and public relations, (2) orientation, (3) counseling, (4) diagnostic testing, (5) assessment, (6) instructional methods and materials, (7) follow-up, and (8) program evaluation. A program's philosophy, the sector in which it operates, the goals it sets for itself and its students, and the nature of its student population will all influence what kind of plan will be formulated for each of these components. It is therefore not the purpose of this section to define a single program design that would be universally applicable.

We will, however, suggest a model for the planning process—examining the factors that must be considered and the options that have proven successful for the programs in the NALP study. We believe that we can identify certain basic principles that will guide practitioners in building effective programs.

Chapter 3
Recruitment and
Public Relations

The goals of a program's recruitment and public relations plan may be any or all of the following:

- to recruit students, whether directly through personal contact or indirectly through referrals
- to recruit volunteer staff
- to elicit community support, which may include support in the form of donations of money, space, equipment, person-time, or in-kind services
- to build a service network with other social service agencies, community groups, and employers to extend the range of services available to program participants

To accomplish these goals, programs may use the media—newspapers, radio, television—or various kinds of newsletters, flyers, brochures, or posters. They may also use personal contacts gained through networking efforts, needs assessment surveys, canvassing, and public speaking engagements, as well as using word of mouth generated by current and former students. Whatever its choice of techniques, a program's recruitment and public relations activities are most effective when they are conscious efforts that result from a deliberate and systematic plan; a once-a-year media blitz will not generate the kind of continuing support that a program will need for its survival.

When discussion turns to the topic of recruitment, the focus is usually on planning for the first of the goals—recruiting students. Yet, especially for programs operating in large urban centers, it may be less than desirable to recruit more students. Many programs are already filled to capacity, and new arrivals can only be told that they will be put on a waiting list for an indefinite period of time. In some cases, adults may be on waiting lists for fourteen to eighteen months. In New York, an outstanding community-based program, Bronx Educational Services, has a recording that begins with the words: "Our reading classes are full. If you want to join in September, you must register in June." One unusual student response to this problem was reported by the coordinator of the Quincy Community School Adult ESL program in Boston. As part of their planning for immigration to the United States, people still in China wrote to request placement on the waiting list for the Quincy ESL program. The letter writers understood from relatives in the U.S. that this request was necessary if they were to avoid waiting for a long time after their arrival to get English language instruction.

For programs that already have or can anticipate long waiting lists, there may well be a need to develop some strategies for limiting applicants and/or for providing pre-enrollment or referral services to those whom the program is unable to serve.

Whether or not a program feels a need to recruit students actively, any planning for other recruitment or public relations activities still begins and ends with a discussion of the needs of the students. Even when the immediate goal is recruiting volunteers, drumming up community support, or building a network of friends and support services, the ultimate goal remains enabling the program to serve the needs of its students effectively. Indeed, without an awareness of and a sensitivity to the needs of adult learners, a program defeats its very purpose. The program must clearly demonstrate this sensitivity in its recruitment message and in its plans for those students who must be placed on waiting lists.

A program's recruitment message—whether targeted directly to the students or to the larger community—must be positive and honest and show respect for the adults the program intends to serve. The formulation of such a message begins with a clear definition of the program's goals and philosophy. The program must objectively define what services it is equipped to provide and whom it is best able to serve. It is simply not enough to *want* to provide adult education services—we can assume that all programs have that desire—the program's financial, human, and physical resources must also enable the program to effectively deliver the services it wants to provide.

Once a program has clearly delineated its services and stated the intended outcomes of student participation, it can communicate that information to potential students without fear of being unable to deliver on its promises. Before a program advertises itself as a high school completion program, for example, it will have thought through to the intended outcomes and will have made provisions for a certification process that allows successful students to receive their diplomas. Clear and honest communication of a program's services and the intended audience for those services also helps potential students match their own needs and goals against what the program can offer them.

We know that many adult students have not had positive experiences with the regular school system in the past and that it will take great courage and a high degree of motivation for them to return to any educational setting. If a program promises such students what it cannot deliver, the program confirms the students' sense of failure or helplessness—it may not occur to the students that it is the program that has failed and not them.

Once the program has clearly defined the services it is equipped to provide and can thus define the target audience for a recruitment effort, it must consider the following five questions.

(1) How will people in the community know about your program? Describe the media and techniques you will use for each of the target audiences of your campaign—potential students, volunteer tutors, community support groups, and other educational or social service agencies.

(2) Does the message that is going out to potential students clearly describe (a) the program's services, (b) any eligibility requirements, and (c) when, where, and how to enroll in the program?

(3) Is that message honest and free of anything that could be interpreted as being patronizing?

(4) At what times in the year do people need to know about your program? What is an appropriate timetable for each phase of your recruitment and public relations campaign?

(5) Who will be responsible for publicizing the program?

The balance of this chapter is devoted to providing you with the information you may need to develop or review the recruitment and public relations plan for your own program. We'll examine the methods that programs in the NALP study use and explore the potential each of these methods has for recruitment and public relations. We'll then focus on the debate over whether and how one engages in selective recruitment. We'll also explore what programs can do in the face of waiting lists. Finally, we'll offer our own conclusions and recommendations for programs building a strong recruitment/ public relations plan. At the end of the chapter, we'll also present an abbreviated and adapted version of one program's twelve-month recruitment and public relations plan. Through the bibliography, we'll point you in the direction of additional resources.

TECHNIQUES THAT USE MEDIA

Within this section, we'll use the term *media* in its broadest sense to include both the sources one normally associates with the word—newspapers, radio, and television— and other vehicles for printed information such as posters, flyers, brochures, news- letters, bulletins, and even special referral forms.

Print Media

Well-written press releases or newsletters sent to local newspapers can serve as the basis for feature articles, editorials, or a topic to be picked up by a regular columnist. Program staff might also submit a letter to the editor or obtain advertising space for anything ranging from full class schedules to simple ads announcing the program's name, general offerings, address, and phone number. Any of these uses of the news- paper can give a program needed exposure, alerting the general public to the program's existence and mission. If a newspaper article is carefully researched and given an attention-grabbing headline, it can enlist the aid of people in the community who might otherwise overlook adult education programs. "Sitting down and writing an article is not going to cost me anything," explains the director of a volunteer program in the rural Northeast. "People come up to me all the time telling me, 'Oh, I read your article and I told so-and-so about it,' and they send someone over!"

Programs also advertise their services or special events through posters, flyers, newsletters, and brochures written in simple, easy-to-read language. In some cases, these media feature clever logos, designs, or photographs that communicate the general message without the use of words in an attempt to circumvent the problem of reaching less fluent readers. Some programs target these media for specific minority populations, distributing them to local community gathering places, supermarket bulletin boards, and local community or special-interest tabloids.

Several programs recruit directly within companies that employ unskilled or semi-skilled labor by distributing flyers, sending information packets to the employers, and even starting classes on the job site.

Yet another use of print is distributing specially designed forms to other community service agencies such as drug and alcohol rehabilitation programs. If these agencies are aware of educational support services their clients have access to, and if they have referral forms readily available, they can easily make appropriate referrals.

In deciding how to use print media, it is important for programs to understand the limitations print may have for meeting certain recruitment objectives. Print media can be an inexpensive and effective means of informing the community at large, private industry, and social service agencies about the educational services a program offers. However, potential students themselves may be unlikely to look to newspapers or even bulletin boards as sources of information. Information disseminated in print form is most likely to reach students indirectly as a result of word of mouth or referral. Print media can, however, produce results in recruiting volunteers, and many programs do use newspapers as their primary vehicle for volunteer recruitment.

Beyond recognizing the limitations of print for recruiting significant numbers of students, programs must be careful of the messages they commit to print. Once that newspaper article, flyer, or brochure is outside the program's offices, it is also outside the program's control. What the program has down in black and white is going to reach a diverse audience across a geographical area that may be larger than the program can serve. Well-conceived and specifically targeted, print media can produce unexpected benefits. Ill-conceived and untargeted, print media can produce unexpected problems. If the message is too vague and general, the program may attract people whose goals and expectations will not be met by the program. Instead of supporting an adult's decision to return to an educational system, inappropriate messages may result in disappointment and frustration for those the program cannot serve well or at all.

Radio

As a requirement of their licenses from the Federal Communications Commission, radio stations must offer a certain amount of free air time each day for public service announcements (PSAs). But PSAs are not necessarily the boon they may at first appear to be. Yours will not be the only organization that submits a PSA to the local station. There may be no problem with smaller stations; indeed, PSAs are widely used in rural areas. But in large urban areas, stations may have such a backlog of PSAs that they may be aired at a time of day when they are least likely to be heard by your desired audience, or they may be postponed until a time when you no longer need them. You might also experience just the opposite problem. As one urban program director commented, "You may just have received 500 calls, and you have to yell, 'Stop, take them off!' because [you] can't cope with the response."

If a lack of targeting can cause problems for users of print media, it can cause even greater problems for users of radio PSAs. Radio stations can reach an unpredictable number of people in a large geographic area. It is not uncommon for programs to receive calls from prospective learners who live thirty to fifty miles from any program site and who do not have the means of transportation to travel that distance.

In an attempt to target their messages for specific populations, many programs choose stations they know to be popular with their intended audience; for example, they choose stations with a format aimed at the Black or Hispanic population or those that exclusively air rock, soul, or reggae. But choosing a station is not the same as targeting the message. As one director of an urban program noted, you may attract the attention of the hardest to reach, but you're not necessarily going to be able to keep them in the program. If potential students come to your program simply because they heard a spot on their favorite station and your program just happened to be in the neighborhood, they may only be acting on impulse and not with the degree of motivation that will be necessary to see them through your program. You cannot lead students to believe through your PSA that you have some quick and simple way of making them fully literate and finding them a good job. You're not writing advertisements for the backs of matchbook covers, and you're not trying to sell some new brand of toothpaste. You can use all the hip language you like and add upbeat background music, but you've got to be honest about what you have to offer and what your program will require on the student's part to benefit from your services.

Although PSAs may be the most obvious use of radio, you can also send the local radio stations the same press releases you send to the local newspapers. They, too, may use the detailed information from your releases in news programs or community bulletin board features; it may not have occurred to them to do the research you can easily do for them. And don't overlook volunteering to be a guest on a radio telephone call-in show or other talk show. If you are invited to participate in a call-in show, listen to the program for several days to get a feel for the kind of audience you're likely to be talking to, and go in prepared to think on your feet.

Television

The use of television in recruitment and public relations efforts is still relatively rare, although television is certainly the medium that most of the target audience turns to for information. And television now means more than three major national networks; it also includes the Public Broadcasting Service stations and a host of independent and cable channels. Press releases may net programs a news or human interest story on local news programs. Some stations also air community bulletin board features that may serve to make announcements of special events or new programs. Almost all stations also have local talk shows on which program leaders might volunteer to appear. And programs should not hesitate to contact television station managers with their ideas for special presentations—perhaps a documentary on the program in operation or a panel discussion involving local community and industry leaders, a local school board member or superintendent of schools, and, when applicable, staff and students from the program.

Because the cost of television production is beyond the means of most literacy programs, only a few programs have produced documentaries or advertisements independently. One postsecondary program in the East produced a one-hour documentary featuring students telling their stories—what prompted them to come to the program, how their feelings about themselves had changed, and what the program meant to them. This documentary not only filled the short-term goals of a recruitment and public relations effort when it was broadcast locally, but it has also been used subsequently in tutor and in-service training sessions. To minimize the costs of production, another program used the donated services of a graduate student in filmmaking at a local university to produce a spot for a local cable channel. (For more information on the use of broadcast media, see the monograph by Marchilonis and Niebuhr cited in the bibliography on page 56.)

Asked to evaluate the effectiveness of television documentaries, the director of a community-based program noted that television can create strong, positive images that people remember. When potential learners can identify with the success stories they see, the medium can be a compelling means of recruitment. And, because television broadcasts penetrate large geographical areas, they may be a useful means of publicizing the program in areas that would be difficult to cover personally. Indeed, in spread-out communities such as those in rural areas, television may be a means not only for public relations but also for instruction.

However, the same cautions we have noted for print and radio apply also to television, perhaps to an even greater degree. Television affords a program the least degree of control over the number of people and the communities it reaches. And, with television, the message viewers receive is not limited to the verbal one the program intends; the power of the message can be either enhanced or destroyed by the visual information supplied by what is in the background as well as by the body language and physical presence of the people on the videotape.

Though we have issued cautions within this section on the use of media, it is not our intention to discourage the use of media. Print, radio, and television can all be very effective means of reaching large audiences. Although these media can serve a thousand purposes, they are probably best suited to the following five:

- conducting large public information campaigns

- soliciting donations of resources, space, person-time, or money

- spreading the word about the opening of a new program and its services to students, tutors, and local community organizations

- spreading the word about the addition of a new educational component—such as adding English as a Second Language—or other significant expansion of an existing program

- targeting a new population or a new neighborhood

TECHNIQUES THAT USE PERSONAL CONTACT

The majority of the sites visited in the NALP study make direct and personal contact with the people and organizations in their communities and view such activities as some of the most effective recruitment techniques they employ. Such contact enables programs to make the message personal, which many think is essential to recruiting and retaining learners. Programs have devised many ways to reach potential students through friends and institutions within their own community. And these same personal contact techniques have rewards that go beyond merely recruiting students or volunteers. Personal contact may yield needed donations, critical support at funding time, and information that helps keep the program tied to the needs of the community. Within this section, we'll examine five forms of personal contact reported by programs in the NALP study: networking, needs assessment surveys, canvassing, public speaking engagements, and word of mouth.

Networking

Networking means tapping the resources and organizations in a community as well as the larger field of adult education professionals. Programs build a network for a variety of reasons, only one of which is the recruitment of students and volunteers. Within this chapter, however, we will concern ourselves with the use of networks in recruitment and public relations.

Information about literacy programs can reach potential students via a network of friends, relatives, and neighbors who belong to community organizations or churches with whom the literacy program has made contact, as well as through employers and social service agencies. In order to establish such a network, literacy programs must make a conscious effort to cultivate ties within their community, whether the community in which the program operates is a civic community, the military, or a correctional institution. Each milieu may place different demands on a program, but, as a program director from the Midwest pointed out, "Programming has to work at the community level and be tied into its institutions."

One way to work within the community is to set up partnerships with organizations that come in contact with the program's potential student population. Corporations and social service agencies are two such targets for partnerships. These organizations may donate space or equipment, as well as much-needed expertise and support services that the program could not otherwise provide.

One literacy system on the West Coast has evolved by organizing class sites in libraries throughout the county, thus serving nearly ten thousand people annually. Although this West Coast system was initiated by the libraries themselves, libraries in many other parts of the country have responded to calls for partnerships initiated by local literacy programs and have offered space, equipment, and materials.

The Prudential Insurance Company of Newark, New Jersey, donates space, typewriters, and supplies to an employment and training program that provides clerical training. The corporate setting is attractive to potential clients who see it as a chance to work (and perhaps eventually get a job) in a large company. Knowledge of such opportunities circulates very quickly through the grapevine and cannot be underestimated as a recruitment tactic.

A third example of a partnership found in the NALP study is a public adult basic skills program in New England. State department of education officials agreed to locate a regional adult basic education (ABE) program in the building of another state agency. This agency was already involved with low-income people in the region, and its ten outreach workers maintained constant contact with the population. The advantage of forming a partnership between a literacy program and this agency was that the agency's outreach workers could provide the literacy program with "instant recruitment"; the agency knew the population well enough to readily identify and contact those in need of the literacy program's services.

Interagency referrals are not uncommon, and they can work both ways. The literacy program may be able to offer other agencies educational programs they might not be able to provide otherwise, and social service agencies can offer the participants in a literacy program a host of services that the literacy program is not equipped to provide.

Needs Assessments and Canvassing

Determining the educational needs and desires of the population to be served is an essential step in the design of any literacy program that hopes to serve its community or interested constituency well. Many programs, however, are limited in their ability to conduct extensive or adequate needs assessment surveys because of funding and staffing restrictions or because the services the program can provide are predetermined by a higher agency to which the program reports.

Despite these difficulties, the findings of the NALP study reaffirm the value of conducting community and/or constituency surveys (a) to determine which services a program is equipped to provide in terms of its financial, human, and physical resources and (b) to determine the extent to which the program is providing the services its community needs and responding appropriately and quickly to any changes in those needs over time. There are other, more subtle benefits to be derived from conducting a needs assessment beyond gaining an understanding of the demographic, economic, and cultural characteristics of the area in which the program hopes to operate. The mere act of getting out into the community and openly asking for its opinion presents the program in the best possible light. The program is demonstrating its desire to be seen as an ally and truly linked to the community. And needs assessments do aid in the formulation of a recruitment plan by answering certain questions: Who should be the target of the recruitment effort? Assuming that you have correctly identified the potential students' needs, how can they be attracted to the program and convinced of its usefulness in meeting those needs?

What follows is a list of questions program operators and planners might seek to answer about their program in order to assess how it may be designed or modified to meet the needs of the community or population it is intended to serve.

Questions about Target Populations and Program Strategies

1. What is your intended target population?

   - youth in school (ages 14–16)
   - youth out of school
   - minority (specify)
   - adult
   - senior
   - other

2. What are the projected educational needs of these groups (e.g., adult basic education, English as a second language, GED preparation, other)?

3. What percentage of persons in each of these groups live within a five-mile radius of your program site/sites?

4. If you already have an operating program, how many persons in each group do you currently serve each year? In what programs?

5. On average, how long does it take students to complete each of your existing programs?

6. What is your approximate retention rate in your existing programs?

7. Do any of your existing programs have waiting lists? If so, which ones?

8. On average, how long does a person stay on the waiting list before gaining entry into the program of his/her choice?

9. Do you offer any pre-enrollment activities for those on waiting lists?

10. What outreach activities do you engage in to draw in your intended population?

11. Do you find outreach activities necessary, or do you have sufficient numbers of learners to fill each of your programs?

12. If you don't now do outreach because you are filled to capacity, can you estimate how many people in your community are still in need of your services?

13. What funding options or other resource options are available to you to support new services should there be a need for them?

14. How will you use the answers to these questions to shape or modify your program?

Questions about Your Agency

1. What services do you or would you like to offer?
   - English as a Second Language (ESL)
   - Vocational Training

- Adult Basic Education (ABE)
- Adult Secondary Education (ASE)
- GED Preparation
- Job-Specific Training
- Other: _____

2. What services are you funded to offer or are you likely to be funded to offer?

3. Where will you offer these services? List all sites if you have a multiple-site program.

4. How would you summarize your program's service philosophy?

5. What prior experience does your agency have in offering these services or related services?

6. What support services is the intended target audience likely to need (e.g., child care, transportation, etc.)? Is your agency equipped to provide these services, or are they readily available in the community?

7. Is your agency involved with other social service providers? What is the nature of the collaboration?

8. How is your agency organized to deliver literacy services?

9. What are your current funding sources?

10. What are your potential funding sources?

11. What services would you like to offer and to whom?

12. What would it take to offer these expanded services should you wish to expand?

Some of these questions may be more difficult than others to answer. Some may involve the use of census data, and some may mean getting out into the community in a canvassing effort. Others may require you to take a coldly objective look at yourself. Basically, the first set of fourteen questions is designed to help you define who is in your service area and determine the extent to which you are providing the services they are likely to need when they need them. The second set of twelve questions is designed to help you determine which services you are equipped to provide in terms of financial, human, and physical resources.

Canvassing efforts are closely related to needs assessments except that the goal is providing rather than soliciting information. Canvassing may include standing on the streets and talking to passers-by (perhaps handing out flyers or brochures as well), knocking on doors, and affixing posters to telephone poles, streetlight poles, and bulletin boards. One community-based program in the Midwest takes to the streets twice a year to stage a recruitment campaign. Program staff divide the town into sectors and then go out to talk to every business and social service agency in town. These canvassing campaigns are planned with census data and personal knowledge of the area. They visibly increase the numbers of recruited students while bolstering the program's public image.

Canvassing is the most direct means of recruitment and may be the most believable one as well. By being on the street and open to direct contact with potential students, program staff have the opportunity for the kind of dialogue that might not take place in the program's offices. The effort may provide just the kind of encouragement someone needs to cross the program's threshold.

Public Speaking

With the current media attention being given to the problem of illiteracy, program directors are in more demand than ever to give public presentations in meetings of local civic groups, charitable organizations, religious organizations, and social clubs. Many program directors interviewed in the NALP study report that meeting with or giving presentations to such groups are reliable ways of providing information, extending the program's network, and raising funds. The presentations may be much more than a speech and include videotapes, audiocassette recordings, slides, and printed handouts. But it is the personal contact with an ambassador from the literacy program that is the most important feature of any presentation.

Public speaking engagements, like any other recruitment or public relations strategy, need to be planned. It is not enough simply to wait to be asked to speak by organizations that may not even know of a program's existence or your availability for public speaking. Some programs plan a yearly schedule of activities and target specific months for personal presentations, luncheons, and meetings.

Word of Mouth

Although word of mouth may not be a deliberate recruitment or public relations strategy, programs need to be aware of its effect in the community. What is said in public speaking engagements or radio or television talk shows and what is written in newspapers, flyers, brochures, and newsletters *do* get talked about. Many directors take care to prepare their staff and volunteers to support the public relations image of the program. As one counselor who works with out-of-school Black and Hispanic youth commented, "In this day and age, the reputation on the street level is extremely important. . . . We are some honest, straight-up people, and we present ourselves that way, and we prove it!"

What happens within the program's walls also gets talked about. Rumors about consistent poor performance by tutors or teachers escapes easily into the community grapevine. But word of mouth is at its best when the words are from a "satisfied customer." When this customer is a friend, relative, or community resident respected by a potential student, recruitment becomes a self-generating process. One program director who sustains a highly successful public relations effort credits word of mouth as her best ally and comments, "Quality sells itself."

TARGETING THE RECRUITMENT EFFORT

Although most programs attest to the usefulness of recruitment techniques, well-established programs often do little or no recruitment because their reputation guarantees them a client population. "We've been here fifteen years now, and the neighborhood knows we are here," says a director of a postsecondary program in the Northwest. In fact, some programs conduct only very focused recruitment campaigns in order to attract specific ethnic groups or particular types of learners. One might view selective recruitment as a sign of a very successful program—a program that has analyzed its strengths, has targeted those learners it can help, and has built its community reputation on delivering what it promises.

Indeed, those programs in the NALP study that reported the greatest successes in learner achievement were those that worked very hard to attract students whose goals and expectations could be met through participation in the program and whose lifestyles (including family and job obligations) did not stand in the way of their meeting program requirements. Such programs use recruitment messages that are explicit about the goals of each of its offerings, the intended outcomes for learners, and the requirements for participation. Prospective students can thus judge for themselves whether a particular program is what they want and need, and the program has established a basis for selecting those students who are most likely to be successful.

Although some may fear that this appears very close to "creaming" the best students at the expense of those most in need of services, others would maintain that these programs are simply being careful to create the optimum conditions for "second chance" learners to achieve rather than fail in an educational setting. This issue of selective recruitment is one of the most controversial issues in the literacy field. However opposed programs may be to the notion of selective recruitment, they are often quite selective about whom they admit. In fact, the word *selective* may be misleading if it is assumed to apply to certain personality traits or blatantly discriminatory practices. The programs visited in the course of the NALP study clearly stated that selective recruitment, to them, implies instead a matching of learners' needs to the capabilities of the program. Perhaps the issue was best described by Mike Fox, director of Push Literacy Action Now, a community-based program in Washington, D.C., who explained his recruitment philosophy this way:

> I am not saying "eliminate" anyone. I think in terms of high risk/low risk. When you have limited resources and you have a feeling who you could work with most effectively, in terms of teaching people how to read, then that's the way to go. Some call it "creaming" . . . creaming to make a program look good for funders and creaming to be effective are two different philosophies. I have never turned anybody away without explaining exactly why. Selective recruitment means that you as a group know what you are best capable of doing and for whom.

Many other practitioners reject selective recruitment in the name of democracy or good works. They enforce an open-door policy and strive, in effect, to be all things to all people. These practitioners argue that students may be permanently discouraged if they are turned away. It is not easy to argue with the motivation behind this opinion. In the best of all possible worlds, programs should serve all the adults who come to them. At least, like Push Literacy Action Now, programs can refer adults they cannot serve to another program or to someone else who *can* help. However, the reality of program and human resource limitations suggests that selective recruitment may be critical to a program's success in helping adults achieve their educational objectives.

POST-RECRUITMENT BLUES— THE WAITING LIST

As mentioned at the beginning of the chapter, waiting lists are a significant and ever-increasing problem for many literacy programs. We'd all like to see waiting lists disappear under the ideal circumstance of having adequate services for all those in need, but the truth is that there may simply be more students who need a program's services than the program is equipped to serve. The waiting list phenomenon is particularly disturbing when one considers that some of these prospective students may be waiting for entry into programs that are not well matched to their goals, needs, and requirements.

Several community-based and postsecondary programs in the NALP study have addressed the problem by creating pre-enrollment orientation sessions. These programs may conduct all of the routine registration procedures and orientation activities and stop just short of placing the students in classes or pairing them with tutors. One program trains former tutors specifically to conduct these special pre-enrollment orientation sessions. They work with groups of up to fifty waiting-list students, explaining program goals, indicating which students are most likely to derive a benefit from the program (including, as applicable, a discussion of any eligibility requirements), and advising participants what they can do to prepare themselves for the program. Participants take some tests and provide a writing sample, and the tutors share some basic reading strategies that the prospective students can begin to use independently even before actual instruction begins. The tutors also act as facilitators in discussion groups between current students and those on the waiting list. The program's director commented that these sessions help prospective students "think about what they want to get out of [the program]."

Pre-enrollment orientation sessions also help programs in their attempt to screen students; it would be reprehensible to place a student on a waiting list with a promise of delivering services when the student might later turn out to be ineligible or ill-equipped to participate in successfully. The program may still lose some of the eligible people on the waiting list, especially if the pre-enrollment session involves a large number of people and therefore does not allow for any individual staff-student contact. If the pre-enrollment session is structured for short one-to-one meetings or small group discussions, the program reduces the risk of losing those prospective students who would be intimidated by participating in large groups or who would "fall through the cracks" because of a lack of personal attention.

It may also be useful to think of recruitment as something more than the recruitment of people; one might think of recruiting services—other service providers and resources needed to address the literacy problems of a given geographic region. To this end, one might consider structuring service consortiums. Programs that belong to the consortium in a given area could help each other identify opportunities for removing people from one program's waiting list and placing them in available spots in another member's program. Too, if one member program identifies students whose needs can be better served by another member program, there will be the kind of built-in referral alluded to at the end of our discussion of selective recruitment.

CONCLUSIONS AND RECOMMENDATIONS

How program practitioners describe what they do best and for whom becomes a determining factor in establishing a recruitment/public relations plan. To many, this means asking some very hard questions about who can best be served and then formulating a plan targeted to recruiting those individuals. The selection of appropriate and effective recruitment strategies is critical to this process.

Before programs select a recruitment or public relations technique, they need to examine carefully the potential of each technique for achieving the desired goals. In a large start-up campaign, multiple techniques may be used, since the goal is to build wide recognition in all sectors of the community. If the goal is solely student recruitment, one must bear in mind that adult students may not be regular readers of print material; the use of audio-visual media and various forms of personal contact will be more effective in reaching potential students. Print materials are effective, however, if the goal is tutor recruitment or community support.

Once the program has chosen the most effective vehicles for its message, it must then carefully consider what message it wants to convey. Well-targeted messages are clear about what services are being offered, who the program is for and what requirements may apply, and where the program is located. In clarifying requirements, a program may only need to make clear that the program offers no quick solutions to life's problems; programs that are specifically funded to serve only a given population may need to specify age, sex, economic, or educational status requirements. Clearly specifying the program's location guards against the problems created when the media used penetrates geographic areas from which students have no access to transportation; it is not enough simply to give a telephone contact number.

The more specific and personal the message, the more effective it will be in reaching the desired audience and reducing the number of phone calls that end in disappointment or discouragement for people who may have found it very difficult to make that phone call. Some forms of publicity may be free, but they may cost a program in human terms—damaging the program's reputation and credibility, straining the workload of program personnel, or discouraging adults very much in need of help. Poorly targeted recruitment efforts can threaten the success of the literacy program, whether it be in the form of long waiting lists created by uncontrolled PSAs or dropping enrollments due to the program's inaccurate representation of itself.

Above all, a program's recruitment and public relations efforts must be the result of a *plan*. It is necessary to distinguish between the need for an initial media blitz and the need for effective methods of ongoing recruitment and public relations. The plan may result in the establishment of a twelve-month calendar of activities that clearly focuses on both the short-term and the long-range goals and needs of the program and that carefully builds in repetition of the program's message and appropriate follow-up.

The plan should include activities specifically designed to strengthen the program's ties to its community. Community support is vital not only to recruitment and retention of students but also to the very survival of the program. Strong ties to organizations, local businesses, and other social service agencies may yield additional funding or needed support services. To build strong ties to the community requires *listening* as well as talking to community leaders and the general public. It also requires a willingness to participate as an educational partner in the community's total social service delivery system.

The recruitment and public relations plan is also inextricably linked to the plans of other program components. It must be built into the overall plan for program management, with some means of evaluating success in meeting stated objectives. Because the recruitment message is the potential students' first contact with the program, any recruitment activities become, in a very real sense, part of the program's orientation and counseling strategies. And public relations efforts can have important results for future program development. Thus, the recruitment and public relations plan cannot be developed in isolation of all other program planning; the plan must be made with the input of all who will be affected—both within the program staff and within the community.

The authors make the following four recommendations to programs that desire to build a solid recruitment and public relations plan.

(1) **Begin with the needs of the community.** A needs assessment survey or other form of early community involvement will help define recruitment strategies, program design, and ultimately the success or failure of the program in serving the needs of its constituency.

(2) **Select appropriate recruitment and public relations strategies.** Define the target audience—are you trying to reach learners, tutors, or community leaders? Define your objectives—are you recruiting for program start-up, maintenance, or expansion of services in new or existing program areas? With these definitions in mind, select those techniques that will best reach the desired target audience and meet the desired objectives.

(3) **Tailor the message.** Be simple and straightforward, keeping in mind credibility, relevance, and accessibility.

(4) **Make recruitment a dialogue between you and the community and other constituencies.** As a communications tool, public relations can enlist the support of citizens, employers, and state and federal agencies. The message must be frequent, believable, and responsive to community needs.

What follows in an adapted version of the first three months of the Lafayette (Indiana) Adult Reading Academy's twelve-month public relations calendar. It was designed to be implemented either by professional staff or by trained clerical staff. It is targeted to student and volunteer recruitment goals as well as public awareness of the program's goals and accomplishments.

EXHIBIT 3.1 Example of Guidelines for Monthly Publicity Activities

JANUARY—Capitalize on the fact that many people use the start of the new year to begin new activities.

1. *Student Recruitment*
   (a) Send out public service announcements (PSAs) to radio and television stations.
   (b) Call the local newspaper's education reporters and offer to provide information for a story on the adult basic education student.
   (c) Contact at least two local social service agencies to renew procedures for student referrals.
   (d) Send program information or announcement to newspaper columns that highlight local news and community activities.
   (e) Call local talk show talent coordinator and offer to appear on the program.
   (f) Send brief information to fast food restaurant for inclusion on food tray liners.
   (g) Take a poster and some brochures to the Food Stamp office.
   (h) Put signs on city buses—if funds are available.

2. *Volunteer Recruitment*
   (a) Results of efforts begun in December to recruit university students as volunteer tutors should now be apparent. Place follow-up calls to university and offer to provide information on volunteering and possible credit or work-study options.
   (b) Call the volunteers network and advertise specific volunteer needs or dates for training sessions.
   (c) Send information on volunteer tutor training sessions to newspaper's community activities column.

3. *General*
   (a) Call state adult education organization and offer to submit an article or news brief for the newsletter.
   (b) Begin work on mailing to area clubs, offering to give a presentation at a club meeting.
   (c) Begin preparation of the quarterly report on public relations activities.
   (d) Give talks as scheduled.

FEBRUARY—Assess program needs for volunteers and students; plan publicity efforts accordingly.

1. *Student Recruitment*
   (a) Send out PSAs to radio and television stations.
   (b) Contact at least two social service agencies to renew procedures for student referrals.
   (c) Work with current students to recruit new students.
   (d) Send information for fast food restaurant food tray liners.
   (e) Take information sheet to welfare department for insertion with monthly public assistance checks.

2. *Volunteer Recruitment*
   (a) Call the volunteer network to advertise specific needs or dates for training sessions.
   (b) Send information on tutor training sessions to newspaper's community activities column.
   (c) Send out PSAs to radio and television stations.
   (d) Mail letters to clubs and religious organizations and offer to give a presentation.

3. *General*
   (a) Begin planning for Volunteer Week (April); select nominees for Governor's Awards and other public recognition awards.
   (b) Compile list of accomplishments to date for an information packet to be sent to school board and other interested groups.
   (c) Update public relations activity files.
   (d) Give talks as scheduled.

MARCH—Student numbers usually peak this month; concentrate efforts on volunteers and community awareness.

1. *Student Recruitment*
   (a) Send out PSAs to radio and television stations.
   (b) Contact two social service agencies or local businesses to renew referral procedures. Begin analysis of effectiveness of referral network.

2. *Volunteer Recruitment*
   (a) Send program newsletter to local university dormitories.
   (b) Send PSAs to university radio station.
   (c) Follow up on letters to clubs and religious organizations.
   (d) Call the volunteer network and list current needs.
   (e) Send dates of tutor training sessions to a volunteer agency.
   (f) Call newspapers and television stations to request coverage of special program activities.
   (g) Contact selected former volunteers who might be likely to return.

3. *General*
   (a) Mail press releases to newspapers and radio and television stations—tell them about staff honors, outstanding student accomplishments, recent presentations or publications, etc.
   (b) Finalize plans for Volunteer Week.
   (c) Plan a coffee/open house for religious and social agencies and for the media as a thank you for services.
   (d) Update public relations activities file.
   (e) Prepare quarterly report on public relations activities.
   (f) Give talks as scheduled.

BIBLIOGRAPHY

Adult Recruitment Practices. Iowa City, Iowa: American College Testing Program, National Center for the Advancement of Educational Practices, 1982.

Esposito, Kathy. *"If Only They Can Be Reached . . .": Strategies for Literacy Program Recruitment*. Louisville, KY: Jefferson County Public Schools, 1983. (ED 235323)

Marchilonis, Barbara, and Niebuhr, Herman. *Broadcasting and Literacy*. Andover, MA: The Network, Inc., National Adult Literacy Project, 1985.

Rossman, M. H. "A Model to Recruit Functionally Illiterate Adults into Adult Basic Education Programs in Massachusetts." Amherst, MA: University of Massachusetts, School of Education (ED 064589)

Walden, B. L. "Recruitment and Retention of Adult Learners." Montgomery, AL: Alabama State Department of Education, Bulletin #32, 1975. (ED 112075)

Way, Max W. "Using Billboard Posters to Promote Adult Basic Education Public Awareness and Recruitment in Ohio: A Program Report." Piketon, OH: Scioto Valley Local School District, 1982. (ED 233237)

Chapter 4
Orientation

Orientation encompasses all activities undertaken by a program from the moment the student first calls or walks into the program's office to the moment that actual instruction begins. During this period, both the student and the program make an assessment of how appropriate the program is for the student. A program's plans for orientation activities will be closely linked to its recruitment strategies, its counseling services, and perhaps its diagnostic testing procedures as well.

As we noted in the last chapter, the recruitment strategy may include some effort at selecting those students who are eligible for participation in the program (assuming that the program has some eligibility requirements) or those whom the program is truly able to serve. In orientation, one major task is to address this issue squarely, matching the students' needs to the goals and services of the program and, as necessary, screening out those students whom the program cannot serve or making appropriate referrals to other programs or agencies that are better equipped to address certain needs. This may involve some level of academic or vocational counseling to help students identify which of the program's services can help them meet their goals; it may also involve diagnostic testing to clearly identify the skills each student brings to the learning process and the skills that need to be the target of instruction. It will certainly involve obtaining any necessary information for the program's records.

If the orientation activities are to truly set the stage for a successful learning experience, however, they must be more than a set of data-gathering and placement procedures. As one program director warned, once students have made the decision to seek education, they want concrete advice and information. They don't want to "sit there and stare around," and they don't want to waste their time. Students want assurance that this experience will not be like "the last time." Ideally, this means making time for some individual attention.

But even large-group orientation sessions can be designed to calm adult students' fear of failure and dispel their suspicion that their personal goals are not going to be addressed. By clearly explaining at the outset the general purpose of the program, the specific goals it is designed to help students achieve, the nature of the instructional process, and the variety of options open to the students, programs can go a long way toward allaying the students' fears and suspicions. Embedded somewhere in the orientation session must be the clear message that the program respects each individual student and is sincere in its desire to serve individual needs, valuing each student "as is" and working with that student toward some mutually agreed upon goals.

Poorly handled, the orientation process can kill whatever motivation brought the students to the program's door. By involving "streetwise" teachers, professional counselors, and even former students in the orientation process, a program can create an atmosphere that the new students will want to return to. Also since a phone call to the program's office may be the first contact a new student has with the program, the office staff also needs to understand their role in the orientation process; their contact with students is important in maintaining the adults' motivation and in creating a positive sense of the program environment.

Though counseling and diagnostic testing are often part of a program's orientation activities, we will devote Chapters 5 and 6 to a full discussion of these vital program components. Within this chapter, we will use the findings of the NALP study as the basis for discussing (1) what programs want orientation to accomplish, (2) how programs structure orientation activities to achieve those objectives, and (3) whom programs involve in the orientation process. At the end of this discussion, we will present our own conclusions and recommendations.

WHAT DO PROGRAMS WANT ORIENTATION TO DO?

Most programs see orientation as serving both a counseling function and a pre-instruction function. It is also the beginning of whatever formal recordkeeping the program needs to document the relative success of its activities and to determine the eligibility of students. Since the first step is usually to ask students to supply some personal information on a registration form, program staff need to be aware of possible student reactions to printed forms. Nonreaders will need assistance; students who ask to take the form home may well be doing so because they need assistance from someone who reads. Once they are away from the program, however, they may not return. Yet it is unwise to press students in offering assistance. It is equally unwise to reinforce any sense of shame or helplessness students may feel by merely handing them a form without any words of explanation. Students need to be told why the information is needed and how it will be used to help the program match the students' needs to an appropriate learning experience. The form must be perceived as serving the student rather than the needs of a bureaucracy. Especially in smaller or more tightly knit communities, students may also need to be assured of confidentiality. Many students will be very sensitive about having anyone know that they are involved in an adult basic education or literacy program.

Once the program has obtained the necessary background information, the orientation process must move quickly into giving direct attention to the students' goals and reasons for enrolling in the program. The quality and content of orientation activities play a significant role in sustaining the motivation of students, clarifying their needs and goals, making appropriate placements, and putting them at ease. While effective techniques may vary widely, the personal element must remain a constant if the orientation is to accomplish its goal of meshing program and learner expectations.

Many programs use the orientation sessions to help students identify the people who will play a role in their lives within the program, setting the stage for the relationships that will be developed. When the sessions are conducted by teachers and counselors, staff can establish rapport with the new students immediately. Students can begin to see staff as people who are there to help, rather than instructors whose role is to move them through a series of prescribed hoops. Directors also usually play a useful role in orientation. They can assure students that, even at the top of the program ladder, there is a person who cares about them and is willing to be a source of information and assistance.

Students interviewed during the NALP study stress the importance of personal contact in helping them make the decision to enter a program. Phrases such as "[they] made me feel at home" and "the teacher was real nice" pepper the stories of how students came to be "satisfied customers" in a program. Although information is essential, students want it to be delivered in such a way as to make them feel comfortable and valued. They also need reassurance that staff members will understand them as individuals and will help them succeed in meeting their educational goals. Using staff who are "streetwise," or familiar with the students' cultural background, lifestyles, and goals, is a helpful approach to accomplishing this objective. Former and current students, too, can be very useful in helping new students decide that the program is as right for them as it was for their peers.

Establishing the fact that program staff are there to help students achieve their educational goals is one step in sustaining student motivation. Students also need to know that the activities in which they will engage have been carefully planned to meet their needs. If the program uses individualized, competency-based, or computer-assisted instruction, the nature of these approaches needs to be explained, and the reasons for using them need to be detailed. Programs need to carefully point out the ways in which their methods differ from those of traditional education and how they have targeted activities for *adults*.

Students may bring to the program only a vague sense of what they want out of the experience, perhaps saying that they want to read better or get a job. Thus, many programs may also use orientation to help students clarify their individual learning goals, matching them to the stated goals of specific classes or services within the program. During orientation, the programmatic and instructional options open to students can be clearly spelled out. For example, information may be provided, as appropriate, in any of the following categories.

Focus of classes—e.g., adult basic education, survival skills, GED preparation, alternative or external high school diploma programs, specific academic or general interest subjects, job training and placement

Instructional modes—e.g., one-to-one tutorials, individualized learning laboratories, computer-assisted instruction, large-group or small-group classes, peer tutoring

Materials—e.g., textbooks, real-life materials, novels, films, computer software

Special program features—e.g., job seminars, workshops, guest speakers, community action training, extracurricular activities

Counseling—e.g., offered both internally and through referral—vocational, academic, personal, crisis, group and peer counseling

Support services—e.g., day care, transportation, referral to other programs and agencies

Schedules—e.g., morning, afternoon, and evening classes; open-ended drop-in learning laboratories

Locations—e.g., program sites and satellite centers (including those in community facilities) or private homes

After a verbal presentation, these options may be summarized for students in the form of a printed handout. Space may be provided on the handout for students to note their choices and the time, date, and place of their first class or tutorial session.

To further help students choose among the variety of options, programs may conduct diagnostic testing or some form of self-assessment as part of the orientation process. Here, the emphasis must be on how the test or self-assessment form is designed to help the program place the students in a class or activity that is right for them. As elsewhere, programs must remain sensitive to the anxieties of adults returning to an educational setting. We'll discuss the ways in which tests might be presented to students in Chapter 6, and a sample self-assessment form is shown in Exhibit 5.1 in Chapter 5.

Many programs use orientation sessions to clarify any rules and regulations. These run the gamut from prohibitions against the use of drugs or alcohol on the premises to procedures for changing classes or teachers that do not suit learners. If the program has any eligibility requirements, these rules will also be explained; however, care must be taken to avoid making those students who are not eligible for participation feel unwanted or as though they had failed an entrance examination. Every effort should be made to make appropriate referrals to other programs that will meet the specific needs of the ineligible students. In their discussion of the rules, some programs will also underscore the responsibility that the students will have to take in their learning experiences, especially noting the time commitment students may expect to make if they are to get the most out of the program.

If the number of students who show up for orientation is greater than the number of students the program can serve, orientation may also be used to make some kind of selection or to advise students of available pre-enrollment activities (these activities were discussed in Chapter 3).

In order to establish an operational plan for successful orientation sessions, the authors propose that programs address the following questions.

(1) How do you plan to handle the logistics of the orientation process? When will you conduct orientation? Where will you conduct orientation? Who will lead the orientation session(s)? Will you meet with students as a group or individually? For open-entry–open-exit programs, how will orientation be accomplished?

(2) What personal background information, including past school records or data from a referring agency or program, do you need from students? How will you gather this information? If you are using printed registration forms or questionnaires, what provisions have you made for providing assistance to students who have difficulty in reading or answering questions on the form?

(3) How will students be screened for eligibility? How will you determine whether such factors as the learners' family obligations and jobs will permit them to participate successfully?

(4) What will you tell students about the program's purpose and goals? Rules and regulations? Schedule? Optional program offerings and support services?

(5) How will you determine if there is a match between the learners' goals and expectations and what the program offers?

(6) How will you describe the instructional methodology of the program?

(7) If appropriate, how will you describe the role of computer software and other special learning materials? How will you describe the students' responsibilities in using these materials?

(8) What materials, if any, will students be expected to buy?

(9) In job-training programs, how will you describe the mix of work and education in the program? How will you explain the interrelationship between the two?

(10) How will you schedule any necessary diagnostic or other pre-instruction testing?

(11) To what extent can you or will you make alternative programs available to students who are not well matched to the demands of the program in which they want to enroll? How will you identify these students, and how will you make any possible referrals? Who will be responsible for counseling such students during the orientation period?

By addressing these questions, enrollees should emerge from the program's orientation sessions with an explicit understanding of:

- the requirements of the program, specifically what is expected of them in terms of attendance, performance, time commitment, etc.
- the services the program offers or can refer them to, specifically support services such as counseling, child care, and transportation
- the outcomes of participation should they successfully complete the program—including the range of activities they will be able to do differently as a result of being in the program and any certification they will receive

WHAT ORIENTATION STRATEGIES DO PROGRAMS USE?

Programs may provide students with orientation information in printed handouts, brochures, phone conversations, large-group orientation sessions (may involve former students), multi-media presentations, or individualized orientation interviews.

Print Materials

To supplement any orientation technique, programs may use print materials such as orientation booklets, information packets, catalogues of courses and services, and other easy-to-read materials. Print materials can be an expedient means of giving at least some immediate response when large numbers of potential students have been attracted by a start-up recruitment campaign. By making such materials available on a counter in the program's office, students have the option of picking up a brochure "for a friend" and studying the program's offerings in the non-threatening atmosphere of their own homes. Print materials may also serve as a screening device, diverting students who need different programs, who do not meet eligibility requirements, or who are not ready to make the necessary commitment. But as we noted in discussing the use of print in recruitment strategies, such materials are of limited value when the program's services are targeted to nonreaders.

When they are carefully planned to dovetail with the sequence of information presented verbally, print materials can be a useful way of summarizing and reinforcing what the program wants students to understand before instruction begins. When the verbal presentation is done by office staff or paraprofessionals, especially in open-entry–open-exit programs, such careful organization of information may act as a safe-guard in ensuring that all students receive the information that program leaders believe to be important. Office staff can use the brochure as a guideline and walk the students through the pages of the brochure.

Print materials can also be designed to serve other instructional or counseling functions. One postsecondary program in the Southwest has developed an information sheet that is also a simple "diagnostic test" that gives teachers clues to what further diagnostic measures to use with individual students. A correctional program gives inmates an orientation handbook that contains an interest survey to help teachers and students identify learning styles and appropriate courses of instruction. An employment and training program uses bilingual flyers and orientation booklets to bridge the language gap for limited English-speaking students.

Phone Contact

Most students make the first contact with a literacy program on the phone. For this reason, the staff person who speaks to interested clients must be sensitive to unexpressed fears and to the difficulties students may have in requesting and digesting information. Directors must take the responsibility of training receptionists to execute this difficult task well. If the first contact is not a good one, it may be the only contact the student makes.

The training office staff members may sit in on orientation sessions. Staff might also be provided with a tip sheet in question-and-answer format that reflects the questions most commonly asked by potential students. This tip sheet might also include referral information to offer the caller after the office staff member has ascertained what general program offerings or services the caller might be interested in. Training might also be extended to include some sensitivity-training sessions or some telephone role-play activities.

A phone conversation with a counselor or other trained adult education professional may produce enough information to determine a potential student's eligibility or general match-up between personal and program goals, and it should reassure potential students that further contact with the program will be beneficial. A structured telephone interview may also yield sufficient information for initial placement. The ultimate goal, however, must remain motivating the caller to come into the program's offices and then into classroom or tutorial meetings.

Group Presentations

When large numbers of students are to be enrolled in a program at the same time, orientation information and pre-instruction testing may be presented in large-group sessions. Most programs try to make individual contacts with students during these sessions, even if it is only by having staff members walk around and speak to them while they are completing forms or taking pre-tests. Care must be taken in large-group environments not to lose members of the student audience by making them feel that they are once again a faceless member of a crowd to be herded from point A to point B and then back out the door. At every point in the formal presentation, students must sense how what is being described will ultimately be directed at them as individuals and how this experience will be different from and better than their earlier experiences with the educational system.

Some programs have found unique ways to make large-group sessions more personal. At Project SCALE in Somerville, Massachusetts, the counselor leads a discussion about the importance of individual learning styles and invites students to express their concerns about returning to school. Because students are airing their concerns with a staff member with whom they will have continuing contact, they can begin to feel that the program is sincere in its stated desire to serve them as individuals. And by comparing their own personal fears and anxieties to those being expressed by other members of the group, they can begin to feel that they are not alone in feeling shame or guilt at not having the reading skills or employment skills they may have assumed everyone else has.

Other programs involve former students in part of the orientation session. As peers of the students in the audience, they can do much to demonstrate how the program is indeed designed to serve the needs of "people like us." We'll have more to say about the use of peer orientation under the section entitled "Whom Do Programs Involve in Orientation" later in this chapter.

Multi-Media Presentations

Slide-tape and, in some cases, video presentations have proven to be effective means of providing orientation information, especially in large-group sessions conducted during heavy enrollment times such as the fall or spring. Scenes of students and teachers give a realistic picture of typical activities. and the visual images reinforce information about programs options that has been provided either verbally or in print. Even the simple addition of colorful overhead transparencies to an oral presentation increases the likelihood of students' retaining information. Just as adult students do not all absorb and process instructional information through the same channels—that is, they all have different learning styles—they will not necessarily understand orientation information if it is presented in only one mode. Programs often view orientation as an extension of the instructional process and employ all the same methods of presentation in orientation that they will use in instruction.

One program on the West Coast uses slide-tape presentations with its English as a second language students. The program maintains a collection of audiotapes in a variety of languages recorded by former students; thus, new students can receive orientation information in their native language and not miss essential information because of their limited command of English. By using former students to do the recording, the program circumvents a host of possible translation problems. These students are familiar enough with the features and services of the program to describe them with appropriate idioms.

Orientation Interviews

Some programs are able to devote time to each individual student in personal interviews lasting from ten to fifteen minutes. The interviews may be with counselors or with members of the teaching staff. During the interviews, the program staff member probes to uncover the students' learning goals and strives to incorporate these goals into individualized learning plans. Students may have difficulty articulating exactly what kind of program they want or need, and these one-to-one discussions with a staff member may help students clarify their goals and choose a program that is best suited to their learning style and needs. The interviewer may explore the students' personal interests, desired practical applications of skills, and areas of perceived strength or weakness.

When programs can give such individualized attention, they can get immediate feedback from the students to ensure that the goals of orientation are indeed being achieved. Informal self-assessment questionnaires such as the one shown in Exhibit 5.1 in Chapter 5 can also structure an individualized orientation interview and provide valuable data for the students' teachers or tutors.

WHOM DO PROGRAMS INVOLVE IN ORIENTATION?

As noted earlier in this chapter, programs often use orientation sessions to introduce students to the program staff with whom they may have contact—the director, counselors, and teachers. In large-group presentations, staff may be assembled as a panel with each staff member explaining his or her role within the program. One-to-one orientation interviews may be conducted by counselors or teachers. Some programs also involve students who have been in the program for a period of time or who have successfully completed the program.

Program Staff

Whether staff make presentations in front of large or small groups or in individualized sessions with students, they should be prepared for their role through an in-service training session. Such a session might ask staff members to address the following questions.

(1) Do I demonstrate empathy for and sensitivity to adult students in a natural and convincing way? There is a difference between empathy and sympathy; students should in no way feel that staff do not respect and value them as human beings just because they lack certain skills.

(2) Do I show a recognition of and respect for community values and cultural mores? This is especially important in working with multi-cultural groups such as those in English as a second language programs.

(3) Am I knowledgeable enough about all phases of program activities to select appropriate and realistic options for students? Am I prepared to field any questions students may have about the program's offerings and support services?

(4) Do I possess strong listening skills? Do I allow students to do some of the talking so that I can avoid making assumptions about what the students want and need?

(5) Will I be alert to patterns in student responses that suggest a need for program modifications and additions? Do I have some way of recording and reporting such information to the program director or others involved in future planning and program evaluation?

Those staff members who can answer yes to all of the foregoing questions will have little or no trouble helping the program achieve the objectives of its orientation sessions.

Current and Former Students

Many programs have begun to use the new students' peers as part of large-group presentations or as part of small-group "rap sessions." Former students share many of the same family or employment problems as the new students and can explain how they dealt with the problems and successfully completed the program. Their personal accounts are real and believable and give new students confidence in the claims of program staff. In their presentations, current and former students can focus on how the program has helped or is helping them achieve their personal, academic, and vocational goals. By carefully selecting the students who will make presentations, the orientation planner can address the variety of viewpoints, concerns, anxieties, and goals that may exist in the audience of new students.

CONCLUSIONS AND RECOMMENDATIONS

A program's orientation activities are designed to set the stage for successful learning experiences by providing students with accurate information about the program's offerings and services and reassuring them that this experience is designed to be different from their past experiences in the traditional educational system.

The activities may be structured in a variety of ways depending on the number of students to be enrolled and the amount of time staff can invest. Ideally, programs will build in some time for one-to-one meetings with students to ensure that best possible match between student and program goals and to clearly demonstrate the program's genuine interest in the success of each individual student. Programs also do well to back up verbal presentations of information with printed handouts and brochures and with multi-media presentations; the use of a number of ways of conveying information increases the likelihood that students will absorb and retain that information.

Everyone with whom the student will come in contact has a role in orientation, including office staff who answer telephone inquiries or obtain information on registration forms. Because the quality of this staff-student contact can sustain or destroy a prospective student's motivation for joining the program, all staff need some form of in-service training that provides detailed information both about the program and its procedures and about the nature of the students the program serves. Giving new students an opportunity to talk to former students can further enhance the staff's efforts to convince prospective students that the program has been carefully designed to serve their needs.

The authors make the following four recommendations to programs that are designing or reviewing their orientation activities.

(1) **Be sensitive to the affective needs of students.** Remember that the students' past educational experiences have not been positive; they will undoubtedly be skeptical or anxiety-ridden during their first contacts with the program. Orientation must offer students psychological reassurance and initiate the process of building student confidence in and rapport with staff. Also, it must demonstrate the value the program places on what the students already know and can do.

(2) **Organize your information needs.** Design easy-to-complete forms and select testing instruments appropriate to the student population. Provide a mechanism for student goal setting. Think ahead to follow-up and evaluation activities, and make sure that the information you gather during orientation is the information you will need at these later points in the program cycle. However, be careful not to intimidate students by requesting information that you do not need or that would be more appropriately collected at a later time.

(3) **Tailor sessions to the program's role in the community.** Demonstrate to prospective students how you have built the program's services on a clear understanding of the education, employment opportunities, and quality of life of the individuals living in the community. Be prepared to change the agenda as changes occur in the community.

(4) **Be alert to changing needs and goals of students.** Build in a means of *listening* to students as well as talking to them. Use the information you receive from students to evaluate how well matched your program's services are to the needs of individual students. Well-developed orientation activities can prevent teachers from wasting the students' time when they are not eligible or otherwise prepared to complete the program successfully. Information gathered during orientation may also be helpful in planning for future program modifications or additional services.

Chapter 5
Counseling

Counseling is the process programs use to support students in their attempts to identify and achieve their personal, academic, and vocational goals. A blend of counseling and instruction enables the program to work with the student as a whole person— addressing the students' psychological or affective needs in order to facilitate their attainment of academic or vocational skill objectives. The importance of counseling for adults who may feel trapped outside the mainstream of society cannot be underestimated. Indeed, practitioners across all sectors in the NALP study have stated that instruction and learning are hampered by the students' lack of confidence, difficult life situations, and inadequate study skills. Some practitioners believe that learning cannot even take place until the overload of personal problems and some of the resulting psychological blocks to learning are addressed. This does not mean that the program itself provides true therapeutic services—although many programs do employ certified counselors. Students with serious problems, such as alcoholism or drug abuse, must be referred to an appropriate social service or mental health agency. However, programs do build strategies aimed at strengthening the students' self-concepts, buttressing their morale and motivation, and drawing them out of any feelings of isolation or alienation.

Counseling may begin during student orientation; in fact, as described in the preceding chapter, orientation is a form of counseling. This first stage of counseling is usually aimed at helping students identify or clarify their goals and match those goals to the goals of specific instructional programs. Goal clarification may grow out of a discussion of the results of diagnostic testing or a discussion of the information students have provided on registration or self-assessment forms. From the beginning, students need a realistic picture of what the program can do for them and what they must do to derive the full benefit from participation in the program. If they are inadequately prepared or unable to assume the responsibilities that participation in the program may entail, students may be counseled not to enter the program and may be referred instead to another agency or program that can better serve their needs.

It is important to remember that counseling a student out of participation need not be a harsh measure or an avenue of last resort. Effective counseling can work to assure such students that the reason for the suggestion is to help them find the conditions or environment in which they will experience success. Enrolling students in a program that is inappropriate or for which they are unprepared paves the way for another experience at failure in an educational setting. Ideally, the counselor would help such students determine what is needed to help them successfully meet their goals and would be able to refer such students to another more appropriate program.

Because successful goal attainment is the object of ongoing instruction, the support service of counseling must also be ongoing and directly tied to the instructional process.

Thus, counseling may be offered as part of whatever assessment techniques the program uses. Discussions at these points are usually focused on how well the students are progressing, encouraging them to continue and boosting their morale by clearly demonstrating how far they have advanced toward their ultimate goals. For those who have been uncomfortable or unsuccessful, alternative instructional strategies or materials may be suggested. Such ongoing counseling support is vital to retaining students in the program. Automatic promotion from one step to the next in the instructional process smacks of the traditional educational system that failed to meet the students' needs earlier in life. Without some kind of reassurance that real achievement is occurring and some means for making adjustments in the methods or materials the program uses, students may well become discouraged or disaffected and leave the program.

Once students have come to the end of the program's instructional cycle, additional counseling support may be offered in the form of one-to-one exit interviews or a wrap-up class session. In employment and training programs, part of the focus of an exit interview may be on job placement. In other programs, part of the discussion may involve suggestions for future training and ways of maintaining the skills that have been learned. Programs that provide post-instruction counseling recognize that although students have acquired new skills through the program, their life situations may not have changed radically. They need to review their accomplishments and be encouraged to use their new skills in their jobs, homes, and communities. Beyond their value to the students, exit interviews can be useful in the program's efforts to evaluate the relative effectiveness of the program from the perspective of the students.

The counseling support offered before, during, or after instruction is generally a responsibility shared by counselors and teachers, though programs without full-time counselors will necessarily rely heavily on the teaching staff. When the counseling function falls to teaching or administrative staff, programs must make some provision to ensure that such staff are sufficiently prepared to deal with counseling issues as well as making some provision for outside support services. As in orientation, professional staff may involve current or former students as part of the counseling effort.

Within this chapter, we will examine the counseling functions that occur at various points during the instructional process and the roles played by teachers, counselors, the students' peers, and outside agencies.

WHAT DO PROGRAMS WANT COUNSELING TO DO?

As we have described it, counseling in most literacy programs is broadly defined to include any activity designed to provide advice or psychological support to students from the beginning to the end of the instructional cycle (and possibly beyond if the program engages in follow-up studies). Internal counseling activities are generally linked to (1) pre-instruction activities of orientation, diagnostic testing, and placement; (2) ongoing assessment; and (3) final evaluation and follow-up. In the following pages, we will examine each of these three phases of counseling.

Pre-Instruction Activities and Counseling

The counseling that programs do before students begin their instructional program may take many forms. Orientation sessions (discussed in Chapter 4) can prepare students for a successful learning experience by carefully matching student and program goals and clearly explaining the way the program works. One-to-one orientation interviews may explore issues beyond academic or vocational goals, helping program staff identify those students who might need to be referred to other agencies or programs for primary or support services. Diagnostic testing procedures (discussed in detail in Chapter 6) can further aid programs in tailoring instruction to the individual skill needs of the students.

Both orientation and diagnostic testing can serve a placement function, but there is some danger in exclusively defining appropriate educational programs and materials in the educators' terms. Students, too, have much to say about what and how they wish to learn, and some programs give students an opportunity to express those desires and opinions. Student-generated information may be obtained by using a self-assessment form; literate students may fill out the form independently, and nonliterate students may provide answers to the questions on the form in an oral interview. Exhibit 5.1 is a sample student self-assessment questionnaire that has been adapted from one used by Jobs for Youth, a jobs training program for out-of-school youth operating in Boston, Massachusetts. To make the form appear nonthreatening and informal, the program has given the form the title "Planning Your Learning" and has deliberately used very simple language.

EXHIBIT 5.1 Student Self-Assessment Questionnaire

(1) What kinds of things would you like to learn in this program?

(2) What skills do you already have? (What do you already know how to do?)

(3) What skills would you like to get better at?

(4) What did you most like learning about in school?

(5) What did you least like learning about in school?

(6) What subjects were hardest for you in school? What was hard about each one?

(7) What are the best ways for you to learn something? (The list below tells some ways a person can learn. Read each thing in the list, and tell us if you like to learn that way. Put a √ under "a lot" if you really like to learn new things that

way. Put a √ under "some" if it would be OK to learn new things that way. Put a √ under "not at all" if you don't like to learn that way.)

A Lot   Some   Not at All

____   ____   ____   working with my hands
____   ____   ____   learning in a group
____   ____   ____   listening to someone explain something
____   ____   ____   reading by myself
____   ____   ____   learning from TV programs
____   ____   ____   seeing something for myself rather than being told about it
____   ____   ____   using a computer to learn
____   ____   ____   seeing films or videotapes
____   ____   ____   listening to a speech
____   ____   ____   listening and taking notes
____   ____   ____   doing work sheets
____   ____   ____   having someone give me examples
____   ____   ____   having someone show me how to do something
____   ____   ____   doing something over and over until I get it
____   ____   ____   practicing something by myself
____   ____   ____   working with another student
____   ____   ____   doing homework
____   ____   ____   explaining something to someone who doesn't know it
____   ____   ____   asking questions
____   ____   ____   listening to a teacher lecturing
____   ____   ____   learning under pressure when there is a deadline
____   ____   ____   memorizing
____   ____   ____   learning on my own—by myself

(8) Do you like to study when
     (Check only the ones that are true for you.)

____   it's quiet
____   there is music in the background
____   other people are around but they are quiet
____   other people are around and they are talking
____   you are by yourself
____   other _____

(9) Do you want your work checked by your teacher right after you do it? (Check one.)

____   yes
____   it doesn't matter

(10) When do you best understand directions? (Check one.)

    _____ when you are <u>told</u> what they are
    _____ when you <u>read</u> them by yourself
    _____ it doesn't matter
    _____ it depends on _____

(11) Do you read just for fun? (Check one.)

    _____ yes
    _____ no

(12) What kinds of things do you read? (Check all that are true for you.)

    _____ magazines
    _____ newspapers
    _____ books
    _____ comics/cartoons
    _____ other _____

(13) If you work, do you read on your job? (Check one.)

    _____ yes
    _____ no
If yes, what do you read? _____

(14) How often do you read? (Check one.)

    _____ every day
    _____ two or three times a week
    _____ once a week
    _____ hardly ever
    _____ never

(15) How long can you read before you get tired? (Check one.)

    _____ 5 minutes   _____ 45 minutes   _____ longer: _____
    _____ 10 minutes   _____ 1 hour
    _____ 30 minutes   _____ 2 hours

(16) Do you like to take tests? (Check one.)

    _____ yes Why? _____
    _____ no Why? _____
    _____ I don't care. Why? _____

(17) When you do not understand something, is it
(Check one.)

_____ easy for you to ask questions?
_____ hard for you to ask questions?
Tell why: _____

(18) Did you like answering this questionnaire? (Check one.)

_____ not really
_____ yes

(19) Do you think you learned anything about yourself as a learner by doing it?
(Check one.)

_____ not really
_____ yes

Once students have been placed in a program that is appropriate to their needs and learning styles, there is at least one other pre-instruction counseling function that programs may provide. Because students have been out of school for a period of time, they may need to be reoriented to the kinds of study skills that will enable them to get the most out of the classes, print materials, and individualized tutoring sessions. However, the kinds of study skills that programs communicate to adult students must take into account the fact that many students work and many live in an environment that is not conducive to home study. The only study time the students may have is the time that they spend in the program's classrooms, and even that time may not always find students well rested and free enough of other worries to give their full concentration to instructional activities. Therefore, a counseling session that helps students with strategies to manage their study/learning time effectively may be important for adult "second chance" learners with family, job, and community responsibilities.

Ongoing Assessment and Counseling

It is unwise to assume that progress will automatically follow once students have begun the instructional program. Many students may be unused to voicing their objections to people they perceive to be in positions of authority, and they may drop out of the program rather than complain that they do not understand the material or are uncomfortable with the way it is taught. If students are not aware that adjustments can be made in the pace or kind of instruction, they may assume that they must either accept what they are being given or leave the program. Students who are bored or uncomfortable may assume that is the way it is supposed to be; they will believe that something is wrong with them, not that something may be wrong with the material or the instructional methodology.

It is important, then, to have counselors, teachers, or others initiate informal as well as formal counseling opportunities in which the learners' views on the program and their progress in it are openly solicited. Until the learners are comfortable with program staff and the program requirements, counselors may need to be more than simply available to students; they may need to be "pro-active" and reach out to them.

There are several points in the instructional process that are also excellent opportunities to check the emotional temperatures of the students. For example, programs often schedule frequent informal or formal assessment tests to ensure that students are indeed mastering the objectives of the instructional program. (These assessment techniques are discussed in detail in Chapter 6.) Teachers can discuss assessment test results, and by listening closely and demonstrating a willingness to hear objections, teachers can elicit information useful in making adjustments for students who are not mastering the instructional objectives. However, even students who *are* successful in mastering the objectives set by the program may have lost sight of the relationship between the steps they have taken and their ultimate goals; they may be vaguely pleased that they have done what they were asked to do, but they are not necessarily interested in or challenged by what they've been doing. Using assessment sessions as counseling opportunities by connecting learning successes to ultimate goals is an excellent way of reinforcing instructional gains and reaffirming the students' goals.

Tying some form of counseling to the program's assessment techniques is also one way of gauging the effectiveness of the program in meeting individual student needs. To further enhance this technique, programs should build and share the total instructional plan with students. If the plan is presented to students in the form of a printed record sheet, they can chart their own progress and see how each step relates to their ultimate goal. Sections for student and teacher comments, including changes in the plan, provide a means of keeping the students actively involved in structuring their individualized instructional program. Exhibit 5.2 is adapted from a form used by a program that has an eight-week instructional cycle with three scheduled counseling interviews.

EXHIBIT 5.2 Student Progress Summary Document

Name: _____   Instructor: _____

Age: _____   Counselor: _____

Home telephone: _____   Work telephone: _____

Dates for goal-setting sessions:

Entry interview: _____

Midpoint interview: _____

Exit interview: _____

Diagnostic summary:

Diagnostic instrument used: _____

Diagnostic test results: _____

Reading grade level: _____

Grades completed in school: _____

Instructional plan:

Segment 1 (weeks 1–3)

Goals:

Skill objectives to be achieved (describe instructional materials to be used):

Skill objectives mastered (describe how mastery was demonstrated and give dates):

Comments:

Instructor:

Student:

Segment 2 (weeks 4–6)

Goals:

Skill objectives to be achieved (describe instructional materials to be used):

Skill objectives mastered (describe how mastery was demonstrated and give dates):

Comments:

Instructor:

Student:

Segment 3 (weeks 7–8)

Goals:

Skill objectives to be achieved (describe instructional materials to be used):

Skill objectives mastered (describe how mastery was demonstrated and give dates):

Comments:

Instructor:

Student:

Summary evaluation at end of program

Evaluation instrument used: _____

Evaluation test results: _____

Reading grade level: _____

Achievement of goals and skill objectives:

Special achievements:

Directions for the future:

The program that uses the form shown in Exhibit 5.2 employs counselors as well as teachers; the form represents one way in which both counseling and teaching staffs can share the same information about individual students and thus work in a true partnership to serve the personal, academic, and vocational needs of the students.

What is clear from this and similar forms found in literacy programs is that teachers are regularly engaged in providing a kind of counseling whenever they invite their students to participate actively in planning an individualized instructional program and evaluating its effectiveness. Therefore, it follows that they should receive some form of training in effective counseling and interpersonal techniques so that they can accomplish these tasks successfully.

Program Exit and Counseling

As noted in Chapter 1 and throughout the text, a central conclusion of the NALP study is that the most effective programs were those that created an educational system that wove all the components of the program into a coherent and integrated design and that located this educational system within the context of a community's overall social service delivery system. Inherent in this concept of effective programs is the notion that these programs can act as brokers, referring their participants to other partners in the system, including community colleges, job training and job placement services, and so on. Also inherent in this concept is the notion that the students' participation in one program is only part of what may be a lifelong learning process.

Thus, as students complete their instructional programs, they may meet with counselors or teachers to review what has happened and to explore what could happen in the future. By using a form such as the one shown in Exhibit 5.2, students can compare the results of their diagnostic tests to the results of their final evaluation tests and cast a backward glance over the skill objectives they have mastered and the general goals they have achieved. At this point, students might be challenged to take their education a step further through other services the literacy program provides or in training programs offered by other agencies or educational institutions with which the literacy program is linked.

In employment and training programs, students may be referred to an employer or promoted within their current places of employment based on satisfactory completion of the program, or they may be given advice on how to go about finding employment using the skills they have learned in the program.

For students who will have no further contact with the literacy program or other educational institutions, there are at least two other kinds of counseling that programs may offer. Students may need advice on how to maintain their skills, and they may need advice on how to cope with possible conflicts in the environment in which they live and work. Programs know from learning theory research and personal experience that skills once learned will be forgotten over time—at least to some degree—if they are not used regularly. Thus, they may discuss with students the opportunities that exist for continuing skill practice; this may be as simple as suggesting that students regularly read the newspaper, subscribe to a magazine, join a book club, or join a religious study group.

From the beginning of the program, some students may have experienced conflicts with their spouses, family members, or peers in their neighborhoods or workplaces, and they have looked to their teachers and fellow students for support in their quest for self-improvement. Once they are out of the program, the support network may disappear. It took great courage for the students to make changes in their lives, and it will take courage to maintain those changes in the face of such comments as "Who do you think you are?" and "I wish you'd never gone to that school." Students may feel very much alone after they leave the program, feeling outside their former environment yet not a part of a new one. Some programs tackle these issues in one-to-one exit interviews or in group "rap sessions" among departing students and other former students. Other programs offer continuing support on a follow-up basis to those that leave the program.

WHOM DO PROGRAMS INVOLVE IN COUNSELING?

The first step in building a counseling plan is to determine what counseling support the program wants or is able to give the students; the second step is to determine who is available to deliver that support. Depending on the staffing pattern of the program and the specific aspects of counseling one is talking about, students may derive counseling support from their teachers, on-site counselors, peers, or personnel in an outside agency. Economic or other constraints may make it impossible to structure a "best of all possible worlds" plan complete with certified counselors who have adult education experience. Programs may therefore need to consider what in-service training they need to supply to equip the available people to do an effective job, as well as to identify agencies that can supply services on a referral basis. Programs also must evaluate the kind of time involved in delivering counseling support from the perspectives of both the student and the program staff. Students should not be shortchanged on counseling support any more than they should be shortchanged on instruction, and program staff need ways of managing the multiple roles they may be asked to perform.

Within this section, we will examine how programs have answered the question of who should or can deliver counseling support as well as what programs must consider when limited human and financial resources necessitate the compounding of staff duties.

The Role of Teaching Staff

Although teachers are seldom formally trained in counseling skills, they occupy the "front line"—they are the people who have the most frequent contact and the closest relationship with the students. Students thus naturally come to their teachers with a host of personal and domestic crises as well as problems related to the instructional program. Some teachers take pride in developing close personal relationships with their students, while others believe that giving advice or guidance in personal matters should be left to highly skilled professional counselors.

The teachers' primary role is to facilitate the students' acquisition of the target skills of the program, and this role is a demanding one—especially in large programs where individual teachers may be responsible for fifty to one hundred students. In order to help students acquire skills, however, teachers will necessarily provide some degree of counseling when they share and act on the results of diagnostic tests, assessment measures, and final evaluative tests. Forms such as the one shown in Exhibit 5.2 or those shown in Chapter 7 ("Instructional Methods and Materials") are a convenient means of managing the delivery of instructional counseling; teachers can set aside time for such counseling as part of their routine, and the program developer can explain to the teachers what minimum counseling support the teachers are expected to provide.

Whether or not programs employ professional counselors, teachers must be able to identify the need for counseling services beyond those they are equipped to provide and must have enough skill to guide students in the direction of professional help. In-service training sessions can offer teachers profiles of possible counseling problems, and presentations by on-site counselors or personnel from outside agencies can make teachers aware of the options that are open to them. During these training sessions, programs should make clear to teachers just how much responsibility they are expected to take on. Because the role of teachers is to facilitate instruction, it is important that they not be overburdened to the point at which instructional time is seriously curtailed.

The Role of Counseling Staff

More than half of the programs visited in the course of the NALP study employ full-time counselors on staff. However, interviews with these counselors revealed that a major portion of their time is consumed with intake procedures (including initiation and maintenance of formal records), orientation activities, and testing responsibilities rather than direct counseling services. Program directors may have no choice but to rely on counselors to perform administrative duties. They may regard counselors as being in the best position to interpret the data gathered from tests and teachers and to make recommendations for the general good of the program, and they may not have a large enough budget to enable them to free counselors from these tasks. Directors recognize that the counselors' time is finite and that time devoted to general administrative duties will limit the counselors' ability to respond to the demand for individualized academic, personal, crisis, and vocational counseling. The challenge is to find ways to tap the counselors' expertise for the benefit of individual students without sacrificing services that the program as a whole may need.

Counselors may have the opportunity to offer advice and support to students as they interpret test scores and recommend class placement. The advice may be communicated directly in one-to-one interviews, or more indirectly through comments on a printed form. Because counselors can anticipate some of the adjustments adults need to make with regard to work, family, and friends, they are the ideal people to address these issues in the orientation session. Their training will also enable them to make comments designed to help students overcome possible anxiety, low self-esteem, a sense of failure, or a lack of confidence.

Beyond giving advice to individuals or groups of students, counselors may be called upon to share their expertise with teachers through in-service training sessions so that teachers can provide some of the direct services that the counselors do not have time to give. They may also conduct sensitivity-training sessions for all program staff who come in contact with the students.

One volunteer effort in Florida, Community Volunteerism sponsored by the School Board of Levy County, has taken a novel approach to supporting learners in a traditional adult basic education program. Volunteers are recruited and trained by professional counselors to provide one-to-one counseling and social support to program participants. Essentially, what has been created is a "buddy system" that ensures that learners have access to the individualized attention of another person who is committed to helping make this educational experience a success.

The Role of the Students' Family and Peers

A number of programs have successfully implemented peer counseling or buddy systems. Such strategies are inexpensive, and they may reduce the amount of time teachers or counselors would otherwise need to devote to an advisor's role. Perhaps their chief value lies in allowing students to share experiences and learn that their problems, though overwhelming at times, are not unique. When other adults reveal how they solved particular problems, all participants derive invaluable personal support while developing critical problem-solving skills. Participating in peer groups also enables students to form friendships that reduce the feeling of isolation and provide a network of support outside the program.

Students can be brought together with their peers in any number of ways. One program on the West Coast organizes two-week to three-week camps to foster group activity and support. Many programs formulate small-group activities as part of their instructional strategy. Such activities might be directly aimed at counseling issues or at such basic survival skills as banking, health care, and legal rights. The teacher's role in such sessions is that of a facilitator or moderator with the real learning proceeding from group problem solving.

Students can also derive support from their spouses, families, or others close to them. If these people reinforce the importance and value students place on their educational attainment, they will provide students with added motivation to accomplish their goals. One way programs may involve these "significant others" in the learning process is to hold an open house, inviting students to bring guests to see the program and to discuss the goals of the program, the instructional philosophy, and the outcomes for the learners. Students might also be encouraged to talk with those close to them about their learning experience or, should they choose, to ask them for help in completing assignments or learning tasks.

The Role of Outside Agencies

Most literacy programs recognize that they cannot provide all the services that students are likely to need. Therefore, they must maintain a strong referral network composed of community, social service, and mental health agencies. These organizations can provide the necessary backup for students who need long-term help, therapy, or other forms of social and financial support. Programs may also gather information about such sources of additional help as crisis hotlines and shelters and make it readily available to students so that the students themselves can take the initiative to seek additional help when they feel a need for it—whether they feel that need while they are still in the program or after they have left it.

Some programs forge a true partnership with an outside agency, such as the state rehabilitation agency, to provide a combination of services for particular target populations. For example, the students of one youth program in the NALP study live together in a group home; the counselor and head teacher in the program find it wise to meet weekly with the social workers who supervise the program's students in the group home.

Whether programs work in true partnerships or merely through referrals, it is important for programs to clarify what counseling services they can provide themselves and to make sure that other agencies within the program's network are equally clear about what the program can do and is doing on a regular basis. When students are referred to the program from another agency in the network, that agency should not assume that the student is receiving counseling support that the program is not providing or cannot provide. Similarly, when the program refers students to an outside agency, the program should be well informed about what services that agency is capable of providing. If the outside agency's activities have a bearing on the student's instructional program, information must flow freely between the program and the outside agency.

CONCLUSIONS AND RECOMMENDATIONS

There is general agreement among literacy practitioners that adult students require counseling support if they are to be successful in achieving their personal, academic, and vocational goals. And practitioners seem to agree that the counseling function is not limited to any single group of people within the program. Teachers, support staff, fellow students, and trained counselors all have an important part to play in helping students succeed. And student success cannot be defined exclusively in terms of the achievement of the specific skill objectives set forth in an academic or job-training program; success also means enabling students to assimilate and use skills within the larger context of their lives.

The question is thus not whether to build a counseling plan but how best to structure that plan using available human and financial resources. Literacy programs must make an honest assessment of the talents of teachers and counselors so that students—the focus of the program—are well served. They must match those talents to the counseling services they can anticipate a need for, delegating responsibility to those best able to shoulder it. In the absence of trained personnel, programs may need to provide training or seek outside services. Programs can anticipate that the closeness of the student-teacher relationship will quite naturally result in students' coming to their teachers with counseling problems, and they may thus assume that teachers will need in-service training in counseling and ready access to sources of counseling support.

Once programs have assessed what counseling services may be needed and who is best able to provide those services, they must consider the issues of time management and information sharing. Staff may find it difficult to provide counseling in addition to their other duties, and they will need a system to help them manage their time efficiently. Such a system will also become essential when counseling becomes a shared responsibility among teachers, on-site counselors, and personnel in outside agencies; each provider needs to know what the others are doing or have done if the students are to derive the benefit of a well-rounded program aimed at integrating academic and vocational skills within the context of their lives.

The authors make the following four recommendations to programs building or reviewing their counseling plan.

(1) **Develop a system for identifying the counseling needs of individual students.** Before, during, and even after the instructional program, students should be given the opportunity to express their counseling needs. Such student-generated information might be obtained through the use of self-assessment questionnaires or through one-to-one counseling interviews.

(2) **Develop a system for responding to the counseling needs of individual students.** Anticipate what counseling needs may surface, and make it clear to all program staff where appropriate help can be found. Tap the talents of those individuals best suited to addressing given counseling needs—teachers, tutors, on-site counselors, and personnel in outside community, social service, rehabilitation, and mental health agencies. Devise printed forms that ensure that staff are routinely eliciting and responding to the students' counseling needs and that provide a means of sharing information among all those who work with the students.

(3) **Explore methods of using peer support.** Peer counseling, buddy systems, class discussions, and small-group activities are not costly or complex, but they help students build an ongoing support network and develop critical problem-solving skills.

(4) **Provide in-service training in counseling techniques for all program staff.** Teachers, tutors, and support staff need some degree of training in effective counseling techniques whether or not they are responsible for delivering the primary counseling support. At a minimum, they need to be able to identify the characteristics of adult learners and the behaviors that suggest a need for some form of counseling. They need strategies for responding appropriately and quickly to the students' problems, whether this means addressing the problem themselves or sensitively guiding the students in the direction of other sources of help. Even if teachers are never confronted with serious counseling problems, their students will derive a greater benefit if instruction is delivered with an awareness of psychological or environmental barriers to learning.

BIBLIOGRAPHY

Ironside, Diana J. *Trends in Counseling and Information Services for the Adult Learner*. Toronto: Ontario Institute for Studies in Education, 1977.

Prosen, Sue. "Counseling Services for Illiterate Adults." Paper presented at the Annual Convention of the American Personnel and Guidance Association, March 1983. (ED 235430)

Chapter 6
Diagnostic Testing
and Assessment

There are two general reasons that literacy programs use some form of testing: (1) to diagnose the students' instructional needs or current levels of performance in an attempt to ensure proper placement in an appropriate class or text or to determine eligibility for enrollment in the program, and (2) to assess the students' levels of mastery of the objectives of the instructional program, whether those objectives are stated in terms of specific skills or more general gains in reading grade level. A comparison of diagnostic and assessment test results also helps programs demonstrate to funding agencies that students have derived some benefit from participation in the program.

In the formulation of the operational plan of a program, the choice of diagnostic and assessment procedures really involves consideration of two separate and distinct program components. The one component, diagnosis, takes place prior to the delivery of instruction and, as such, may be closely tied to registration, orientation, and counseling activities. At their best, diagnostic procedures feed into the instructional process, providing teachers, counselors, and students with information necessary for individualized instructional plans.

Assessment, on the other hand, takes place after the student has undertaken at least some instructional activities and is therefore closely tied to the overall evaluation activities that are part of program management. At their best, assessment procedures provide a means of monitoring student progress, providing students with essential feedback, and ultimately measuring the success of the program in achieving its stated goals.

Both components grow out of the design of the instructional process, and the methods a program selects will be based on the stated goals and objectives of the program. Despite the separateness of the two components in terms of when and why they come into play, the issues that surround the process of selecting appropriate testing procedures for both diagnosis and assessment are so similar that we have combined the discussion of testing procedures in general into a single chapter.

The use of tests has always been a given in educational programs. After all, tests are supposed to tell us what the student knows and does not know, as well as how to target instruction for the remediation of any skill deficiencies the student demonstrates. It is therefore not surprising that all the programs in the NALP study use some kind of diagnostic test. Indeed, almost one-third of the 225 programs queried rank diagnosis as the most important component of their program. The diagnostic tests used are quite commonly standardized tests developed by commercial test developers; however, with the exception of GED preparation programs, ongoing assessment during the instructional cycle tends to be accomplished through less formal testing procedures.

Despite this universal use of tests for both diagnosis and assessment, program directors and teachers alike expressed ambivalence about the virtues of many of the tests they currently administer. Tests that yield reading grade level scores may or may not be viewed as helpful in selecting materials written at an appropriate level of difficulty, but no instructors believe that such results can tell them anything about what specific skills they should include in a student's instructional program. Instructors seem to have an intuitive sense that some tests, especially standardized achievement tests, do not really measure the instructional goals they set with students. And, given that inability to tie achievement test scores to the students' educational goals, instructors often view the feedback that can be given to students as too abstract to be meaningful.

Beyond the instructors' reluctance to confront students with abstract scores is their reluctance to expose students to an experience that produces high levels of anxiety. Adult students almost certainly view tests with some degree of fear; after all, the test results they received in their past educational experiences often served to confirm their sense of failure. There is also a widely held belief among instructors that adult students simply don't test well and that means other than paper-and-pencil tests provide much more valid and reliable measures of the students' abilities. Instructors are often frustrated when they know students have made progress but cannot demonstrate that fact with the results from the assessment test instrument that they are required to use to measure achievement. Instructors are further frustrated when the program schedule dictates the administration of tests with such frequency that they know true progress cannot really have been made, let alone measured. This frustration is counterbalanced by the instructors' need to know that they are not leaving students behind and to find out whether adjustments need to be made in the rate of progression or level of difficulty of the skill instruction.

Ultimately, then, programs *do* want diagnostic and assessment measures, but opinions vary as to which kinds of tests wil! serve the intended purposes. Commercial test developers are viewed with a high degree of suspicion. Program staff wonder how statisticians or publishers, not classroom teachers, can design and norm tests for a population with which they have had little or no direct contact. On what basis do they write the questions and decide if they are appropriate for adult students? And how can programs evaluate the claims made by the developers? The technical manuals that accompany commercial tests often do little to clarify what the tests are designed to measure, how well the tests do what they claim to do, and how results are to be interpreted; the jargon used in the technical manuals is largely incomprehensible to practitioners in the classroom.

Within this chapter, we will attempt to demystify the process of test selection and to provide guidance in evaluating which of the possible procedures is most appropriate to the needs of their students and the goals of their program. We will begin by defining the terms used to describe tests. Next, we'll examine what programs want tests to do and which tests programs use to meet those objectives. We'll then explore the problems and issues that surround testing and suggest some ways of circumventing problems.

Finally, we'll offer our own conclusions and recommendations for your consideration. At the end of the chapter, you'll find a reference list of commercially available tests and a bibliography for further study of testing and measurement issues.

DEFINITION OF TERMS

Exhibit 6.1 is a reference guide to the terms used in this chapter. Some words used to describe tests—especially *reliability* and *validity*—have very specific meanings when applied to tests; these meanings may be very different from their meanings in more general contexts. Interviews conducted during the NALP study revealed that not all programs mean the same thing when they use such terms as *diagnostic test* or *standardized*. To ensure that you understand the intended meanings of the terms used in this chapter, read through the list and note any terms that we define differently than you do. This should also help programs define more precisely what kinds of tests they really want.

EXHIBIT 6.1 Reference List of Terms Used to Describe Tests

Formal Testing—Testing done at set times, under prescribed conditions, and with set procedures for administration, scoring, and interpretation of results. Such tests are usually but not always commercially prepared paper-and-pencil tests.

Informal Testing—Testing done at the discretion of the teacher and designed to monitor student progress or assess student needs through direct observation. Usually done to determine necessary adjustments in the instructional process. Such tests are often non-commercial, teacher-developed tests, though programs may set procedures for how and when informal tests are given.

Norm-Referenced Tests—Tests that compare the general performance of students to the general performance of some norming group. The Tests of General Educational Development (or GED) represent one well-known norm-referenced test battery; the adult students' scores are derived based on the scores achieved by a norming group of high school seniors—thus, one can describe the level of performance of the adult student on the GED in terms of the performance one would expect of a "typical" high school senior. Norm-referenced tests are not designed to yield data on the students' ability to perform specific skill objectives; they are intended only to describe the students' level of achievement relative to some norming group. In using norm-referenced tests, it is helpful to know who was in the norming group as well as when the norming was done; some tests in use in adult education were normed against a population of children, and some might well be regarded as dated.

Criterion-Referenced Tests—Tests designed to measure students' ability to perform specifically stated skill objectives. Mastery level of the skill objectives is described in terms of some absolute standard—the number of items a student must answer correctly on each given skill objective. For example, a student who correctly answers three out of five questions that involve a given skill may be described as having demonstrated mastery of that skill. The data obtained from criterion-referenced tests can be extremely helpful in determining whether a student has the prerequisite skills needed for a given program as well as in planning an individualized course of study targeted at only those skills over which students have not demonstrated mastery.

Achievement Tests—Tests that measure students' degree of knowledge or skills as opposed to attitudes or values. Such tests may be either norm-referenced or criterion-referenced.

Diagnostic Tests—Tests that evaluate students' abilities to perform a specified set of subskills and yield data that can be used to diagnose the need for instruction and formulate precise objectives in an individualized learning plan. Tests that have diagnostic capabilities are not necessarily exclusively used prior to instruction; they may be used as part of ongoing assessment to ensure that any skills that have not been mastered as a result of instruction can be targeted for further instruction. By definition, diagnostic tests must be criterion-referenced; however, they may be informal, teacher-prepared tests as well as standardized, commercial tests.

Informal Reading Inventories—A set of graded word lists and graded paragraphs used to assess students' decoding skills and processing errors, approximate reading level, and comprehension skills. Under this testing procedure, a student first reads lists of words aloud so that test administrator can note decoding errors and choose a reading passage at an appropriate reading level. The student then reads the passage aloud and answers comprehension questions about the passage. In some procedures, students may then be asked to read another passage silently and again answer comprehension questions. As a final step in still other variations of this procedure, students may be asked to listen to the test administrator read a passage and then answer comprehension questions about what they have heard. In this way, a comparison of the students' listening comprehension and reading comprehension can be obtained. Students' performances are judged against 100 percent accuracy, not against norms established by other students.

Validity—A test is said to be valid when it can be demonstrated that it measures what it claims to measure. A test may have *face validity*—it physically appears to measure what it says it measures. Face validity may be very important in enabling students to see the connection between the test-taking task and their personal educational goals. It may have *construct validity*—the test developers clearly constructed the test items in accordance with a clear and logical plan. And it may have *concurrent validity*—it compares favorably with other tests of the same subject(s) in current use. A test that claims to be a reading comprehension test but is limited to items that require no more than simple word recognition skills would not be called a valid reading comprehension test.

Reliability—A test is said to be reliable when the results obtained from it are consistent enough to be trusted. This means that an individual student's score would remain similar if the test were retaken after a short time interval and that similar groups of students would achieve similar results. It also means that enough items are provided to rule out the possibility of chance errors that result either from ambiguities in the wording of the item or in simple carelessness or misreading. Test developers will usually report the statistical evidence of their test's reliability. The fact that a test can be shown to be reliable does *not* imply that the test is also valid.

Standardized Test—A test is termed standardized when it has been subjected to full-scale field-testing and has been rigorously analyzed for statistical reliability and validity. By definition, all norm-referenced tests must be standardized; however, not all commercially available tests are standardized.

NOTE: To defend yourself against the array of statistical data commercial test developers may provide or to investigate the wide variety of informal testing techniques, you may wish to consult the texts cited in the bibliography.

WHAT DO PROGRAMS WANT TESTS TO DO?

During the interviews conducted in the NALP study, program directors and staff offered a variety of reasons for their use of tests. Most frequently, the reasons offered centered around the link between information obtained from the tests and the instructional process. "We need to know as much as we can about individuals when they come here and also what skills they have. . . . [We need to] get them through the program and out of here onto something else in a reasonable period of time . . . and not put them in here just for the heck of it," commented one interviewee. This comment strikes to the heart of what adult education attempts to be. Instruction is not offered as an end in itself; it is aimed at helping students achieve some larger goal. Adult students can and will leave a program if they do not clearly see that their needs are being served and that their time is not being wasted. One teacher from a community-based program explained: "If we fumble around, it's an indication to them of our own uncertainty. . . . We need to show them what we are doing and [that] they can trust our judgment."

The use of tests can help programs overcome the negative self-concept that adult students bring to the program. They can also help programs deal with the unfortunate possibility that teachers themselves may hold their students in low esteem or underestimate their abilities. A program director in the East emphatically states: "There can be no assumptions made. One of the cruelest assumptions made is that when students come in to learn to read, they in fact don't know how. . . ." Without a clear picture of the skills that students do and do not possess, programs can waste valuable time and impede the progress that students are capable of making. Students as well as teachers derive benefits from a clear knowledge of the students' skills. As the director of a correctional program stressed: "One of the goals that we have is to show [the student] that he isn't a failure. . . . [He] didn't know it then, [but he] knows this now!" A test administered prior to instruction can help a teacher say, in effect, "OK, here are the things you have trouble with, and we'll work on those; but look at how much you *do* know." Tests administered as part of ongoing assessment provide valuable feedback to the students and clearly tell them that their efforts are paying off.

Tests also help programs guard against exposing students to the possibility of not succeeding in achieving the goals of the program. For an instructor in an employment and training program, testing identifies the skills a person needs to be successful in the training program. "This is why diagnostic testing is important. The worst thing you can do is put an underemployed person into training, and they fail . . . and they are right back in the same situation." Programs that have a test as the exit criterion for awarding a credential or promotion often find that the use of practice tests can prevent students from attempting the final test before they are ready. For example, the use of such predictor tests as the *Official GED Practice Test* in a GED preparation program simulates the experience students will face on their test date, thus reducing some of the anxiety they may feel and demonstrating the likelihood of passing the actual full-length test.

Finally, programs find tests useful in overall program evaluation and program management. A director of a community-based program noted: "I like to see a standardized evaluation of what I'm doing. . . . It gives me a nice picture, not something I made up. . . . I'm getting an evaluation of me."

Effect of Program Philosophy on Test Selection

It appears that programs choose tests that reflect their teaching methods or philosophy of instruction. In programs that are driven by specifically stated educational objectives or competencies, truly diagnostic tests that isolate specific skill strengths and weaknesses are the general rule. Writing samples, specific phonics inventories, and competency-based pre-tests are frequently used before any instruction is attempted. These instruments measure student mastery of certain learning tasks and help teachers select specially designed modules or targeted sections of texts to teach those skills over which students have not demonstrated mastery.

In competency-based approaches to instructional design, programs may devote a great deal of time to helping students define goals and therefore choose diagnostic and assessment procedures that will measure those goals in a concrete and meaningful way. The ultimate goal may be defined by the nature of the program (as in a job-training program), or the students themselves may be asked to state their personal goals. The teacher then chooses appropriate learning sequences built on sets of behavioral objectives that reflect the prerequisite skills for the achievement of the stated goals. Pre-tests are used to diagnose which of the prerequisite skills need to be the target of instruction, and individualized plans are then developed with the students. The plans may lay out daily or weekly goals with specifications for the methods and materials to be used. Upon completion of each assigned task, students make an assessment of their level of mastery. In this way, achievement of each objective in the learning sequence is carefully monitored. Students are getting frequent feedback on their progress toward their ultimate goal, and any necessary adjustments in the methods or materials being used can be made quickly.

The diagnostic pre-tests and assessment measures used with this system, often referred to as a Management of Instruction System (MIS), will vary, depending on the nature of the specific skill objectives. Such measures may include teacher observation, student self-assessment, teacher-made or textbook unit tests, role-plays, simulations, or the demonstration of some behavior such as writing a paragraph or counting out change. For more academic objectives, commercial tests may be used. The required level of mastery will also vary depending on the nature of the specific skill objectives; usually students are expected to demonstrate eighty percent accuracy, but for some critical skills, students might be expected to perform with one hundred percent accuracy.

The philosophy of other programs may lead them to select tests that will yield general reading grade level scores rather than a diagnosis of the students' abilities to perform specific skill objectives. Such programs know that these standardized group tests are not valid for individual diagnosis, but they doubt the claims of any commercial test as a truly diagnostic measure. Because they do not believe that tests can provide the information they seek, few of the programs that administer standardized tests speak in passionate defense of the tests they use. The grade level scores obtained are viewed only as a starting level for the teacher, who is expected to do further and daily diagnosis in the classroom through informal testing procedures or simple direct observation. The scores represent ballpark figures to place students in classes or match them to appropriate materials, though always with the knowledge that students may later be moved into other classes or other materials as the teacher's or students' own assessment suggests. The teacher's job, as one ABE director explained, is to "explore the ballpark." That exploration takes place in what we will call later in this chapter *diagnostic teaching*.

Whether or not they are convinced that diagnosis is not the job of formal tests, programs may choose to use standardized tests in the belief that a comparison of pre-instruction and post-instruction reading grade level scores represent better hard data for reports to funding agencies. Indeed, some funding agencies require programs to report such scores and may even go so far as to specify which test must be used.

Community-based programs affiliated with Literacy Volunteers of America (LVA) or with Laubach Literacy International often follow the guidelines set by those organizations. In LVA's case, this includes the READ Test, which is an informal reading inventory designed to measure word analysis and comprehension skills. LVA tutors are encouraged to use the resulting diagnosis and tutor-student contact to explore a variety of teaching techniques suited to the individual learner's needs and learning style. In Laubach programs, learners are not diagnosed or subjected to any form of testing; rather, tutors follow a prescribed instructional program beginning with Book 1, which covers basic sound-symbol relationships.

Effect of Sector of Operation on Test Selection

The NALP study revealed that community-based, correctional, postsecondary, and local adult basic education programs tend to be the heaviest users of standardized tests such as the Test of Adult Basic Education (TABE), the Wide Range Achievement Test (WRAT), Botel Reading Inventory, the Stanford Diagnostic Reading Test, and the California Achievement Test in reading (CAT). Since the goal of literacy programs in these sectors is to raise the academic literacy level of the students, it is not surprising that most of these programs use standardized tests to document their success in achieving that goal.

When the program's goal is helping students obtain a high school equivalency credential through the GED Test, the two forms of the standardized, norm-referenced *Official GED Practice Test* are widely used as pre-instruction and post-instruction tools for predicting student success. Some programs may also use the simulated GED practice tests found in commercial textbooks for the same purpose; however, these tests are neither standardized nor norm-referenced and therefore should be carefully evaluated for validity.

The programs targeted for site visits in the NALP study reported using a diversity of testing techniques in a number of different combinations. They do not rely exclusively on standardized tests. Some thirty to forty percent of community-based and local ABE programs use criterion-referenced instruments for specific instructional objectives. In California, a consortium of forty ABE, community-based, and postsecondary basic skills and English as a second language programs are implementing a competency-based assessment system called the California Adult Student Assessment System, or CASAS (this system will be described in Chapter 7 under the heading "Teaching Competency Applications of Literacy Skills").

Using packages of different tests to obtain different kinds of information is not an uncommon practice. One community-based program designed a pre-enrollment program for prospective students. At the end of the fourth session, a specially trained tutor administers the LVA READ Test, specifically to obtain what is known as a miscue analysis. The student then takes the Adult Basic Learning Examination (ABLE) or the Degrees of Reading Power test, depending on his/her level, as a measure of reading comprehension skills. Finally, a writing sample is requested. This session prepares the student for instruction and provides the sort of diagnostic information the program requires. Both reading and writing skills are diagnosed because writing and reading are seen as complementary modes for teaching reading.

The goals of military programs lead them to a different kind of packaging decision. Such programs not only want to raise the general literacy level of their students but also want to ensure the achievement of the basic reading and math skills necessary for military duty assignments. At the beginning of the program cycle, students usually take a standardized test such as the TABE, the WRAT, the CAT, or the Armed Services Vocational Aptitude Battery (ASVAB) to determine eligibility for the program. Students are then pre-tested on specific competency-based learning modules. These pre-tests are often supplied by an agency that has been contracted by the military to provide custom-designed educational testing and curriculum materials. For example, a pre-test and accompanying learning material may be developed based on a section of a repair manual to determine whether the learner can put directions in a logical sequence. Before program exit, students' achievement is assessed with a combination of a standardized test, usually the same test administered at program entry, and military-specific, criterion-referenced tests.

The goals of employment and training programs generally lead them to favor criterion-referenced tests over standardized achievement tests. Their focus is on developing specific skills that enable their students to get and keep jobs. For example, reading instruction may be focused on filling out applications, reading manuals, and writing a resume. Math skills might focus on such money-related topics as making change, keeping a checkbook, or simple bookkeeping. Because instruction is targeted to job-specific skills, program staff often design their own criterion-referenced tests both for diagnosis and for assessment to ensure that students can get and hold on to the jobs for which they have been trained.

Effect of Level of Students on Test Selection

Beyond matching the tests they use to the goals of the program, programs often select tests based on the reading levels of students the program serves. In fact, many commercially available standardized tests have separate forms to reflect different ability levels.

Informal reading inventories, the Woodcock Reading Mastery Tests, and the Slosson Oral Reading Test (SORT) are often favored for beginning-level students. These tests must be administered on a one-to-one basis. Thus, testing can be halted as soon as the test administrator has enough information to start the student in an appropriate program of instruction. Students need not be frustrated by being asked to take a two-hour paper-and-pencil test when it can be determined in a matter of minutes that a student is a true nonreader.

Tests such as the Gates-MacGinitie Reading Test or the Stanford Diagnostic Reading Test are perceived by some programs as less frustrating than most standardized tests and are therefore favored for use with middle-level ABE students. Comprehension sections on these tests include shorter reading passages, and the format is clean and clear. Similarly, one Midwestern ABE program has designated the Stanford Achievement Test for use with GED candidates because they feel its more sophisticated format and more complex comprehension passages accurately measure the skills a GED candidate must possess.

Generalizations

Although there are variations in what programs want tests to do and what tests they choose to support their individual philosophies, there are some generalizations that can be made based on the NALP study:

- The TABE is the most widely used standardized test; it can be found in programs in all sectors.
- The ABLE is used almost exclusively in community-based programs and is rare in other sectors.
- The *Official GED Practice Test* is widely used in all sectors.
- Interest or vocational inventories and learning style assessments are rare. This is true despite the frequency with which educators mentioned tailoring instruction to student interests and learning style.
- Intelligence testing is not done except in two correctional programs.
- Group testing is common, though many programs are able to provide individual testing and counseling.
- In most programs, counselors or staff are responsible for testing.

ISSUES AND PROBLEMS IN TESTING

Just as any discussion of teaching methods cannot result in defining the "right way" to teach adult students, no discussion of testing procedures can result in defining the ultimate model for diagnosing students' needs and assessing their progress. As we have seen, part of the answer to selecting an appropriate method or combination of methods lies in what a program wants a test to do both for the students and for the program. However, the interviews conducted as part of the NALP study also reveal a number of things that tests should not or can not be. Certain procedures and certain tests themselves present problems that can be avoided.

Sensitivity to Adult Students

Most programs use some form of pre-test soon after a student's entrance into the program, often on the first day. Yet many program staff speak of the negative connotations testing holds for learners. A student in a Midwestern ABE program expressed it this way: "I was scared . . . the first day. I just came in, did what I had to do, and took off." And a woman who is now a GED teacher in an East Coast community-based program from which she graduated spoke for herself and her students when she said: ". . . one of the similarities of all adult students is that they are real scared. It doesn't matter what sex they are, what color they are . . . they all come back to the classroom really scared because their last memory of education was through a system, whatever system that was. . . . They come in with a lot of real negative attitudes, a lot of blaming themselves, . . . feeling like failures because they quit school. . . ."

Programs have devised a variety of ways to ease learners' fear. Sometimes teachers carefully explain to students the purpose of the test they are about to take. They may scrupulously avoid the use of the word *test* in their description and emphasize that it is an evaluation or skills check to help the teacher find the best class or material for the student. The student is reassured that there is no way to "fail" the test. Teachers often follow up by discussing the test results with the student, taking care to show how much the student *does* know as well as what skill weaknesses the program will address. By emphasizing what the student already knows, the teacher can demonstrate how the program will not waste the student's time in unnecessary instruction. In programs that use competency-based pre-tests, the results may be described in terms of some desirable life-related or job-related skills, and students are shown either how well they have already demonstrated the skill or how the program will help the student achieve mastery.

When programs are sensitive to the vulnerability of the students, the students generally express much less anxiety after the testing experience is over. One student in an urban community-based program commented simply: "It was a test to see . . . where was your reading and where was your math . . . it wasn't that tough. It was just to see what grade you were in, what level." The grade level designation given to this student apparently doesn't bother her, perhaps because the level was not seen as any personal judgment, but simply as a convenient way of finding the right class for her.

The more disadvantaged the learner, the greater the need for sensitivity. Teachers say that the surest way to drive away the most disadvantaged learners is to give them a long test (which, in some cases, might mean up to two hours of testing) and a test they can't read. In one urban ABE program, the registration process helps to identify this special learner. Those who have difficulty completing the registration form are directed to the beginning level class where the teacher uses informal measures to diagnose skills. Often, these diagnostic measures are integrated into the teaching process. Parts of informal inventories and word lists are introduced slowly as the teacher gets to know the student. Because the diagnostic procedures are short and informal, the students do not perceive them as frustrating or negative. Instead, they see the procedures as tied to their learning and progress.

Some programs delay the testing procedure for several class sessions so that students can feel some sense of accomplishment and success from their initial encounters with the program. These initial encounters can take the form of pre-enrollment orientation sessions, observation of classes, simple trial lessons, self-selection of material, or language experience stories (these last two methods are discussed in detail in Chapter 7). In one urban ABE program, the educational counselor meets with low-level students for counseling and administers some very basic tests in a private and comfortable setting. In some programs, the counselor may use specially designed interview forms as an informal means of obtaining information about the students' oral and written language skills.

Reliability and Validity

The reservations and complaints heard most frequently are about the questionable reliability or validity of the tests in current use. One ABE program director told us bluntly, "There is no reliable test in adult education on the market." She added that many programs using standardized or diagnostic tests use those normed on the K–12 population. This same director was quite candid about how test scores can be manipulated for funding support. Staff can simply choose tests that will produce higher scores and show greater gains as a post-test; tests that yield lower scores can be used as pre-tests.

For many programs, the true job of diagnosis and assessment is borne by the teachers—". . . they know what their problems are, and I know what their problems are; we don't need to test." A teacher from an ABE program adds: ". . . just because a person goes through an evaluation, that's not the be-all and end-all. We take those scores with a grain of salt. There are people who don't test well." Many program staff imply that the fear most students have of testing may be the cause of unreliable test results. Others add that available testing instruments just aren't specific or flexible enough to diagnose learning disabilities or to measure the skills of beginning readers.

Balanced against this opinion that available tests may not be valid or reliable is the desire for an objective analysis of student ability. Many would take strong exception to the statements quoted in the last paragraph. Students may well underestimate or overestimate their abilities, and teachers can't claim to know what the students' problems are without asking the students to demonstrate their skills. We'll have more to say about the role of the teacher in the section entitled "Diagnostic Teaching" later in this chapter.

Although many of those interviewed expressed dissatisfaction with the tests they use, few could articulate the technical aspects of tests that might make them unsuitable for use with adult students. And thus few could construct a test that would be a valid and reliable measure of student ability. Because the technical aspects involved in test selection require a level of expertise that few adult educators possess, we strongly urge that readers consult the texts cited in the bibliography. The Indiana Department of Education has also recently completed a review of tests appropriate for adult education programs and can provide a summary of their recommendations.

Frequency of Testing

For students to remain in programs, they must see a payoff for their efforts. Effective diagnostic and assessment procedures allow programs to give their students the kind of feedback that demonstrates that payoff in concrete and meaningful terms. Immediate feedback through frequent assessments also allows teachers to make any necessary adjustments in the methods or materials being used to help students attain their goals. Despite the value of frequent assessment, the NALP study did not uncover any consistent assessment routine across programs. The frequency with which programs used some kind of assessment measure varied from daily, weekly, and monthly cycles to such schedules as every thirty to sixty hours, every five weeks, or every three months. Some programs tested after 150 hours of instruction, and in many programs, standardized tests are given on an annual basis. For new students, the annual tests serve as a pre-test, and for continuing students, they serve as assessments of progress. Similarly, progress reports may be issued to students daily, weekly, monthly, or after a term of eight or nine weeks. In some programs, there is no formal assessment strategy.

About half of the programs interviewed in the NALP study reported that they attempt to tie pre-testing to post-testing, often by using the same instruments. Yet many programs never reach the post-test stage because students leave the program before the scheduled time for post-testing. Programs with schedules calling for the administration of standardized tests only in the fall or at the start of a new term miss many students if they also have open-entry–open-exit policies. The programs most successful in conducting post-test assessments are those that tie assessment to the students' completion of tasks on each individual skill objective or competency, often making demonstration of mastery a prerequisite to moving on to the next step in the sequence of instruction.

The questions of when, how, and even whether to use assessment post-tests are closely tied to the same issues we discussed under the heading "What Do Programs Want Tests To Do?" The philosophy and goals of the program will largely dictate the answers. When programs see tests only as rough measures for initial placement and sources of data for funding agencies, they are unlikely to use formal tests as part of ongoing student assessment and rely instead on the teaching process as the means of monitoring student progress and providing feedback. Programs that model themselves after some competency-based model, such as the New York State External Diploma Program, are more likely to engage in frequent assessment activities, which include many forms of assessment besides printed or software-generated tests. Simulations of real-life problem-solving activities are frequently used in such programs.

Diagnostic Teaching

Despite the variations in testing procedures noted within this chapter, we have frequently mentioned programs' reliance on their teaching staffs to overcome the shortcomings of formal tests. A director at an employment and training site explains: "My staff learns from individual work. Diagnosis is part of every lesson if you are teaching one on one." Adds a director of a community-based program: "We have seen so many 'plans in a can' where the person jumps in at point A and plods along to point Z . . . so what we try to do is continuously investigate with the person. Do you need to back up and review? Do you need to branch out there?" A staff member at a military site concludes, "I think what the student is getting in the classroom with the teacher is probably more beneficial and more meaningful than testing."

Most students, when asked how they knew they were making progress, replied that they could "feel it" or that they could "read more words" than when they started.

Teachers, too, are in tune with these real, but hard-to-measure, signs of progress. Consequently they rely heavily on observation, informal conversations, and diagnostic teaching to monitor and assess progress. Unlike formal tests, teachers can be flexible and tailor both instruction and assessment to the individual goals and learning styles of their students.

Given experienced, high-caliber teachers, program directors might be more comfortable in this reliance on teachers and the concept of diagnostic teaching. However, especially in programs that use volunteer tutors, the teaching staff may not have a level of expertise that equips them to be the sole judge of student needs and student progress. And students' feelings about what they know may not be reliable unless they have the opportunity to apply their skills in different contexts. Students are quite likely to be very hard on themselves and underestimate how much they have learned, or they may not be skilled enough in objective self-criticism to go beyond very general statements meant more to reassure the teacher than to guide the instructional process.

Even given a high-caliber teaching staff, we would stress that documenting student progress in ways that are explicit and can be affirmed by those outside the teacher-student relationship is important for several reasons. First, it makes learning gains or successes concrete and observable for the students. Also, it provides a record that can be understood and followed by those who may need confirmation of student progress and program effectiveness.

Although diagnostic teaching is valuable and underscores the importance of competent and committed instructional staff, it can be idiosyncratic. The value of the teacher-student relationship cannot be denied, especially in evaluating the more abstract or affective and personal goals of the students, but it is necessary to strike a balance between the measurement of concrete skill objectives through formal tests or through carefully designed informal tests and ongoing assessment through daily student-teacher interactions. To achieve this balance and to make the most of the teacher's role in diagnosis and assessment, one needs to do two things: (1) clearly state both program and student goals and define how mastery of those goals can be diagnosed prior to instruction as well as assessed after instruction, and (2) provide in-service training for teachers and volunteer tutors in both formal testing procedures and the wide variety of informal testing techniques. With a combination of diagnostic teaching and appropriate assessment, students can externalize their accomplishments and teachers can confirm or discover what they should help the student attend to as they progress through the instructional program.

CONCLUSIONS AND RECOMMENDATIONS

The variety of program philosophies and program goals in the field of adult education make it impossible to make definitive judgments in such hotly debated areas as testing and instruction. Yet the NALP study does help us identify the issues that need to be considered in a program's selection of appropriate diagnostic and assessment procedures. Some method of placement needs to exist if a program is to address the real needs of each individual student and avoid the frustrating experiences of placing students at so low a level that they become bored and leave or at so high a level that the students' sense of failure is reinforced. In the former situation, the program has failed the student by not addressing real needs, and in the latter, the student can only fail in the attempt to meet the desired outcomes of the program. This placement of students can be accomplished through the use of criterion-referenced instruments, the criteria of which are determined by the goals and objectives of the program and the students. Or it may be accomplished through the use of standardized achievement test scores for rough placement paired with subjective judgment and informal instruments used by carefully trained teachers as an integral part of the teaching process.

Once students have been placed in classes or instructional materials, there should be some plan for ongoing and systematic assessment, both for feedback to students—demonstrating to them that they are making progress or signalling to teachers the need for adjustments in the methods or the materials being used—and for overall program evaluation. It would appear that the frequent use of criterion-referenced measures may be the best means of monitoring student progress and ensuring the greatest possible degree of individual student success, though the use of learning gain scores obtained from standardized tests may well be the most convenient way of reporting data to funding agencies.

No single commercial test or teacher-generated technique could be designed to yield the variety of data that might be needed. Programs would do better to use a mix of tests and informal assessment procedures and select what goes into that mix based on the specific goals of the students and the program. A test may be termed valid because it measures what the *test* sets out to measure, but the kind of validity a program must seek is in terms of what the *program* sets out to measure. And that means developing very clear specifications of the objectives of the program. Once the objectives are down on paper, the program can go down the list and select appropriate measures for each individual objective.

Whatever procedures a program selects, the selection ought to be based on a recognition that the students are adults. On the one hand, this means remaining sensitive to the characteristics and anxieties of adults returning to an educational setting. For students on the lowest ability level, this may mean avoiding any formal testing altogether. On the other hand, it means carefully investigating norm-referenced tests to ensure that program staff are fully aware of the norming group used by the test developer and will consciously bear in mind the limitations of any test that compares adult student performance to the performance of children. The inspection of any commercial test will also involve an evaluation of the extent to which the test measures the application of skills in adult contexts.

The authors make the following four recommendations to programs formulating plans for solid diagnostic and assessment procedures.

(1) Clearly define the instructional mission and goals of the program.
Any tests or set of procedures the program adopts should reinforce the

philosophy of the program and be tied to the goals of the program. They should also be devised to serve *adult* students.

(2) Develop expertise in educational psychology and measurement. Because testing is a technical area and most adult educators do not have an extensive background in the field of testing and measurement, programs might well seek additional information from consultants, sources of test reviews, textbooks, or university courses. Once diagnostic and assessment procedures have been determined, staff should be regularly involved in in-service training activities to ensure the most effective use of any formal tests and the appropriate use of informal procedures.

(3) Translate the students' and the program's goals into sets of clear and measurable objectives. Without statements of objectives, diagnostic and assessment measures cannot effectively aid the instructional process. Diagnostic measures should ensure that students (a) are not being exposed to instruction they don't really need and (b) are not being placed in classes or materials for which they do not have the prerequisite skills. Assessment measures should provide feedback to both students and teachers to ensure that any necessary adjustments in the materials or instructional methods are being made.

(4) Build a regular and frequent schedule for assessment. Ideally, some form of assessment should be employed after a student completes each learning task in the instructional sequence. This will document student progress and required levels of mastery and ensure that the student is being moved along neither too rapidly nor too slowly.

EXHIBIT 6.2 Commercially Produced Tests

The following tests are listed in decreasing order of use in each category as reported by the programs we visited. This list does not imply that these are the most useful, valid, or reliable tests to use, nor does it imply any endorsement by the authors.

STANDARDIZED ACHIEVEMENT TESTS

Test of Adult Basic Education (TABE)—CTB/McGraw-Hill, Del Monte Research Park, Monterey, CA 93940

Adult Basic Learning Examination (ABLE)—Harcourt, Brace, Jovanovich, 5 Sampson Street, Saddle Brook, NJ 07662

Stanford Achievement Test–Reading—Harcourt, Brace, Jovanovich, 5 Sampson Street, Saddle Brook, NJ 07662

Gates-MacGinitie Reading Test—Riverside Publishing Company, 8420 Bryn Mawr Avenue, Chicago, IL 60631

California Achievement Tests—CTB/McGraw-Hill, Del Monte Research Park, Monterey, CA 93940

Slossen Oral Reading Test (SORT)—Slossen Educational Publications, Inc., 140 Pine Street, P.O. Box 280, East Aurora, NY 14052

Stanford Diagnostic Reading Test—Harcourt, Brace, Jovanovich, 5 Sampson Street, Saddle Brook, NJ 07662

Woodcock Reading Mastery Tests—American Guidance Service, Inc., Publisher's Building, Pines, MN 55014

CRITERION-REFERENCED TESTS

Botel Reading Inventory—originally published by Follett Publishing Company—Modern Curriculum Press, 13, 900 Prospect Road, Cleveland, OH 44136

Reading/Everyday Activities in Life (R/EAL)—CAL Press, 76 Madison Avenue, New York, NY 10016

Standard Entry Assessment—This test may be obtained by writing to Joe Cooney, Vocational Education Special Project, San Mateo County Office of Education, 333 Main Street, Redwood City, CA 94063

INFORMAL READING INVENTORIES

Reading Evaluation–Adult Diagnosis (READ)—Literacy Volunteers of America, 404 Oak Street, Syracuse, NY 13202

BIBLIOGRAPHY

Allen, Virginia F. *What Does a Reading Test Test?* Philadelphia: Temple University, 1975.

Anderson, Beverly L. *Guide to Adult Functional Literacy Assessment Using Existing Tests.* Portland, OR: Northwest Regional Educational Laboratory, 1981. (ED 210317)

Bloom, Benjamin; Madaus, George F.; and Hasting, Thomas. *Evaluation to Improve Learning.* New York: McGraw-Hill Book Company, 1981.

Brown, Frederick Gramm. *Guidelines for Test Use: A Commentary on the Standards for Educational and Psychological Tests.* Washington, DC: National Council on Measurement in Education, 1980.

Buros, Oscar K. *Seventh Mental Measurements Yearbook.* Highland Park, NJ: Gryphon Press, 1972.

Green, Bert F. (Ed.) *Issues in Testing, Coaching, Disclosure, and Ethnic Bias.* San Francisco: Jossey-Bass, 1981.

Kryspin, William J. *Developing Classroom Tests: A Guide for Writing and Evaluating Test Items.* Minneapolis: Burgess Publishing Company, 1974.

Lerche, Renee S. "Competence Assessment: A Model for Matching Adult Learner to a High School Completion Program." Ed.D. Thesis, Harvard University, 1983.

Nafziger, D. H. *Tests of Functional Adult Literacy: An Evaluation of Currently Available Instruments*. Portland, OR: Northwest Regional Educational Laboratory, 1975.

Newman, Anabel P. *Adult Basic Education: Reading*. Boston: Allyn and Bacon, 1980.

Pikulski, John J. (Ed.) *Approaches to the Informal Evaluation of Reading*. Newark, DE: International Reading Association, 1982.

Rossman, Mark H.; Fisk, Elizabeth C.; and Roehl, Janet E. *Teaching and Learning Basic Skills: A Guide for Adult Basic Education and Developmental Education Programs*. "Chapter 5: Creative Testing." New York: Teachers College Press, Columbia University, 1984.

Vonderhaar, K. *Tests for Adult Basic Education Teachers*. Kansas City: University of Missouri School of Education, 1975.

Chapter 7
Instructional Methods and Materials

The instructional methods and materials that programs use are the tools designed to help students achieve the levels of literacy necessary to meet their personal, academic, or vocational goals. The choice of methods and materials will depend on how programs define:

(1) **The desired outcomes of instruction**—What should students be able to *do* when they complete the program?

(2) **The sequence of subskills that lead up to those outcomes**—Are there identifiable steps that can be the focus of discrete units of instruction? Is there any order in which students should learn the steps?

(3) **The ways in which adult students acquire and integrate those subskills**—How do adults learn to perform each of the steps? In what ways do adult learning styles or preferences differ from those of children, and how might those differences affect instructional design and delivery? How and when do adult students put the steps together to perform the task as a whole? What kinds of materials provide appropriate kinds of practice for skill development?

One might get programs to agree that the *ultimate* goal of literacy education is to enable students to extract meaning from the kinds of print material they are likely to encounter in their jobs, their homes, and in their communities. If students are to function in these settings, this definition of goals must include applicable objectives in mathematics and writing skills. However, these comprehensive goals are unlikely to be the stated goals of the first "course" in which students enroll.

The stated goals of the first weeks or months of instruction will depend largely on how programs answer the other questions suggested above, and, especially with respect to reading instruction, these questions are the subjects of considerable debate. Often programs are left with the rather unsettling advice, "Use whatever seems to work." Unfortunately, what works for some students will not necessarily work for others, and what works for one program may not be successfully replicated by a different program with different personnel and a different mix of students.

It seems clear from a review of the findings of the NALP study that the most consistently successful programs are those that structure and systematize their instructional design. They closely link instructional objectives to materials and methods and to assessment of student progress. Further, these programs individualize instructional plans to reflect learner strengths and to address learner deficiencies. To monitor learner progress and to provide frequent feedback to learners on their progress, they also include an instructional management and documentation system. Thus, in formulating an effective instructional design, a program must not only wrestle with the larger systemic issues but also attempt to accommodate what it perceives to be the nature of the students in its service area and the abilities of and time constraints on its teaching staff.

To accommodate individual differences among students and to maintain an adult focus, program designers must consider at least five variables: (1) life and employment goals; (2) educational background, including current skills, prior knowledge, and linguistic abilities; (3) life experiences and cultural background; (4) personal preferences and interests; and (5) learning styles or special learning problems. In designing individualized learning plans for each program participant, teachers and tutors are thus challenged to be extraordinarily flexible in choosing methods and materials that optimize each learner's potential for achievement.

Program designers must balance the desire to arm teachers with the variety of instructional methods and materials they may need to accommodate a diversity of students against the reality that many teachers and most volunteer tutors, however well intentioned, may not have either the time or sufficient expertise in adult education for the kind of analysis, preparation, and monitoring required to implement truly individualized educational plans. Staffing patterns or educational philosophy may also lead program designers to structure their system for large or small group instruction, as opposed to individualized, one-to-one tutorial sessions. Programs may also choose to adopt a packaged model for individualizing instruction in which instructional objectives are linked to diagnostic instruments, given sets of materials, and assessment strategies. Two such models are the California Adult Student Assessment System (CASAS) developed by the San Diego Community College District and the CASAS Consortium (a system discussed in the section entitled "Teaching Competency Applications of Literacy Skills") and the Comprehensive Competencies Program (CCP) developed by the Remediation and Training Institute in Washington, DC.

Whatever the process, program designers should develop a well-defined, step-by-step curriculum to ensure that teachers can manage their time and yet be held accountable for helping students achieve certain minimum goals or standards. Such a set curriculum design does not necessarily imply a rigid adherence to a single methodology or the use of only one kind of material; in fact, different goals or standards suggest different instructional activities or materials.

Within this chapter, we cannot settle the debate over the issues we have just raised or suggest that there is a single "right way" to structure an instructional program. The important point is that there is structure; programs do create educational systems. The NALP study can help programs examine the issues and make informed choices about the methods and materials available.

We maintain that program designers as well as teachers and tutors ought to have some knowledge of the variety of methods and materials for literacy education from which they can choose. To that end, we will begin by examining the variety of instructional methods the programs in the NALP study have found successful for teaching reading, noting how the different methods address the questions set forth at the beginning of this chapter. Although subsequent sections on materials selection and instructional management systems embrace any skills that might be the focus of instruction, we have chosen to devote the discussion of instructional methods to methods of teaching reading. We have done so chiefly because it is in this area that the choice of options seems most controversial. Experts in the field of reading can offer some advice, but even they cannot agree on definitions of what cognitive processes are involved in reading or in learning to read. There is also no agreement on how to define levels or degrees of reading proficiency. Many professionals view the concept of a reading grade level for out-of-school adults as next to meaningless and as demeaning to the students' adult status. Other practitioners dispute the segmentation of reading comprehension skills into hierarchical arrangements. Frustrating as it may be, it appears that one simply cannot define the steps to becoming a skilled reader as easily as one can define the steps to becoming proficient in such disciplines as mathematics.

Although mathematics education tends to follow fairly well-established guidelines, interested readers may do well to contact such organizations as the National Council of Teachers of Mathematics, 1906 Association Drive, Reston, VA 22091, to investigate current practice. Writing skills instruction for basic education students has begun to attract considerably more attention in recent years, and we would strongly urge readers to stay in contact with such organizations as the National Council of Teachers of English, 1111 Kenyon Road, Urbana, IL 61801, for research and development in this area.

In the second major section of this chapter, we will turn to the issues involved in choosing materials that are appropriate for adult learners. We will suggest guidelines for evaluating the potential usefulness of materials for an adult audience—though here, too, programs will ultimately find a need to have a wide variety of materials available. Finally, we will discuss the issues involved in designing a full instructional management system that will benefit both the teachers and their students. Within this discussion, we will address the factors involved in deciding whether to structure the program for group or individualized instruction. At the end of the chapter, we will offer our own conclusions and recommendations. As further assistance, we have provided a list of commercial suppliers of adult education materials and a bibliography of sources of information about the teaching of reading to adults.

WHAT INSTRUCTIONAL METHODS DO PROGRAMS USE?

In order to describe the methods programs use to teach reading to adults, we will discuss three basic methods for beginning reading instruction—phonics, sight word, and language experience—and two issues that programs address—how to teach reading comprehension skills and how to address life skill or competency applications of basic literacy skills. At the end of the section, we will summarize the modes of presentation programs may use to deliver instruction. However, it should be noted at the outset that programs do not necessarily use the methods described in the following pages in their pure form, and many programs use variations on or combinations of these methods. Although any attempt to categorize instructional methods necessarily creates some artificial boundaries, it may be useful to describe a program's choice of methods as resting on the program's definition of learning to read either as the accumulation and integration of discrete subskills or as the mastery of a holistic process.

Proponents of approaches based on the accumulation of discrete subskills might liken learning to read to assembling a jigsaw puzzle. Under such an approach, one defines the whole in terms of its parts and teaches how the parts are put together to form the whole. For example, in a phonics-based approach, one begins with the smallest possible element—the individual letters of the alphabet—and teaches students to associate particular sounds with particular letters or combinations of letters. Gradually, one builds a knowledge of a wide range of possible sound-to-symbol correlations; theoretically, students can learn to decode virtually any word they may encounter. (In fairness, it must be noted that even the most passionate believer in phonics accepts that students must be taught to recognize some words on sight; the rules and exceptions in phonics cannot cover every word in use in English.)

As an extension of such a discrete skills approach, one might also view the development of reading comprehension skills as a sequence. The most elementary comprehension skills, such as recalling a specifically stated fact, are taught first (the student reads, "The book is red," and is asked to tell what color the book is), and the student is gradually introduced to more and more sophisticated comprehension skills with increasingly more difficult material. Proponents of this philosophy reason that skilled readers actually select and apply those strategies that are appropriate to a given piece of reading material from the full range of comprehension skills, but they do so almost subconsciously and with such rapidity that they appear to be applying the skills simultaneously. Beginning readers, they would argue, must be taught each skill in isolation and build toward integration of each part of the process of comprehension. Under this approach, even the difficulty of material may be controlled as part of some kind of sequence, beginning with reading passages made up entirely of simple subject-verb-object sentence patterns that may use a limited number of simple adjectives or adverbs.

Proponents of holistic approaches take strong exception to what they view as the artificial, abstract, or overly simplistic lessons to which phonics teachers expose their students. They fear that students lose meaning when they focus on sounding out words, and they are frustrated by the inability of phonics to tap the interests, life experiences, and oral vocabulary of adults from the very beginning simply because the sound-symbol correlations of certain high-frequency words will not be taught until later in the skill development continuum. They may even argue against phonics instruction because it resurrects the ghost of the students' past failure; if phonics did not work for the students in elementary school, they ask, why would it be any more effective now?

Both the sight word method and the language experience method discussed in this section are holistic approaches that begin instruction with whole and meaningful words.

These approaches are based on the idea that, given repeated exposure to words within meaningful contexts, students will develop a useful and relevant sight vocabulary and will discover for themselves the processes involved in reading. (It should be noted that some programs use the sight word method or the language experience method in a much more controlled manner than we may have just led the reader to believe. Such programs may include phonics instruction, though the emphasis will remain on whole language instruction.)

Practitioners who use holistic approaches to reading instruction may also view reading comprehension skills from a slightly different angle. If one assumes that reading is a holistic experience in which many processes occur simultaneously, and if one assumes that adults are capable of reasonably sophisticated analytic skills in activities other than reading, there may be no reason to artifically segment instruction in reading comprehension. From the very beginning, one might expect students to be able to extract literal, interpretive, and evaluative levels of meaning from a reading passage (a more detailed explanation of these three levels of comprehension skills can be found under the section "Teaching Reading Comprehension Skills"). Indeed, rather than thinking of reading as a process of selecting and applying discrete comprehension skills, one might describe reading more holistically as a three-part problem-solving process: (1) *prediction*—the reader makes tentative decisions about meaning while reading, (2) *confirmation*—the reader tests hypotheses or guesses to see if the prediction is valid, and (3) *integration*—the reader incorporates the new knowledge into the existing storehouse of his/her knowledge and experience. Under such a philosophy, one might be more concerned with the complexity of the concepts in a reading passage than with the complexity of sentence structure or the number of syllables in the words used in the passage. (The issue of readability will be discussed in the section entitled "Choosing Appropriate Materials for Adults.")

Related to the issue of how students comprehend the meaning of material is the issue of what material one finds essential for students to comprehend. That is, if most of the reading that adults ultimately want to do is reading for a purpose—reading for information rather than reading for entertainment—one must decide how and when one introduces reading material that addresses life-related or job-related skills or competencies. Within this section, we'll explore the implications that adult students' need to connect reading instruction to meaningful applications may have for one's choice of methods, though this issue will surface again in the section entitled "Choosing Appropriate Materials for Adults" as well as in the section entitled "How Can the Instructional System Be Managed?"

The NALP study found holistic approaches common in community-based and local ABE programs, while correctional and military programs tended to rely more heavily on phonics and sequential skills approaches. However, most programs reported that they are flexible and will use whatever works. In practice, this usually results in a combination of phonics, sight word, and language experience methods of reading instruction. One teacher we interviewed stated that the ideal teacher "has to be willing to dig in with the individual student and to explore different types of curricula, strategies, and learning styles . . . and to have an arsenal . . . of techniques." One program teaches students about the different ways of practicing reading skills and encourages them to choose the methods that suit them best. "... After a month, my students know the repertory of things we can do. We can read together, we can write language experience stories, we can work on words, all these things! ... And then you have the student coming in saying, 'You know, I should work on *this* now. ....' " Indeed, the choice of approach may well be decided by the teacher's analysis of the cognitive style of the individual students.

The description of specific methods that follows is necessarily abbreviated and thus somewhat simplified; it is not our purpose to offer the level of understanding of each method that would be required before using that method with students. For such detailed information, the reader should consult the texts cited in the bibliography.

Phonics-Based Method

Phonics, more than other method, relies on the development of auditory and visual perception and discrimination skills as the basis for learning to read. On the auditory level, students are taught to associate certain letters or combinations of letters with certain spoken sounds, and they are helped to sound out the words that they read. Along with this instruction, students are taught such important visual skills as recognizing the differences among letters (as, for example, recognizing that turning a *b* around will create a *d*) and properly sequencing the letters within words (and thus telling the difference between *was* and *saw*).

As students learn to recognize the letters and the sounds they make, the teacher helps students put together the letters they have learned and blend the sounds; the letters may be combined either as meaningful words or as nonsense syllables. Phonics instructors defend the use of nonsense syllables with the thought that individual syllables within longer words may in themselves be nonsense (as, for example, the syllables in the word *phon-ics*). With the addition of a few simple sight words, students can begin to read full sentences early in the instructional process when they may know only one vowel sound and a few consonants.

A variation on the pure letter-by-letter phonics method is the word pattern method. In this method, students are taught a word part, such as *-it*, and are then given a family of words that contain this part (*bit, fit, hit, lit,* and so on). With the addition of a few sight words, one can develop simple stories (the resulting stories are reminiscent of the characteristics of such Dr. Seuss books as *The Cat in the Hat*).

Though phonics has its detractors, it is a very popular method of teaching reading. Laubach Literacy International's philosophy is firmly grounded in phonics, and that organization has done much to spread the use of phonics in adult education. (For more information, interested readers may wish to contact that organization directly or contact New Readers Press, the publisher of Laubach materials, at the address given at the end of this chapter.) Because Laubach tutors can be trained and sent out into the field fairly quickly, programs may accept phonics instruction as an expedient yet effective means of responding to the high demand for literacy education. The educational background of teachers also contributes to the popularity of phonics; most ABE teachers have been trained in this traditional reading method, and many adult educators began their careers in the public school system in which basal readers and phonics workbooks are the centerpiece of reading instruction.

The most often cited drawback to phonics-based instruction is that students must go through the lengthy process of decoding skill development before they finally reach the day on which they can read the meaningful prose that they want to read. It may be true that the early reading books in commercial phonics programs tend to be either bland or juvenile, but many creative programs such as Bronx Educational Services have developed reading materials of their own that manage to be mature and reasonably interesting within the limitations imposed by the number of letters and sounds a student may be able to decode. It takes some ingenuity on the part of the program designer in sequencing the phonics skills and some creative brainstorming on the part of the materials developer in deriving the words that can be generated from that sequence and then putting them into a meaningful story, but programs need not settle for puerile materials. A literacy program in Atlanta circumvented this problem by using both the sight word method (described below) and the phonics method of instruction. They chose sight words that occur frequently in the language of adults and those that would help the materials developers tap topics of genuine relevance.

Sight Word Method

Programs that use the sight word method (also often referred to as the "Look-Say" method) reject the notion that reading is a letter-by-letter decoding process; from the very beginning, students are taught whole words as the basic unit of meaning. Through a progression of lessons, students are taught to recognize whole words on sight. In each lesson, the teacher presents a few new words, often in combination with a pictorial representation of what the word stands for. The teacher reads each new word to the students, and the students repeat the word after the teacher. Students are drilled on recognizing the words in isolation and in the context of whole sentences. Through deliberate and systematic repetition of new words and words learned in previous lessons, students memorize the sight vocabulary they will need to read meaningful stories.

Students do receive instruction in visual and auditory perception and discrimination, though not in quite the same manner as in phonics-based instruction; this training is always done using whole words. Activities may focus on getting students to see or hear similarities in the beginning, middle or final letters or sounds within words (e.g., noting that *stop* and *start* both begin with *st*) or to see differences in the sequences of letters within words (e.g., discriminating between *soup* and *soap* or among *stop*, *pots*, and *tops*). Other activities may ask students to trace and copy whole words to help them feel the shapes of the letters that combine to make up the words. In a pure sight word method, students are never asked to practice this with individual letters (as they might be under a phonics-based method); the skill is always practiced within the context in which it is assumed to be actually used during the process of reading—with whole words.

One of the chief advantages of the sight word method over the phonics-based method is the ability to teach students those words that occur most frequently in written language early in the sequence of instruction. One can thus focus on language that is relevant and useful to adults and build meaningful and interesting stories much more rapidly.

Instruction does require a considerable amount of repetition and drill for students to internalize the sight vocabulary, and it is important to remember that such repetition is rarely as boring for the students as it is for the teacher. Teachers become bored because they already know the words; students who are reading these words for the first time may demand much more repetition than teachers may assume necessary and will remain alert as they face the challenge of remembering the thousands of words they will need to read proficiently. To provide such repetition, teachers often use lengthy worksheets, software drill-and-practice programs, and flashcards or other mechanical devices that students can use either alone or in practice sessions with a "buddy."

Language Experience Method

The language experience method derives its name from the fact that instruction is based on the oral language that students already have. Under this method, students dictate stories in their own words, and the teacher transcribes the stories for use in the reading lessons. The lesson may begin with the teacher's reading a student's story back to him or her and pointing to the words as they are read. The student then reads the story one line at a time with the teacher, again following along with the written text as each word is read. The teacher may then select words from the story as the basis for phonics lessons, word pattern drills, or sight word drills. Because the written language being taught is transcribed from the students' own language, it is assumed that students will bring to bear what they know (their transcribed experiences or feelings and their oral vocabulary) on what they do not know (the conventions of written language) and thus acquire reading skills much more quickly than would be possible when the language is controlled by the instructor or program designer. Too, reading instruction can be closely related to what the student wants to be able to read. For example, one student in an urban program who works in a garage repairing cars is writing and learning to read his own repair manual.

A variation on the use of individualized language experience stories is the generation of reading passages based on group discussions in the classroom. Such a strategy extends the instructional process into speaking and listening skills as well as critical thinking skills. This group discussion technique is a staple of the Lutheran Settlement House Women's Program in Philadelphia, which provides education, employment, and social services to women in a low-income area of the inner city. One teacher in the program explained the value of the technique this way: ". . . [The students] should be able to take the same concepts they learn and apply them to a life situation. The same processes they use in reading comprehension [exercises] . . . need to be applied to their lives . . . to enable them . . . to bring about constructive change in their lives." The teacher begins by suggesting an issue critical to the lives of the students. "[Then] one student would start off with an opening statement, and each student would have to build on whatever had been given and develop it that way. . . . It's taking an issue and [having them] express how they feel about it, their opinions."

The NALP study revealed evidence that such holistic approaches as the language experience method are very much a trend in adult literacy education, and its supporters are quite enthusiastic about its virtues. ". . . Students create their own curriculum," commented one volunteer. "It seems to apply to anyone. It's a good way to go when you're trying to find out something about them, their needs and wants and interests," adds a teacher who was trained in this method at a Literacy Volunteers of America (LVA) workshop. Indeed, the critical difference between LVA and Laubach is LVA's support of the language experience approach backed by an eclectic array of techniques that tutors draw upon depending on the needs and learning styles of the students. (For more information, interested readers may wish to contact LVA directly at 404 Oak Street, Syracuse, NY 13203.)

The language experience method is not without its detractors. One issue is what to do with the possible ungrammaticality of the students' own language. Some practitioners insist that the students' own words be used verbatim since these are the words and the word order that the student will recognize and since it is this recognition that will lead the students to connect meaning to print. Others argue that one should correct the students' language so that they are presented with a model of standard English usage—a skill they will also need if they are to compete in the mainstream of society. Related to this issue is the concern that the students' stories may not contain enough repetition of words or similar word patterns to build adequate lessons for the development of auditory and visual perception and discrimination skills. A third concern is how and when one adds to the students' store of vocabulary to include those words likely to be found in the kinds of materials students will ultimately want to be able to read.

Some language experience teachers have overcome the last two objections by carefully selecting reading materials for oral reading and discussion in class. Teachers in all the youth programs we visited argued forcefully for some group reading and discussion. One teacher described her young students as "mesmerized" when she read them *Occurrence at Owl Creek Bridge*. Other teachers might argue that adult students have a richer store of vocabulary than some teachers give them credit for having. One teacher in a community-based program on the East Coast argued this point: "I had a student [who] made a comparison between the treatment of females within his own Native American society to . . . civil rights. He said, 'It's parallel to the civil rights [issue].' The vocabulary and the understanding is there!" She commented that the student's task is "just being able to identify what he knows with the written language."

Teaching Reading Comprehension Skills

Whichever of the methods we have just described a program uses to teach beginning reading skills, instruction must evolve to the development of the students' abilities to extract meaning from sentences, paragraphs, and ultimately multi-paragraph reading passages and whole books. Traditionally, reading teachers have described three levels of comprehension of such extended prose: (1) the literal level, (2) the interpretive level, and (3) the evaluative level. Exhibit 7.1 is an attempt to list the skills on each of these three levels that we assume proficient readers bring to the reading process. The list is necessarily artificial, as the lines between skills and even levels of skills blur. Which skills the proficient reader employs will depend on any number of factors. Certainly the overriding factors will be the reader's purpose for reading and the nature of the reading material.

If it does nothing else, this list is intended to illustrate the wide variety of things that skilled readers can do with a piece of reading material and the challenge we face in adult education if we are to help our students become skilled readers. It is simply not enough to give students decoding abilities or a large sight vocabulary—our mission must include the kinds of thinking skills required to obtain, interpret, evaluate, and apply information presented in print. (By extension, such thinking skill development can be applied to information taken in through other channels such as radio or television.)

EXHIBIT 7.1 Comprehension Skills of the Skilled Reader

I. LITERAL COMPREHENSION SKILLS

A. Stating the main idea/purpose—both recalling from memory and pointing to statement(s) that directly state the main idea

B. Retrieving directly stated facts—both recalling from memory and locating fact on printed page (in the case of tabular data and other such material, proficient readers would not be expected to recall the specific facts from memory but would recall the general categories and could use that recall to scan the material and locate the desired facts)

C. Skimming to locate desired facts or to see whether material contains information relevant to the information that is being sought—this shades into evaluative comprehension, as in determining whether a fact is likely to appear and thus evaluating relevance of the material to the question at hand

D. Paraphrasing stated facts

E. Stating sequence of facts/events

F. Stating interrelationships among facts (cause-effect; comparison; contrast) based on directly stated conjunctions or other connectors

G. Stating literal meaning of words from word-part analysis or from such directly stated context clues as definitions, examples, and restatements

H. Predicting content from directly stated clues ("The title of this chart says X, so I know the chart is about X"; "The menu lists several dishes under the heading 'pork,' so I know all those dishes contain pork")—this skill shades into inference skills

I. Translating abbreviations of words into complete words—this skill shades into inference skills

J. Translating sentence fragments and other abbreviated sentence structures into complete sentences—this skill shades into inference skills

K. Relating details of text to details of an illustration and vice-versa ("I see a peculiar thing X in the diagram and can find an explanation of what it is in the text"; "I read an explanation of putting X and Y together in the text and can locate these two points in the diagram")

L. Recognizing organizational pattern of material—used especially in conjunction with B, C, and H above and in classifying the type of material

II. INTERPRETIVE COMPREHENSION SKILLS

A. Stating the main idea of material in which the idea is only indirectly stated

B. Identifying writer's assumptions:
   1. through knowledge of conventions of format (the numbers after chapter titles in the table of contents are the page numbers on which the chapters start)
   2. through personal life experience ("The author assumes natural phenomenon X because he mentions Y, and X and Y always occur together")

C. Making inferences about:
   1. what something is
   2. who someone is (including characterization; recognition of use of stereotype)
   3. where something is/was/occurred
   4. when something happened
   5. why someone did/said what they did/said (motivation; probable cause)
   6. implied cause of a stated effect; implied agent of stated action
   7. (rare) implied effect of a stated cause
   8. implied relationship between two things or people
   9. the condition (state of being) of something or someone

D. Drawing implied conclusion from stated facts—this skill shades into evaluative comprehension skills

E. Inferring word meaning from context clues (implied by repetition of key words, through use of connectors, through parallel structure, through restatement, through use of antonyms or contrast)

F. Inferring meaning of figurative language—either through familiarity with idiomatic use or through internal logic of the language

III. EVALUATIVE COMPREHENSION SKILLS

A. Evaluating writer's attitude toward subject (recognition of tone, irony, sympathy, disdain, and the like through evaluation of writer's choice of words)

B. Evaluating writer's intent/purpose (including recognition of propaganda and rhetorical devices)

C. Evaluating logic of writer's reasoning and/or reliability (accuracy) of stated or implied details

D. Distinguishing fact from opinion

E. Evaluating usefulness of material for a specific purpose

F. Applying ideas to related but unstated situations (transfer of knowledge, especially to the reader's life situation)

Leaving aside any debate over whether the skills listed in Exhibit 7.1 are inclusive enough, one must ask whether any such array of skills represents a sequence that suggests discrete units of instruction. In some programs, students progress from the literal to the interpretive to the evaluative level of comprehension over a sequence of lessons, and one does not ask questions about a reading passage that would require a comprehension skill that had not yet been the target of specific instruction. Some practitioners would argue that there is nothing wrong with artificially segmenting the instruction in order to bring isolated skills to the forefront for discussion and analysis, but they would object to keeping comprehension exercises at the literal level over the first umpteen lessons. They would reason that we are dealing with adults who have skills, albeit not reading skills, and that we can therefore structure whatever activities or ask whatever questions a given reading passage may suggest are appropriate to extracting such meaning as may exist. A compromise position would be to expect students to be able to employ skills that have been the target of instruction and to present activities that require other skills in the form of "challenges" or discussion questions.

Once one defines the set of skills that are the target for development, one must consider what activities will help students acquire and use those skills. Just as students must be given practice in reading with proper left-to-right progression and making smooth eye movements from one line to the immediately succeeding line, they must practice "seeing" the verbal and organizational cues that skilled readers rely on to extract meaning from print. Imagine, for example, that you are reading a table of contents or an index for the first time. How would you as a new reader be able to answer such seemingly simple questions as, "On what page does Chapter 2 begin?" or "Where would you find information about X?" Someone would have had to clue you in on the facts that the numbers parading down the left-hand side in a table of contents are chapter numbers, the numbers after the chapter titles are the page numbers on which the chapter begins, the words in an index are in alphabetical order, and the numbers after the entries in an index are the pages on which information about the entry can be found. Even underlying the assumptions that you understand these conventions are the further assumptions that you understand and can use the concept of alphabetical order and that you would be able to call up a synonym for X if it were not listed in the index as X or call up a more generic category if X were listed as a subentry under a larger category. Mathematics and cross-referencing skills might come into play if the question were to be, "In what chapter will you find information about X?" You would have to know how to relate information found in the index to information provided by the table of contents, and you would have to know enough about the number system to be able to determine the chapter in which a given page number would fall. As this simple illustration demonstrates, especially in early lessons, one must be careful to avoid activities that assume that the student already has the background and linguistic ability that could only come from *experience* with printed information.

To guard against making such assumptions, skills are best introduced with several sample passages and a step-by-step walk-through of the application of the target reading comprehension skills. It is never enough to give an abstract explanation of reading comprehension skills—students need to be shown, not told, how to use skills. If one is using commercial textbooks that do not provide sufficient demonstrations, it may be necessary to use the activities that the publisher intended for independent practice as oral exercises done in class. Another way of making many reading comprehension skills more concrete is to help students draw parallels to the kinds of reasoning they use with non-print media or with events that take place around them. Such introductions enable students to understand how they perform such skills as making an inference in their day-to-day lives and thus reassure them that reading skills are not as arcane as their academic labels may imply.

Even with such concrete introductions, it may still be wise to structure the first exercises with pre-reading activities to preview what the students are about to read and to set up what they are expected to look for. Well-constructed activities, through their very sequence, should lead students through the reasoning involved in deriving the writer's intended meaning. Such activities are not limited to multiple-choice or short-answer questions—though these may be the easiest to construct and score. (See the article by Herber and Nelson cited in the bibliography for an interesting critique of teachers' reliance on traditional comprehension questions for unskilled readers.) One might also ask a student to paraphrase or criticize the ideas presented in the reading passage, perhaps using what the student generates as a further language experience story or as the basis of a classroom discussion. One might ask the students themselves to construct their own questions—after all, this simulates what we do when we read independently in the "real world." If the passage were a practical how-to-do-it article, it might be the best possible measure of comprehension to ask students to do what the article describes.

The bottom line for post-reading activities is to give students some mechanism for checking that they have extracted the meaning that a skilled reader could reasonably be expected to extract and that they can use print sources of information for the purposes they were designed to serve; it is not to ask students to recall insignificant details or to perform feats of memory that they will never have to perform outside the classroom. One must remember that skilled readers do not read material word for word or retain every word they read. Thus, when one does use a question-and-answer strategy, one must be careful to ask only those questions that readers might logically want to ask about a given piece of reading material.

And, in structuring multiple-choice questions, one must take care to provide answer choices that are based on logical misreadings of the text—thus building in a means of assessing what kinds of comprehension errors students are making. Further, because incorrect answer choices have been constructed to reflect likely errors and will therefore be attractive to some students, students should be provided with complete explanations of the correct answers and should not be presented with a simple answer key. An answer key may tell the students whether they are right or wrong, but it leaves them without any means of understanding why they were wrong and of avoiding similar errors in the future. Complete explanations provide vital reinforcement to the instructional process, helping those students who answered incorrectly understand the reasoning they should have used. (The American Council on Education, GED Testing Service, One DuPont Circle, Washington, DC 20036, has developed useful guidelines for reading comprehension question writing that are available for purchase.)

In summary, the factors one must consider in designing an instructional program in reading comprehension are:

- selecting the major reading comprehension skills that are to be the target of instruction

- determining the sequence, if any, in which these skills are to be taught

- analyzing the major skills to determine what underlying assumptions may exist about the students' prior experience with print and providing such necessary background as unskilled readers may require—appropriate diagnostic measures will also prove valuable in determining what skills students do and do not have

- providing ample demonstration of the use of skills before asking students to apply the skills independently

- constructing appropriate reinforcement and assessment activities to help students check their comprehension—any activities presented in question-and-answer format should be limited to questions that are truly essential to understanding the writer's messages and that proficient readers could be expected to answer

- providing adequate feedback, including explanations of the answers to all reinforcement and assessment activities

As we will suggest in the section entitled "How Can the Instructional System Be Managed," once one has developed the components of the instructional process, it is wise to write up the instructional plan and share it with students. Students would see in some chart form a list of the reading comprehension skill objectives, the materials and activities they will use to reach those objectives, and the assessment measures they will be expected to use to demonstrate mastery of the skills.

Teaching Competency Applications of Literacy Skills

Adult students generally do not return to education to learn to read for entertainment; rather, they have very practical reasons for wanting the skills that literacy programs can provide. They recognize that limited reading, mathematics, and writing abilities may mean limited employment opportunities, and they know very well how vulnerable they are in such matters as money management, shopping, and health care as well as in any encounters with the civil or criminal justice system. Students may have developed compensatory mechanisms for dealing with such matters, usually through dependence on a helper who can read, but students need and deserve the skills that will make them independent.

For this reason, opportunities to apply basic skills to real-life situations are built into the curricula of most programs. The movement toward the incorporation of such opportunities gained considerable momentum in the late 1970s with the wide dissemination of the Adult Performance Level (APL) study that came out of the University of Texas at Austin. Though the study has been criticized in more recent years, it remains a benchmark study in its identification of the need for functional abilities in five domains:

- occupational knowledge
- consumer skills
- health and safety
- community resources
- government and law

Within each domain, one can specify the basic tasks a fully independent and competent adult would be able to perform and the requisite reading, writing, speaking, and computational skills that underlie the performance of these job-related or life-related tasks.

The concept of establishing such objectives is rarely questioned, but there is considerable debate over (a) what these functional competencies are and (b) when and how they should be introduced into the curriculum. The second question also holds implications for a program's diagnostic and assessment procedures: Does one create separate instruments for academic skills and for competency-based applications; does one use tests of competency-based applications as the sole criteria of student achievement of the ultimate goals of the program; or does one integrate both academic and functional competencies within the same tests?

Obviously, the incorporation of job-related and life-related skills into the curriculum will influence a program's choice of materials. But at what level does one present students with such real-life materials as job application forms, Social Security applications, other government forms (income tax forms, Medicaid applications, etc.), insurance forms, apartment leases, bank forms, telephone books, driver's manuals, roadmaps, transportation schedules, food and medication labels, and the host of other print materials involved in the lives of adults? Too, does one present such materials "as is," or does one present simplified versions to students on a lower reading level? (We'll have more to say about materials selection in the next section on "Choosing Appropriate Materials for Adults.")

Ultimately, then, the decision to attempt to guarantee that instruction will help students do those things that are essential to functioning well on the job and in life will mean the development of an instructional management system. One such system is the California Adult Student Assessment System (CASAS). This system is administered through the CASAS Project Staff of the San Diego Community College District, but it represents a consortium of ninety districts and agencies in California and five other western states. At present, one can obtain the following through CASAS:

CASAS Competency List—a common core of competencies included in ABE and ESL programs, encompassing 26 competency areas and 132 specific competency statements

CASAS Curriculum Index and Matrix—a list of readily available curriculum materials coded to the specific competencies and classified by level; updated annually

CASAS Item Bank—a bank of over 2,000 items designed to measure student performance of specific competency statements—items can be assembled to form diagnostic or assessment tests

Curriculum and Data Management Services—sample recordkeeping forms; system for scoring tests and reporting results

Technical Assistance—CASAS project staff and consultants will work with districts and agencies in developing an assessment system tailored to their own existing curriculum

Additional information about CASAS can be obtained by writing: California Adult Student Assessment System, San Diego Community College, 3249 Fordham Street, San Diego, CA 92110.

The inclusion of life skill objectives does not mean the exclusion of academic objectives. For example, the Adult Diploma Program (ADP) of the Lowell Adult Education Program, Lowell, Massachusetts, requires students to complete eighty credits, a minimum of forty in academic disciplines (e.g., English, mathematics, science, U.S. history) and a minimum of fifteen in life skills. To help students apply academic skills to practical, everyday living situations, program staff developed competency-based modules in reading, mathematics, and English; these modules have also been used to supplement instruction in the regular ABE program.

Another program, Caldwell Community College and Technical Institute in Lenoir,

North Carolina, obtained a federal grant to examine the competencies needed for adult basic education, adult high school diploma programs, and the vocational, technical, and college curricula. The goal of their study is to design a spectrum of competencies from level zero through college in reading, mathematics, and English and to define which skills are needed for entry into an ABE or GED program or for transfer into vocational training and college. (At this writing, the study has not yet been completed.)

The New York State Department of Correctional Services has also recently developed a curriculum guide that includes 214 competency statements that are to be integrated into the traditional curriculum. Its "Adult Functional Competencies Curriculum" lists the required reading, mathematics, writing, and reference/study skills for each of the four levels of instruction (ABE I, reading levels 0–2.9; ABE II, reading levels 3.0–4.9; Pre-GED, reading levels 5.0–7.9; and GED, reading levels 8.0–12.9) and suggests the development of "learning activity packets" as a means of pairing content and skills objectives. Each packet is to contain: (1) instructions to the student, (2) a checklist of activities, (3) instructional materials for content, (4) instructional materials for skills, and (5) a pre-test and a post-test.

All the programs cited in the foregoing paragraphs—and the countless others in the field—share one common factor. They are all based on clearly stated behavioral objectives that drive a true system of diagnosis, instruction, and assessment (we'll return to the concept of instructional management systems later in the chapter). Lists of competency-based behavioral objectives can be very useful tools for programs that want to investigate what skills they might incorporate into their curricula, yet the field of competency-based adult education is still a field in evolution. Perhaps the best way to stay abreast of research and development in the field is to contact: The Competency-Based Adult Education Network, Division of Adult Education Services, U.S. Department of Education, Room 5610 ROB #3, 7th and D Streets, S.W., Washington, DC 20202-3583. (At this writing, the network is headed by Mr. Richard Eason.)

Modes of Presentation

In planning the delivery of instruction, programs have a number of options open to them. The worksheet shown as Exhibit 7.2 presents a listing of possible instructional practices; from these, teachers can select those practices they will use to introduce new information or skills, reinforce the presentation of skills, and have students practice the new skill, review all skills, or apply skills to job-related or life-related material.

EXHIBIT 7.2 Instructional Strategies Planning Document

Instructional Modes

Instructional Practices	Introduce New Information or Skills	Reinforce Information or Skills	Practice New Skills	Review	Apply New Skills or Knowledge
1. Teacher presentation to group					
2. Teacher presentation to individuals					
3. Group drill and practice					
4. Individual drill and practice					
5. Students reading aloud					
6. Students reading silently					
7. Students working in pairs or threes					
8. Film or video presentation					
9. Computer-assisted instruction					
10. Small-group role-play or simulation					
11. Large-group role-play or simulation					
12. Students' presentation in group					
13. Handouts with some instruction, some practice					

Instructional Practices	Introduce New Information or Skills	Reinforce Information or Skills	Practice New Skills	Review	Apply New Skills or Knowledge
14. Book or booklets with some instruction					
15. Teacher-led student discussion					
16. Teacher-led Socratic method instruction					
17. Individual student desk work					
18. Group work					
19. Teacher demonstration or modeling of skills					
20. Guest presentations					
21. Homework					
22. Other					

CHOOSING APPROPRIATE MATERIALS FOR ADULTS

Assuming that a program has determined the target skills and the sequence of skill development, the program must then seek to match appropriate materials to the statements of skill objectives. The skill objective statements and the instructional methodology of the program will largely determine what materials the program chooses; after all, the materials should help the students achieve the desired objectives. However, if materials are to be of genuine help to adult students, programs must evaluate whether the materials they use accommodate different backgrounds, interests, goals, learning styles, strengths and weaknesses, and reading levels. To be most effective, materials should include or be clearly correlated to diagnostic/placement mechanisms, afford ample opportunities for practice, and include assessment mechanisms.

Critical Factors in Materials Selection

The International Reading Association's "Checklist for Evaluating Adult Basic Education Reading Material," reproduced as Exhibit 7.3 in this chapter, provides a very useful means of determining whether given material includes the features one might demand of adult education material. The fifty-one questions of the IRA checklist are focused on four critical factors—readability, relevance, manageability, and accommodation of special needs—each of which needs some preliminary discussion.

Readability

It may go without saying that, to be useful, materials have to be readable. Unfortunately, it is not always clear what we mean by the term *readability*. The most common means of describing the readability of material is to apply one of several readability formulas to determine a reading grade level. The Gunning Fog Index (detailed in the IRA checklist in Exhibit 7.3) and the Fry Graph (a source for which is also cited in Exhibit 7.3) are two popular formulas in use in adult education; both are based on the average number of syllables and the average number of sentences in 100-word samples taken from the reading material, and both are quite simple to learn to use. Other formulas, such as the Dale-Chall and the Spache, use lists of words that are assumed to be familiar to readers on various levels; if words that occur in the reading material do not appear on the list, these words are assumed to be unfamiliar and are counted and multiplied by some numerical factor to derive the reading grade level.

Despite the usefulness of such formulas in categorizing the general level of material (it is somehow nice to be able to say of a story, "This story is written on a second-grade level"), even the developers of readability formulas caution that there are some serious limitations to relying exclusively on a statistical measure of readability level. For example, formulas that rely on syllable counts and sentence length alone will find such sentences as "Black is the color of my true love's hair" or "Do not go gentle into that good night" to be on a low readability level. Yet the inverted structure of the first and the level of abstraction of the second will make both sentences difficult for many new adult readers to comprehend. The frequent use of a polysyllabic word such as *Mississippi* will inflate the readability level of a reading passage, yet it may not make the material particularly difficult to read. On the other hand, one-syllable words (such as *ewe, urn, shard*) or words with multiple meanings (such as *run, walk, set*) may introduce comprehension problems that will not be reflected by the statistically low readability level of the passage in which they occur. (Imagine confronting a new adult reader with the sentences, "His pet ewe has the run of the yard," and "The urn fell on the walk and broke into a dozen shards." Obviously, readability level does not necessarily equal comprehensibility.) The concept load of reading material also cannot be reflected by a readability formula. For example, Hemingway's *The Old Man and the Sea* may be on a low readability level, but the concepts it develops are much more complex than some new readers may be prepared to handle.

Beyond attempting to describe the readability level of given reading materials, it is also useful to think of students as being able to operate on several levels. Reading teachers generally speak of three levels: (1) the *independent* level, material that can be easily read by the student without any form of assistance; (2) the *instructional* level, material that is something of a challenge but can be read with some limited assistance; and (3) the *frustration* level, material that is too difficult to be read with comprehension. The personal interests or background of a student may make these levels shift depending on the material to be read. For example, an auto mechanic may find an auto repair manual written at a tenth-grade reading level to be well within the independent level and yet find a short story written at a sixth-grade level to be at the frustration level.

We do not suggest that adult educators abandon the use of readability formulas. It is useful to group collections of materials by their levels of relative simplicity or complexity in order to choose materials appropriate to the educational levels of students. Nevertheless, we suggest at least two cautions. First, do not rely on a publisher's advertised readability designation as a criterion for purchasing material (even if the publisher specifies the formula used). You should still inspect the material to determine how easy it will be for your student population to read. Second, do not hold students back by assigning materials only on the reading grade level determined by the students' scores on a standardized test. The students' interests, background, and motivation may enable them to read at a much higher level. Further, students may be challenged by materials that are somewhat more difficult than those they could read easily.

Relevance

The words *relevant* and *meaningful* are often invoked by adult educators to describe the difference between materials that are appropriate for adults and materials that were designed for children or adolescents. "We are working from materials that students identify in their own lives," explains one director. "I talk to [my students] about topics *they'd* like to explore," adds a teacher at one ABE program. Many commercial publishers have responded to the call for materials relevant to adult students, but not always with success. The most serious indictment we heard of some commercial materials is that they "write off" the poor and the disenfranchised because they don't talk about things that are real in their lives. "A lot of books show them what to do with checks and phone bills. . . . [Our students] don't have either! Life skills for whose life?" questions a director whose students come from a decaying neighborhood in a large Eastern city. One must be careful to define *meaningful* in the students' terms.

Language experience stories, especially those generated from one-to-one or class-room discussion, can be extremely useful in tapping the interests and information needs of students and guaranteeing that information is presented in the detail, in the terms, and in the contexts that the students' experiential background indicate are appropriate. Another useful technique is to allow students to choose their own material from the program's library or to bring in materials from their jobs or their homes that they want to learn to read. Students can tell teachers what is of most concern to them and can quickly determine if a given text or lesson on that topic is genuinely helpful in fulfilling their need to know. If the materials on the library or resource center shelves have been chosen to reflect the wide range of information needs of adults, the materials themselves may suggest topics that the students might not have thought of requesting on their own.

Teachers often draw on the context of events in the community or their students' lives to demonstrate the practical applications of reading, math, and writing skills. For example, a math instructor in a military program uses articles from the local newspaper as the information base of word problems. At income tax time, he designs lessons to assist students in filing their tax forms. He also teaches a module on contracts in which he uses two real contracts so that the students can pick them apart and learn to interpret terminology. In the U.S. Army's Job Skills Education Program (JSEP), reading and math lessons are drawn from soldiers' field manuals or typical military situations so that skills can be applied directly to daily tasks.

An inmate tutor at a correctional institution, when asked what students want to know, replied, ". . . one of the main things students want to do right off the bat is writing letters. . . ." He described how he deviates from scheduled lesson plans to help inmates write letters, even if he has to print them out for the inmates. In prison, where waiting lists to use the telephone can be a month long, writing letters is "one of the major forms of communication," explained the tutor.

Materials that center around any of the practical items listed below can provide meaningful contexts for reading practice or sight word recognition drills as well as the development of important survival skills. However, care must be taken in using any such list. For example, a menu from the teacher's favorite French restaurant is hardly as appropriate as the counter menu from a fast-food restaurant, yet one must also guard against being condescending.

advertisements	measuring devices
application blanks	menus
ballots	money
bank statements	newspapers (including national
billboards	tabloids)
bills	occupant mail
bumper stickers	owner's manuals
calendars	packages and containers
catalogues	political campaign literature
checks	recipes
contracts and leases	sales slips
coupons	signs
	statement stuffers from utility and
	phone bills

driver's manuals	tax forms
guarantees	telephone book
insurance policies and claim forms	television and movie schedules
labels	tickets
magazines	travel schedules and timetables
maps	warranties

In choosing real-life materials, one is instantly confronted with the question of whether or not to adjust the readability level. To be sure, such legal documents as insurance policies and apartment leases are written at levels far beyond beginning level students, but one must ask whether simplified versions of such documents actually serve the purpose of preparing students to be informed consumers. Students who have been taught to read only simplified versions of the labels on over-the-counter medicines will still be bewildered by the warning and dosage labels they'll find in the drugstore—perhaps to their detriment. One solution is to present a simplified version side by side with the real article and to give students strategies for extracting the general meaning of the real article without being able to read every word.

The concept of meaningfulness extends beyond such practical material to include fiction, biography, general-interest features from newspapers and magazines, drama, and poetry. Many program leaders feel that learners must go beyond narrow goals that serve an immediate need, such as filling out employment applications, to using reading skills in a broader context. If the program teaches nothing but life skills, "[students] just don't develop the kind of fluency they really need," comments a director in a large urban program. Some educators feel strongly that students want and need exposure to literature and the great thinkers of the past. "They want poetry, they want Karl Marx, they want whatever we can get them," explains one director who frequently sits down at his typewriter to adapt material for his beginning readers.

Whether or not one uses Literature with a capital L, using familiar and compelling topics is one way to relate reading and writing instruction to real-life situations and thereby enhance the students' ability to acquire skills. For example, a teacher in a community-based program describes how she uses the story of the breakup of a marriage to encourage the development of thinking, discussion, and writing skills. Students are invited to take sides in the debate and justify the positions of both the man and the woman. By contrast, stories that are meaningless—that is, outside the life and language experience of the students—may actually slow the development of reading comprehension and critical thinking skills. This does not mean that students don't want or won't read materials that will "expand their horizons," though the decision to use such materials is probably better left to the students themselves; it does mean that a story about a divorce is better suited to skill development than an article about pre-Columbian art or stories that barely rise above the level of the old "Dick and Jane" readers.

Since students have varied interests, there must be a variety of materials to appeal to those interests. This may mean ordering two or three copies of many types of materials, going to a public or university library to track down something on a topic suggested by a student, ordering free government pamphlets, or maintaining files of the language experience stories and poetry written by former students. "Out of the thousand books in our resource center, there is not one book that we would put a student into on a regular basis," states one director. He is opposed to the practice of routinely placing every student in the same skillbooks or series as the means of instruction; skill objectives may be fixed, but the materials used to help students achieve those objectives do not have to remain fixed.

Manageability

Effective educational materials must be more than readable and relevant; they must also include those features that will help both the student and the program manage the instruction the materials are designed to deliver. This will mean that material should include very clear statements of its objectives and some means of measuring the extent to which students have achieved those objectives. If the material includes a diagnostic pre-test, that pre-test must be clearly correlated to the instructional portion of the material. It should help the student and the teacher pinpoint the level or other point in the sequence of the instruction at which individual students should begin. To avoid wasting the students' time studying material over which they have demonstrated mastery on the pre-test, the pre-test results should tell the students both what portions of the material they should plan to study and what portions may be safely eliminated. It is important to inspect any pre-test carefully to see that there is a sufficient number of items for each specific skill objective for reliable results and that items validly measure the skills they purport to measure. (The information we presented in Chapter 6 should prove helpful in checking reliability and validity.) If the material contains no pre-test (as, for example, in a set of supplemental readers), the instructional objectives and the level of the material (including assumed prerequisite skills) should be clear enough to permit programs to construct some formal or informal means for student placement.

Once students begin using the instructional material itself, they should find frequent and reasonably extensive practice activities, and they should clearly see how the activities relate to the goals and objectives of the program. Instructions should lay out what the students are expected to do and how they can evaluate their performance. When a student does not successfully complete a given exercise, there should be some provision to allow the student to reread the instructional material and then work on a supplemental practice exercise to demonstrate mastery of the target skills. Some commercial materials do not provide for this common occurrence, though some publishers do prepare supplemental workbooks for their basic texts and some computer software programs are designed to recycle students until they demonstrate mastery. Literacy programs often correlate practice activities from a number of different materials to accomplish this same purpose, a task made easier when all of the materials have clear and identifiable objectives. When programs share the instructional plan with students, clearly labeling the objectives and the variety of different sources of instruction and practice for each objective, students themselves can initiate supplemental work when they feel a need for it.

In addition to having practice activities on specific subskills, material should include cumulative practice activities to ensure that students are retaining all the skills that have been developed up to a given point in the instructional sequence. We know from learning theory and from experience that skills will be selectively forgotten if they are not reinforced periodically. In math material, cumulative practice exercises would challenge students to work multi-step problems that might involve any of the four basic operations (addition, subtraction, multiplication, and division) and a mix of different kinds of figures (whole numbers, fractions, decimals, and percents). In reading material, cumulative practice exercises would help students integrate discrete subskills and develop reading fluency, drawing on whatever skills may be required to extract the meaning of reading material. An additional benefit of cumulative practice exercises is that they closely simulate real-life situations in which students will have to decide independently which skills to use. Real life has a habit of not neatly falling into textbook-like compartmentalized areas, and instructional material that does not help students become problem solvers adept at choosing appropriate strategies from the range of possibilities is simply not fulfilling the ultimate needs of the students. At the conclusion of a cumulative practice exercise, all the skills that were involved should be identified so that students can go back to earlier points in the material and reread explanations of those skills they may need to review.

If material is to fit into a program's instructional management system, it must have not only diagnostic or placement mechanisms and ongoing, cumulative assessment mechanisms but also some form of final evaluation with a clear indication of what the students are equipped to do upon completion of the material. One will need to inspect the evaluative measure for reliability and validity in exactly the same way one inspected the diagnostic pre-test. If the pre-test was appropriately constructed to reflect all the skills covered in the material, there should be a strong (perhaps one-to-one) correlation between the post-test and the pre-test. And if ongoing assessment measures included cumulative exercises, students should be prepared to perform successfully on the post-test. Indeed, a post-test should not hold any surprises; students should know from the beginning of their work within the material what criteria they will be expected to meet and should understand how the objectives of each lesson relate to those criteria. The post-test should serve to confirm students' mastery of the objectives of the material, yet it should still include a detailed item analysis to guide students who may need to review some portions of the instructional material. To accommodate students who do not perform successfully, it may be wise to have a second, parallel form of the post-test.

Accommodation of Special Needs

Material that can be evaluated positively with respect to the foregoing three factors—readability, relevance, and manageability—will have the flexibility to meet the individual needs of most adult students, yet a small percentage of the population has special learning problems that require special materials. Considerable attention has been focused on the topic of learning disabilities in recent years, but the field of research on adults with such disabilities is still extremely limited. The occurrence of severe visual or auditory acuity problems and developmental disabilities (we long ago abandoned the unkind and inaccurate terms *mental retardation* and *mentally handi-capped*) is a fact; unfortunately, such labels as *dyslexic* have often been freely applied to those who only appear to have such disabilities. (See the article by Gerald Coles cited in the bibliography for more on this unfortunate phenomenon.)

It was not within the scope of the NALP study to explore current practice in the education of developmentally disabled adults, but we do recognize the importance of obtaining accurate information for some readers. Interested readers should contact the Network of Adult Education Programs Serving the Disabled Person at the address cited in the bibliography.

Commercial Print Material

The number of commercial materials targeted for adult education has grown dramatically in the past several years, and adult educators now face the welcome challenge of choosing from the wide variety of available materials those best suited to students in their programs. (A list of twenty-four publishers active in the field of adult education is presented at the end of the chapter beginning on page 156). Well-constructed commercial material can be a boon to those programs that cannot devote the amount of time involved in developing truly diagnostic pre-tests, extensive and varied practice exercises, and reliable and comprehensive assessment and evaluative measures.

Purchasing commercial material extends beyond such clearly educational material as phonics workbooks, collections of controlled readability stories with comprehension exercises, and GED or pre-GED preparation texts to include the same fiction and nonfiction published for the general public. Especially for some content areas in the social or natural sciences, programs may even find high school or college textbooks useful. Programs that do design their own core curriculum materials still find it necessary to supplement such self-developed material with commercial materials that match specific objectives or that provide additional opportunities to read. As the director of a volunteer program in a correctional institution commented: "You don't want thirty books at the beginning level, because the person needs to read two hundred! If someone is in the program for a year or so, they run out of books before they can advance to the next level of materials. . . . [and] books that are interesting to read are hard to write [yourself]." This director acquired 20,000 volumes that were being discarded when a local library closed its doors, thus providing her students with a wide choice of books written with varying degrees of difficulty.

Rarely do programs adopt a single series as the sole instructional tool, yet the evaluation and correlation of the countless volumes currently available and the new texts that flood the market each year can be a time-consuming task. Assembling a panel of teachers can be a means of reducing the workload, but is essential that all members of the evaluation team are using the same evaluation criteria. In Exhibit 7.3, we present a useful model evaluation checklist for adult basic education reading material; it is reproduced with permission from the May 1981 issue of the *Journal of Reading* (Volume 24, Number 8; a publication of the International Reading Association). As explained in that publication, this checklist was developed by the IRA's

Committee for Basic Education and Reading during the years 1977 through 1980 and represents the combined efforts of adult educators across the United States through several revisions.

EXHIBIT 7.3 Checklist for Evaluating ABE Reading Material

Demand for basic skills reading material to meet the concerns of adult learners continues to grow. In the United States, this demand has especially been fostered by the U.S. Adult Education Act of 1966 which encouraged establishment and expansion of adult basic education programs. However, because the many materials now being published do not always satisfy ABE teacher/learner needs, this assessment checklist has been developed. Where possible, material should be evaluated by those who understand the special problems of ABE students and are familiar with the principles, processes, and rationale for selecting educational materials.

This checklist should help you:

- Select material that will meet the special needs and interests of adult basic education learners;
- Make objective judgments based on a clear evaluation process;
- Assist in staff development by providing a mechanism for sharpening staff judgments;
- Provide individualized instruction that relates to the particular knowledge, abilities, and informational needs of ABE students—especially those far from mastery of basic skills; and
- Identify and classify material for placement in a filing/retrieval system.

Instructions

When reviewing reading material for adults, consider these points: cost, dustcover, preface, table of contents, introduction, instructions, print, graphics, content, index, and any supporting addenda. An easy-to-apply readability-level determiner is an additional aid. Robert Gunning's Fog Index is included here, but, of course, other readability formulas, such as the Fry Graph, are acceptable options.

In the columns on the right, circle the symbol that most clearly represents your response to each of the 51 questions:

$$+ = yes$$
$$- = no$$
$$u = undecided$$
$$na = not\ applicable$$

Space for written comments is provided after each set of questions.

Appeal

1. Is the material
   a. fresh?   +   −   u   na
   b. enjoyable to read?   +   −   u   na
   c. of interest to adults?   +   −   u   na
   Comments: _____

Relevance

2. Does the material
   a. pertain to adult life experiences?   +   −   u   na
   b. add to general knowledge of adults?   +   −   u   na
   c. present factual, up-to-date information?   +   −   u   na
   d. use language in a natural way?   +   −   u   na
   Comments: _____

Purpose

3. Does the content
   a. state (or imply) broad goals and specific
      objectives?   +   −   u   na
   b. address the functional needs of ABE students?   +   −   u   na
   Comments: _____

Process

4. Does the material present
   a. prereading experiences?   +   −   u   na
   b. word-analysis exercises?   +   −   u   na
   c. well constructed reading passages?   +   −   u   na
   d. a clear progression of ideas or story line?   +   −   u   na
   e. comprehension exercises?   +   −   u   na
   f. appropriate vocabulary?   +   −   u   na
   g. opportunities for silent reading?   +   −   u   na
   h. passages suitable for oral reading?   +   −   u   na
   Comments: _____

Human relations

5. Does the material
   a. depict cultural, racial, or ethnic groups and the
      sexes in a positive way, avoiding stereotypes?   +   −   u   na
   b. depict characters without sexist bias?   +   −   u   na
   c. avoid male nouns and pronouns when content
      refers to both sexes?   +   −   u   na
   d. show the sexes in nonstereotypical work roles?   +   −   u   na
   e. show individuals in various current occupations?   +   −   u   na
   f. stimulate discussion?   +   −   u   na
   Comments: _____

Evaluation

6. Does the material
   a. suggest ways to continue evaluation of a student's progress? +   −   u   na
   b. provide for pre-tests and post-tests? +   −   u   na
   Comments: _____

Function of the material

7. Does the material
   a. encourage wide reading? +   −   u   na
   b. suggest resources and activities for student exploration? +   −   u   na
   c. promote inductive as well as deductive reasoning? +   −   u   na
   d. offer clear and understandable instructions? +   −   u   na
   e. offer opportunity for continuous success and mastery? +   −   u   na
   f. provide an answer key for the teacher? +   −   u   na
   g. provide an answer key for the student? +   −   u   na
   Comments: _____

Format

8. Does the format of the material
   a. appear usable with adult students? +   −   u   na
   b. appear attractive? +   −   u   na
   c. include suitable illustrations (drawings, photographs, graphs, maps, etc.)? +   −   u   na
   d. present an easy-to-read type size? +   −   u   na
   e. provide ample margins and spaces between type lines? +   −   u   na
   Comments: _____

Teacher directions

9. Are instructions
   a. offered the teacher where needed? +   −   u   na
   b. offered the student where needed? +   −   u   na
   c. clear, so that special training is not needed to understand them? +   −   u   na
   Comments: _____

Content

10. In content,
    a. do the authors provide adequate reinforcement? +   −   u   na
    b. are selections short enough to hold interest but long enough to develop ideas? +   −   u   na
    c. does the material provide appropriate reading-level experiences? +   −   u   na

    d. does the material's readability level increase appropriately?   +   −   u   na

    e. does the material promote literal comprehension (exactly as stated)?   +   −   u   na

    f. does it promote inferential comprehension (reading between the lines)?   +   −   u   na

    g. does it promote evaluative comprehension (making judgments)?   +   −   u   na

    h. does it promote other types of comprehension?   +   −   u   na

    i. are there problem-solving exercises?   +   −   u   na

    j. are there writing activities linked to reading selections?   +   −   u   na

    k. does the material provide reference and study skills?   +   −   u   na

Comments: _____

Totals: _____

Quantitative evaluation

Often a simple checklist—though its yes/no procedure may not fully assess a material's value—is sufficient to determine the item's usability with particular students. If a quantitative assessment is desired, the following formula may be helpful. Note: The *undecided* and *not applicable* responses are not used in the calculations.

$$\frac{\text{POSITIVE responses divided by}}{\text{POSITIVE plus NEGATIVE responses}} = \underline{\qquad} \times 10 = \quad \text{Numerical evaluation}$$

Scale

10	9	8	7	6 (or less)
Superior	Very good	Good	Poor	Unacceptable

Other data
(Circle appropriate dots)

Type of material
- Single volume
  Textbook
  Workbook
- Multiple volume (series)
- Hard cover
- Soft cover
- Pamphlet
- Consumable
- Group centered
- One-student centered
- Teacher centered
- Programmed
- Supplemental only
- Pleasure

Content intended for
- Adult Basic Education (ABE)
- General Educational Development (GED)
- Coping skills
    Adult performance level
    Vocational
    Employability skills
- Level I   (Grades 0–3)
- Level II   (Grades 4–8)
- Level III   (Grades 9–12)

Age-group designation
- 16–29   • 50–65
- 30–49   • Over 65

Material designed for
- General population
- Rural population
- Urban population
- Regional USA (region: _____)
- Canada
- Other: _____

Specific background or need
- Linguistic
- Cultural/ethnic
- English as a Second Language
- Socioeconomic
- Technical

A readability determiner

Robert Gunning's Fog Index—based on the average number of sentences and poly-syllabic works in selected 100-word passages—is a formula for estimating the reading level of materials. The following, though different in wording, shows the steps in Gunning's Index as outlined in his *Techniques of Clear Writing* (New York: McGraw-Hill Book Co., 1968, p. 38. See also: Robert Gunning, "The Fog Index After Twenty Years," *Journal of Business Communication,* vol. 6, pp. 3–13, Winter 1968).

1. Select three 100-word passages, one each from the beginning, middle, and end of the reading material. (One such passage is sufficient if the material is short.)

2. In each passage count the number of words with three or more syllables. Do NOT count proper nouns ("January"), easy compounds ("bookmaker"), or three-syllable verbs ending in *ed* or *es* ("promoted," "progresses").

3. Determine the average sentence length for each passage by dividing the number of words by the number of sentences. (Estimate if a sentence left incomplete at the 100th word might be counted as a full sentence; i.e., is the fragment an independent clause, or only a few words short of the period?)

4. Add together the number of polysyllabic words and the average number of words in a sentence in each passage.

5. Multiply each total by 0.4. The result is the Fog Index—the years of schooling, or grade level, needed to read the passage.

6. Add together the reading levels for the three passages and divide by three. This is the Index for the complete material—that point where intelligibility gets fogged in!

Note: Another helpful and easy-to-use formula for assessing readability is the FRY GRAPH. For a discussion of the graph and how it is applied see: Carl B. Smith, Sharon L. Smith, and Larry Mikulecky, *Teaching Reading in Secondary School Content Subjects: A Bookthinking Process* (New York: Holt, Rinehart and Winston, 1978), pp. 9–10. Also, preceeding this is an outline of the FOG INDEX.

Reference data

Title of material _____

Author/editor _____

Publisher _____ Copyright date _____

Number of pages _____ Cost _____ Numerical evaluation _____

Fog Index (if computed) _____ General Comments _____

_____

_____

_____

_____

_____

_____

_____

_____

Computer Software

In their investigations of the possible uses of computer-assisted instruction (CAI), programs face a number of decisions. If one cannot budget over the long term, leasing or buying computer hardware and educational software may not be as economically feasible as investing in print material. Even when funds are available, the array of microcomputers on the market is bewildering to educators who themselves may not be "computer literate." The decision in favor of any particular microcomputer is made all the more difficult when one discovers that software designed for one manufacturer's machine will not necessarily (and almost never does) run on another manufacturer's machine; the same problem may also occur with different models in the same manufacturer's product line. One must also face the fact that, desirable as the concept of CAI may be, there may not be software available to perform the tasks that the program wants to have computers deliver. As of this writing, there is very little software on the market designed specifically for adult education. Therefore, the best way to make the investment decision is to define the tasks the program wants the hardware and the software to perform and then to determine whether there are systems that will do those things. Once this decision has been made, some programs have softened the economic crunch by forming cooperative relationships with businesses who loan or donate hardware and software. One program located near a military base shares computers with a military program.

Beyond the issues of finding funding and then finding appropriate hardware and software, programs must also face a host of human issues. Teachers will need to be persuaded of the value of CAI and given training in the operation of both the hardware and the software. As one director commented, "If [the teachers] don't like it, it will fail." Some teachers may actually fear that the use of microcomputers may reduce the need for the current level of staffing within their program; they will certainly be resistant to the notion that they are being "replaced" by a machine. Some students may also react negatively to the idea of working with a machine, though many more see it as an enjoyable encounter with the world of high technology. (For programs still in the decision-making process, we recommend the text by David Gueulette as well as the monograph entitled "A Statewide Approach to Computer Application for Adult Literacy Programs" cited in the bibliography.)

Although computers certainly are not the major tool for instruction in the adult education programs we visited, we did note trends within certain sectors. Computers were being used or being introduced in most of the local ABE programs and in half of the correctional institution programs, and both programs that have adopted the Comprehensive Competencies Program (CCP) use computers as one mode of delivering instruction. Given employment trends in many communities, students often eagerly welcome the opportunity to become computer literate, and many programs have developed courses in basic programming and word processing.

The software on the market includes programs for extensive drill and practice, student recordkeeping, and diagnostic/prescriptive testing. With the exception of programs in mathematics, however, there are very few complete instructional programs delivered solely by microcomputer that are suitable for adult basic education students. With appropriate cautions, some programs have used basic reading and writing skills programs originally developed for children, and some programs have designed their own software. (A list of nine software publishers whose materials have been used successfully in adult education programs is presented at the end of the chapter.)

In evaluating software, one must first determine whether all the necessary hardware, including a printer, is readily accessible to the students and teachers. One may also need to evaluate other technical considerations, such as whether the software can be used with a network of computers serially connected to a master console controlled by the instructor. One then inspects the features of the software much as one would for print material to see that it has all the elements of a good instructional design, appropriate readability level, and adult content. Unlike a book, a software program is not necessarily designed to be opened or closed at any point the student desires, and thus one must determine how easily students can enter and exit the program. If students are expected to use the software independently, one must know how much knowledge the students must have, including knowledge of the operation of a computer or required command keys (that is, those keys on the computer's keyboard that teachers must instruct students to use to operate the various features of the software). Software developers generally aim to make their programs "user-friendly," that is, easy to operate by those unfamiliar with the technical jargon; nevertheless, it is wise to ask a few students to experiment with the software before making a decision to purchase in order to determine just how "friendly" the software is.

Well-designed software can offer distinct advantages over traditional print materials. From a set of diagnostic exercises, the computer can generate an individualized prescription for instruction and immediately place students in an appropriate part of the program. After presenting instruction, the software may cycle students through as many or as few problems as they need to demonstrate mastery and may present additional instruction or "skill reminders" for those who are experiencing difficulty. The problems presented during the instruction may be presented step by step so that the software can help the students determine where they may be going wrong. For example, students may be asked to work a division problem one place at a time, and the software will stop the student at any step that is performed incorrectly. The interaction that takes place is very much like one-to-one work with a tutor (indeed, such software is usually referred to as a tutorial program), and the computer is an always patient tutor who never becomes bored with the amount of practice or repetition of instruction a student may require. Some software has built-in flexibility or customizing features; teachers can control the difficulty level and the rate of presentation and may even be able to add their own material or delete or alter existing material.

Computer software may need supplementation. Thus, publishers of software programs may correlate their individual programs to available pre-tests and post-tests and to commercially available print materials or to other appropriate software programs. If the software developers have not made such correlations, adult education programs may make the correlations themselves as long as the developers have provided clear and detailed lists of the objectives of the software.

Exhibit 7.4 is an evaluation form developed through a project funded by the Massachusetts State Department of Education, Bureau of Student, Community, and Adult Services; we reproduce it here as a possible model.

EXHIBIT 7.4 Evaluation Form for Adult Education Software

PROGRAM TITLE:_____ Software Producer:_____ Version:_____

Hardware Requirements:_____

Cost, if known:_____ Includes Back-Up Disk:_____

Comment on Typical Runtime:_____

INSTRUCTIONAL PURPOSES AND TECHNIQUES (check all that apply)

Appropriate Uses:

___ABE (0–4); ___Pre-GED (5–8); ___GED (9–12); ___ESL; ___Pre-Voc.

Specific Subject/Skill Area_____

_____Basic Skill Remediation   _____Drill and Practice

_____Skill/Knowledge Development   _____Tutorial

_____Enrichment   _____Game or Simulation

_____Learning Tool   _____Diagnostic/Prescriptive

_____Administrative/Teacher Tool   Other_____

INSTRUCTIONAL CHARACTERISTICS   Yes   No

Learning objectives are clear and worthwhile for adult
   learners.   ____   ____

Typical runtime is commensurate to educational value.   ____   ____

Tone of address is acceptable to adults.   ____   ____

Format is challenging, not frustrating.   ____   ____

Feedback is appropriate, useful, and timely.   ____   ____

CONTENT CHARACTERISTICS   Yes   No

Content is error-free and factually correct.   ____   ____

Difficulty level may be adjusted.   ____   ____

Presentation is logical and well-organized.   ____   ____

Vocabulary, concepts, and examples are relevant to adults. ____   ____

Content can be changed or added by instructor.   ____   ____

Content avoids ethnic, racial or sexual discrimination and
   stereotyping.   ____   ____

TECHNICAL CHARACTERISTICS	Yes	No
Documentation is concise, readable, and adequate.	___	___
Screen directions are concise, readable, and adequate.	___	___
Adult learners can operate program independently.	___	___
Program may be entered and exited with ease.	___	___
Program is user friendly and apparently error free.	___	___
Screens and/or text are readable and uncluttered.	___	___
Sound and graphics enhance the program; are not demanding.	___	___
Rate and sequence of program operation can be controlled.	___	___

Management/Record keeping system: _____ None; _____Optional; _____ Required for program operation

PROGRAM QUALITY SUMMARY   RECOMMENDATIONS

4 (high) to 1 (low)

_____Instructional Characteristics

_____I highly recommend this program for use with adult learners.

_____Content Characteristics

_____I would use this program, but with some reservations or changes.

_____Technical Characteristics

_____I would neither use nor recommend this program for adult learners.

Comments: (Strengths, weaknesses, suggested uses, training requirements, etc.)

_____

_____

_____

_____

Evaluator's Name: _____ Date: _____

Position: _____

Organization: _____

Self-Developed and Real-Life Material

Despite the availability of commercially produced material, programs often find it necessary to custom design at least some of the material to be used. Employment and training programs or military programs are especially likely to develop their own material so that highly specialized or constituency-specific goals can be addressed. Other programs base their decision to develop their own material on the concept that students learn best when material directly addresses the students' personal needs and concerns; such immediate relevance may not exist in commercial materials designed to appeal to a broad national public.

The Lutheran Settlement House Women's Program in Philadelphia believes that all teaching must be centered on the learners' life experiences and interests. The program develops its own material to "focus on those issues or those underlying themes which may emerge from class discussion." Several manuals, as the materials are called, were in use in GED classes, and at the time of the NALP interview, a manual on oral traditions was being developed for use in ABE classes. The manuals are used in reading classes and are supplemented with other manuals, both commercial and teacher-made.

The director of curriculum development explained: "We found that students liked to talk about their families and how things used to be. . . . In this [ABE] manual, we deal with the history of the family. . . ." To compile the manual, instructors and paraprofessionals interviewed senior citizens in the Fishtown-Kensington area of Philadelphia, the same area in which most of the program's students live. The oral histories document the themes of women's lives and roles, men's lives and roles, discrimination, hard times, and growing up. In addition, the editors were incorporating some geography to enrich the understanding of those who had never traveled beyond the boundaries of their small community. Language arts exercises and comprehension questions, which are based on material in the text, are all geared to the level of the ABE student. "[We] find students want to learn . . . [because the manual] . . . is something they can relate to, something they helped create, and it helps them take part in the learning process. They take responsibility for their learning and they have input into it. . . . It gives incentives. . . . they can take that same story and build on it generation by generation."

Curriculum development of this kind requires a huge commitment of time and money, but the Women's Program feels it is worthwhile. As the curriculum developer explained: "The average student who goes to a program is not aware that there are alternatives, whether with materials or a life situation. That's why this program is so special. We present the alternative teaching methods, materials, and alternatives that they can take to apply to their lives."

Another common practice in adult education is maintaining files of materials related to specific learning objectives. For each objective, teachers may pool clippings taken from commercial materials (or a checklist citing specific pages in commercial texts and references to applicable software or video-based programs) together with self-developed activity worksheets to form a ready resource file of possible instructional strategies and community-specific applications of skills. As we will discuss later in this chapter, these files can be assembled with activity log sheets and pre-tests and post-tests to form complete learning modules.

A program's files may also contain clippings from newspapers and magazines arranged by topic and difficulty level for use as reading passages. Teachers might develop comprehension activities to be filed along with these clippings. Photographs clipped from magazine articles and advertisements are frequently filed for use in sight word drills or as stimulus material for language experience stories. Because commercial materials that focus on such real-life materials as job applications may be too generic and not a close enough match to the idiosyncracies of local customs, programs often collect materials such as those detailed in the list on pages 122 and 123 so that students can apply their skills to materials drawn from the real life of the community. Such a collection can be especially useful because commercial publishers avoid reproducing facsimiles of such things as food and drug labels, largely to avoid copyright or trademark infringement.

HOW CAN THE INSTRUCTIONAL SYSTEM BE MANAGED?

Our description of instructional methods and materials in the preceding sections demonstrates that, because of the very nature of the adult students they serve, effective programs are eclectic. Yet eclecticism does not imply chaos or a lack of instructional management. As we suggested in the beginning of the chapter and under the heading "Manageability" in the section on choosing appropriate materials, effective programs do develop true systems that are based on clearly stated objectives. Indeed, we have described all components of effective programs as resulting from systematic plans designed to optimize the chances for both the program and its students to meet their goals successfully.

The planning process begins with a critical self-evaluation of the effectiveness of current instructional practice in helping students achieve both the goals of the program (e.g., for an employment and training program, one must ask how effectively students are prepared for performance on designated jobs) and the personal goals of the students. We suggest that programs evaluate the following eleven factors.

(1) Appropriateness and relevance of learning sequences and objectives
(2) Appropriateness of entry-level, interim-level, and exit-level performance standards

(3) Appropriateness of provisions to accommodate learners' individual needs

(4) Extent to which learners participate in setting their own learning objectives

(5) Appropriateness of instructional methods, given learners' needs and program objectives

(6) Nature and quality of relationships between learners and instructional staff

(7) Reliability and validity of assessment and feedback procedures

(8) Appropriateness of indicators and measures of learning objective attainment

(9) Quality of instruction, including amount of individual attention

(10) Efficiency of administrative and recordkeeping procedures

(11) Quality and use of counseling and other learner support services

As we will suggest again in Chapter 9, "Program Evaluation," evaluation and the resulting decision making should be a joint effort of all program staff. When the target of such evaluation is curricular decision making, however, some practitioners do not welcome having ultimate decisions made by anyone other than the classroom teacher. They would argue that the teachers are the experts and are competent to make all curricular decisions. And since teachers have the most direct and frequent contact with students, they are in the best position to judge when and how to vary from a given sequence of objectives to suit the individual learning goals or learning styles of their students.

Others feel that the director has a responsibility to participate in curricular decisions so that the result of planning sessions will be a curriculum design that reflects the overall program philosophy. Participation also allows the director to remain up to date on instructional methods and materials and to facilitate appropriate adjustments in other aspects of program operation when changes are made in instructional methods, material, or delivery systems. In some way, the decision for or against involving themselves is a reflection of the directors' management philosophies; directors must decide whether they include direct involvement in monitoring the instructional process as part of program administration. One director told us that she feels she would have no credibility in staff evaluation unless she were involved in curricular decisions. Another director feels that if the "art of teaching" is valued, *all* program staff must involve themselves in curricular decisions.

During the NALP site interviews, it was teachers, not directors, who most often stated a desire to include administrators in curricular decision making. Because so many programs employ part-time staff and volunteers, there is often a need for assistance in planning instruction and choosing materials. Yet there is no ready avenue for advice and guidance in curriculum if programs publish no set of guidelines. One teacher in a postsecondary program noted that it is an "overwhelming" experience for a new teacher to have to choose materials from the huge stock in the curriculum library independently. Another teacher felt strongly that the choice of curriculum and of methods and materials is a philosophical statement and that the whole staff needs to be involved in choosing and implementing that philosophy.

However, not all programs in the NALP study have designed structured curricula as part of their systems or plans for instructional management. Some openly oppose the idea of a structured curriculum in the beliefs that such structure will lead to a lock-step progression through a prescribed series of workbooks and that students and teachers will lose the ability to be flexible, to control instruction to serve the individual needs and goals of the students. Yet many of the teachers we interviewed expressed a need for some structure. One teacher complained that there had never been any supervision in her program. Since no one was really monitoring what skills teachers were covering, she feared that some students might be falling through the cracks. "There are skills and objectives that need to be met," she declared; there is some need for a sequence that can be used as a "jumping off point" at least.

A curriculum framework does not mean a slavish adherence to materials or methods. It *does* mean building in accountability. For programs in which students move from teacher to teacher through a series of levels or "courses," accountability is reasonably extended to include the expectation that teachers of lower level students will have given them the foundation for work that will be undertaken at intermediate and higher levels or, at a minimum, that all teachers will have carefully documented the objectives over which individual students have demonstrated mastery. And as we suggested under the headings "Teaching Reading Comprehension Skills" and "Teaching Competency Applications of Literacy Skills," there are skills one might list as appropriate outcomes if the aim of literacy education is to develop proficient readers and functionally competent adults. Without a specification of such outcomes, one has no way of designing a diagnostic/prescriptive plan for instruction that serves the long-range needs of students; one is left only with short-term plans based on immediate needs.

A structured curriculum framework, we would suggest, does not imply inflexibility. For example, in one community-based program, the director expects instructors to teach a core set of concepts but leaves them free to choose methods and materials. An employment and training program encourages students to choose from given sets of objectives. In this way, student needs and interests are met, yet the objectives define structured plans for diagnosis, instruction, and assessment with documentation of student achievement. And in an ABE program, teachers are writing down the sequences of instruction that seem to work for various types of students who enter the program at different stages of literacy. These sequences will become a guide for other teachers who are planning for similar students.

It is not within the scope of this book to formulate an exhaustive list of objectives from which programs could select those appropriate for their students. The formulation of objectives will depend on how a program answers the questions we posed at the outset of this chapter. However, in the next section, we will argue that programs must develop a system for setting goals and documenting each individual student's achievement of those goals. We will then explore two other issues in program design and management—group versus individualized instruction and modularized instructional systems.

Goal Setting and Documentation

Whether or not a program's self-evaluation results in the establishment of a core set of prescribed objectives that all teachers must include in the learning plans for their students, we urge programs to derive and distribute lists of objectives appropriate to the goals of the program and the characteristic goals of learners in the program's service area. For each objective, the program should suggest possible instructional methods, materials, and diagnostic and evaluative measures. The benefits that can be derived from such a curriculum planning document include:

- clearly stated behavioral objectives can communicate to learners what they are expected to do and why
- counseling can be facilitated; individual needs assessments can be made more specific and concrete
- diagnosis, whether formal or informal, can be tied to the range of objectives that can be assumed to underlie program or student goals; programs can evaluate the reliability and validity of diagnostic instruments based on criteria set by the program rather than those outside the program
- individualized instructional prescriptions can include basic skills, life-related skills, and job-related skills assembled in whatever combination may be appropriate; the students themselves may contribute their own suggestions for life-related or job-related skills that they want to have included
- instruction can be outcome-based rather than time-based, allowing learners to set their own pace and use whatever resources may be necessary to reach an appropriate level of mastery—this is especially relevant for open-entry–open-exit programs
- teachers have access to and can use a variety of activities and modalities (individual deskwork, group work, interaction with audiovisual or computer software programs, etc.)
- assessment mechanisms or other indicators of learning objective achievement can be designed in concrete and measurable terms rather than subjective terms
- documentation of student progress and program effectiveness can be systematized and standardized so that all who may need access to information about students can easily interpret that information

The course of action we have just recommended is not an easy one, but it is one that we believe can lead to optimum program effectiveness. Once a resource list of objective statements has been derived, student-generated or program-generated curriculum plans can be developed and implemented under a Management of Instruction System (MIS), which we first described in the chapter on diagnostic and assessment testing. In that description, we noted that programs using such systems begin with statements of program goals and student goals and then define the sets of behavioral objectives that reflect the prerequisite skills for the achievement of the stated goals. All parts of the instructional cycle—diagnosis of which prerequisite skills need to be the target of instruction, individualized learning plans with specifications of the methods and materials to be used, and assessment of student progress and achievement of mastery—grow out of the statements of behavioral objectives.

Programs that have adopted systems driven by behavioral objectives and competency statements are convinced that such systems best reflect the unique characteristics of *adult* education. The director of a military program that has adopted such a management system declared: "Adult learners really don't like going back to a traditional classroom approach. They like the idea of being more in control of their own educational process. I think they like to choose the way they spend their time. . . . and to me, one of the big advantages with this program is that students have that control, they can work at their own pace. . . . they can get one-on-one tutoring assistance from the teacher instead of being one of the group."

The director at a program for out-of-school youth exclaimed: "The objectives are clear. They're sequential! That's the way people learn. [We] have a developmental education philosophy." She continued: "This kind of system allows teachers to do what they do best. [In other systems] . . . a lot of a teacher's time is not time engaged with a student on a specific learning task. . . . It's in marking papers." She ended with a sincere endorsement: ". . . although I never would have said this two years ago, I have come around to thinking that it is the individualized, self-paced component that is the most successful means of instruction for this population."

Despite the obvious virtues of doing so, not many of the sites visited during the NALP study had implemented a self-developed objective-driven or competency-driven system. Rethinking goals and processes in order to derive specific learning objectives as well as correlated diagnostic, assessment, and evaluative measures requires a large commitment in time and financial resources as well as technical know-how. It also means making some hard choices about what subskills and functional competencies should be classified under given general goal statements. As we suggested in the introduction to this chapter, some programs have alleviated part of the development burden by adopting flexible pre-packaged curriculum designs such as the California Adult Student Assessment System (CASAS) or the Comprehensive Competencies Program (CCP). Programs have also chosen well-designed commercial materials that clearly label the elements necessary for instructional management—such as GED preparation texts that follow a diagnostic/prescriptive design with specific statements of objectives—and have developed supplementary materials for such additional skill objectives or competency statements as the program has deemed necessary.

One issue that programs must resolve is the extent to which students are to be involved in the development of their individualized instructional plans. On this point of instructional philosophy, the director of one Midwestern community-based program declared: "You cannot develop a program for a student. . . . in other words, you have to look at the student and develop a program around his needs. . . . the adult knows his problem basically . . . because of his realm of experiences." As we suggested in the chapter on counseling, students should be given the opportunity to express what it is they want to learn as well as how they believe they learn best. Such student input can be solicited through such self-assessment questionnaires as the one we illustrated in Exhibit 5.1 in Chapter 5. The students' goals are important to them, and every effort should be made to integrate instruction targeted to those goals within the total instructional plan. This desirable practice is made easier under the kind of instructional management system we have been describing. However, the dialogue with students about goals and objectives to be included in the instructional plan does not end with a discussion of the immediate goals that students bring to the program. Students may not be able to articulate precisely what they need a program to do for them, and the experience of program staff will undoubtedly suggest objectives that are critical to student success in academic, life-related, or job-related tasks. Appropriate diagnostic procedures and a discussion of the results can help students and their teachers identify these learning needs.

An additional benefit of engaging students in the instructional planning process is the possible discovery that a given student may be better served by some program other than the one the student is enrolling in (a possibility we also discussed in the chapters on orientation and counseling). One employment and training program interviewed in the NALP study uses an individualized, competency-based instructional system but provides a consultation to all clients to determine their learning preferences. Those who would prefer to participate in a different type of program (e.g., a traditional high school completion program) are referred to a program that suits their needs. To aid in this process, the program has compiled a directory of all programs in their large urban area that offer educational services to youth and adults. Information about the programs includes everything from subway stop and neighborhood to types of credentials offered. This same directory also helps other educational and social service agencies make accurate and efficient placements.

Once the program has determined how goals and their underlying specific objectives are to be set, there remains only the issue of how to design the documentation system. One youth program in the NALP study has implemented a contract system. The contracts worked out between the students and their teachers detail objectives and learning activities and are used to chart student progress. In a similar program, the teacher and the student prepare a master record sheet that lists the student's broad goal and the first set of subgoals. The record sheet is designed to cover a three-week span, and all subgoals are written as specific tasks, complete with specification of materials to be used.

In developing a documentation system, we recommend that programs consider designing forms for each of the following:

- monitoring the composite progress of the group of all learners
- monitoring individual students' progress in meeting their goals
- maintaining attendance records, when appropriate, for each learner and for the group as a whole
- detailing an individual learning plan for each student
- documenting the agreements and observations of goal-setting sessions with individual students
- allowing students to assess their own learning styles and preferences

- collecting evaluation data on the appropriateness of the instructional materials and assessment strategies

We suggest further that programs answer the following seven questions in order to complete an operational plan for instructional management and ultimately program evaluation:

1. What form or software program will you use to keep track of the skill objectives each student has begun and mastered?
2. Does that form or program include the means to track skill objectives
   - mastered through demonstration in a pre-test?
   - currently being worked on by the student?
   - mastered through demonstration in an assessment test?
3. What means will you use to give students regular feedback on their progress in the program?
4. What means will you use to record information on students'
   - attitude?
   - motivation level?
   - preferred learning style?
   - special achievements?
5. What means will you use to keep track of students as a group and their performance in mastering skill objectives?
6. What means will you use to keep track of group attendance?
7. What means will you use to keep track of individual student's attendance?

In Chapter 5, Exhibit 5.2 illustrated a possible model for summarizing a student's individualized learning plan. The following pages illustrate other model documents that programs might adapt to reflect the characteristics of their system. Exhibits 7.5 through 7.7 all relate to detailing instructional plans and progress. The designation "Competency Area" refers to general clusters of related skills. For example, in reading, one might designate the following five competency areas:

Area 1—recognizing words and identifying their meanings
Area 2—applying literal comprehension skills
Area 3—applying interpretive comprehension skills
Area 4—applying evaluative comprehension skills
Area 5—interpreting illustrations

The document shown in Exhibit 7.5 is designed to assist teachers in planning individualized instruction by recording each student's performance level on designated sets of objectives or competencies. In effect, the document is a master checklist of the complete set of objectives within the program, reflecting both those skills the student could already perform upon program entry and those that the student mastered upon completion of targeted instruction.

The document shown in Exhibit 7.6 is designed to communicate to the students what skills they will be working on during given time periods. By specifying the "Goal Statement" at the top of the form and the specific competency objectives in the first column, teachers can show students the relationship between the students' goals and the activities they will be undertaking. By listing specific "Learning Activities," teachers can provide a checklist of materials that students can seek out independently, thus freeing teachers to provide assistance only when students actually need help. The column labeled "Describe Competency Mastery Activity" enables the teacher to tell students what performance criteria will be used to evaluate their mastery of each specific skill objective or competency statement. The "Comments" column might be used to recommend supplementary activities to be undertaken by the student as well as words of encouragement and praise.

The document shown in Exhibit 7.7 is designed to assist teachers in monitoring the activities of all the individual students within the group under their guidance. A number code system for competency statements is extremely useful in filling out this document. On a weekly basis, teachers will record each student's activities, specifying both the numbers of the specific objectives being worked on within each general competency area and the level of material being used. Such a composite profile is also useful in planning small-group activities for groups of students who are working on the same objectives.

The documents shown in Exhibits 7.8 and 7.9 are attendance logs for groups of students and individual students. Beyond the obvious use of these documents in recording data for reports to funding agencies, they can alert teachers to the fact that certain students may have fallen away from the program. As we will suggest in the next chapter, a follow-up phone call to such students may result in encouraging them to return to the program.

EXHIBIT 7.5 Individualized Instructional Planning Document

Name:

Site:

Instructor/Counselor:

Competency	Demonstrated Mastery In Initial Diagnosis	Demonstrated Mastery In Pre-test	Demonstrated Mastery In Post-test	Date Competency Mastered
Competency Area:				
Competencies				
•				
•				
•				
•				
Competency Area:				
Competencies				
•				
•				
•				

EXHIBIT 7.6 Individual Student Activity Form

Name: _____

Site: _____

Instructor: _____

Goal Statement: _____

Date: From _____ To: _____

Competency: _____

Competency Area: _____

Competencies	Date Begun	Date Completed	Learning Activities	Describe Competency Mastery Activity	Comments

EXHIBIT 7.7 Weekly Composite Progress Profile

Site: _____

Instructor: _____

Week: _____

On the chart below, please indicate whether the student is working on the Basic, Intermediate, or Advanced competency level.

B = Basic
I = Intermediate
A = Advanced

Students' Names	Competency Area 1	Competency Area 2	Competency Area 3	Competency Area 4	Competency Area 5

EXHIBIT 7.8 Group Attendance Log

Date: _____

Teacher: _____

STUDENT	Week 1						Week 2						Week 3						Week 4						Week 5						Week 6						Week 7						Week 8						Total
	1	2	3	4	5	T	1	2	3	4	5	T	1	2	3	4	5	T	1	2	3	4	5	T	1	2	3	4	5	T	1	2	3	4	5	T	1	2	3	4	5	T	1	2	3	4	5	T	

EXHIBIT 7.9 Individual Student Attendance Record

WEEK OF: NAME: _____   CLIENT No.: _____

		MON.	TUES.	WED.	THURS	FRI.	Hrs./Wk	Attendance /Wk.
___	Time In							___
	Time Out							
	Total Time							
___	In						___	___
	Out							
	Total							
___	In						___	___
	Out							
	Total							
___	In						___	___
	Out							
	Total							
___	In						___	___
	Out							
	Total							
Schedule:							Ttl./ Mo.	Total/ Month:

Group versus Individualized Instruction

The system we have just described is customarily used to develop individualized learning plans with instruction being delivered via independent work and one-to-one assistance. However, the system may be used with some modification by programs that deliver the majority of instruction in large-group or small-group classes, but with allowance for students to do some independent work on specific skill weaknesses outside regular class sessions in independent learning laboratories or resource centers. In designing the system, one must thus address the issue of whether one-to-one or group instruction should be the primary mode of instructional delivery, an issue on which practitioners interviewed in the NALP study are divided.

The following statement from a teacher in an ABE program is typical of those we heard in support of one-to-one instruction:

The adults who come to our program have a history of problems . . . a history of needs, and . . . different abilities. There is no way . . . a teacher standing in front of the classroom [can] say, "Today we will work on X." . . . I have never found people who are that close in every respect that they can be matched. . . . When you have adults, you have to meet their emotional and psychological needs as well. Some of them are very embarrassed to be here. They don't want to work in a group with other people. I don't think that's something you can force. . . . They also have different work styles.

The chief advantage of individualized, one-to-one instruction is the ability to customize instruction to match the skill strengths and weaknesses, the learning styles, and the personal goals of each student. One volunteer went so far as to claim that "an hour spent with a tutor is worth more than a whole semester with a teacher." For students who have experienced lock-step movement from one grade to the next in the traditional school system, there is genuine appeal in being able to take whatever time may be necessary to achieve mastery of desirable academic, life-related, or job-related skills. There is also an appeal in not having to sit quietly through instruction that addresses skills over which the student already has mastery or skills in which the student has no interest.

Some practitioners who work with young adults emphasized that individualized, one-to-one instruction gives students time to talk quietly and positively with an adult, provides students with a good work model, and encourages the characteristic adolescent search for independence. One director at an employment and training program commented, "Young adults are exploring. . . . and they need to change their minds a lot. . . . and you need to have a system to respond to that."

Yet several of the practitioners we interviewed objected to the use of individualized, one-to-one instruction as the sole mode of instructional delivery. For example, the director of an all-volunteer program that provides one-to-one tutoring commented: "We are kind of unhappy with the one-on-one tutoring. . . . The sutdents tended to develop a real dependency. . . . [When we] found a tutor who we felt wasn't doing very well. . . . it was this huge problem of trying to tear them apart. . . . [The student] wasn't developing self-confidence, independence, assertiveness—so we thought small-group [instruction] would be beneficial in terms of developing independence."

The decision to use small-group activities or traditional classes is often based on a reaction against the isolating experience of one-to-one instruction. One teacher in an inner city, community-based program saw group instruction as a socialization issue: "It's an idea for developing a cohesive unit. . . . They . . . have a lot to learn about themselves as a group. . . . Part of what we do is . . . to help them recognize that they are part of the community. . . . They feel a sense of attachment for each other . . . a connectedness." The director of an ABE program in Massachusetts seemed to concur: ". . . You have to have unity. . . . People need to work together towards a common goal, and a common goal is to learn something."

A program director in Pennsylvania shared this opinion and noted the benefits to be derived from group dynamics: "It doesn't matter what their reading level is . . . they are all adults, and each one has something different to contribute to the class . . . a different background . . . a wealth of knowledge that . . . they share, and everyone gains from that person's experience. . . . We try to learn from each other." This emphasis on the importance of group dynamics was echoed by one employment and training program. This program finds that group activities help students build cooperative interpersonal relationship skills as well as problem-solving skills that are important in the workplace; the program designed activities so that "people could meet each other's needs and feel more comfortable with each other."

Some programs use small-group activities as part of initial or ongoing counseling support. For example, one educator in a correctional institution stages rap sessions before beginning academic instruction. "Before you can get to [reading and writing] and make them count for yourself, you have to believe in yourself. You have to know you're worth it."

Several programs have designed peer tutoring activities using pairs of students or small groups. One instructor in a military program who uses the technique declared, ". . . peer tutoring works fine; . . . I don't care who teaches them as long as they get it!" A community-based program that uses an individualized, competency-based system is experimenting with student team learning. In their model, students who have independently completed the same learning module are assembled as a group. Members of the group employ a variety of techniques to review the material in the module, quiz one another, or otherwise reinforce the skills that have been studied independently. The students themselves seem to like the technique, as demonstrated by this comment: ". . . once you find out you learned something, you feel important. So I'm going to get up and show it to somebody else. . . . Everybody basically helps each other. It's like a family group. Everybody sticks together."

After a long outside evaluation, one community-based organization has concluded that group processes produce better results, both academically and socially. Although the program was originally designed to offer one-to-one instruction through volunteer tutors, the program now encourages students to join groups and trains volunteer tutors in group processes. Most importantly, the program has found that group techniques are more cost-effective and enable the program to offer instruction to more students.

There is logic to the arguments for both one-to-one and group instruction, and both can be effective modes of delivery as long as one does not lose sight of the learning needs and preferred learning styles of the individual students. Regardless of the primary mode of instructional delivery, we would maintain that provisions must be made for diagnosing individual student needs and for allowing at least some time in which students can work independently in addressing those needs. As we noted at the beginning of this discussion, the use of individualized instructional plans does not necessarily imply one-to-one instructional delivery.

The Use of Learning Modules

In our discussion of self-developed materials under the section entitled "Choosing Appropriate Materials for Adults," we noted that programs often maintain files of materials coded to specific objectives. These files may contain clippings of relevant pages from commercial materials (or a checklist citing those pages) together with self-developed activity sheets that teachers have found useful. By adding a pre-test and a post-test to each file, the program can design learning modules that can be sequenced in a variety of different ways to build custom-designed programs for individual students.

By handing a student a simple file folder of materials on a small set of subskills rather than a large text or workbook that includes everything in the curriculum, teachers can give students a greater sense of achievement. Once they have worked through the folder, the students have actually finished something and have experienced the joy of success; they are not instantly confronted with how much further they have to go.

The availability of learning modules on specific topics that might not be part of the core curriculum allows programs to build "mini-courses" that can be delivered to individual students or small groups of students who have shown an interest in such extracurricular topics. Similarly, students who are enrolled in traditional large-group classes but who have demonstrated a special need can easily be given an appropriate learning module for supplementary independent work outside the classroom.

Modular curriculum designs have been applied to a host of different programs. The GED preparation curriculum being used by Jobs for Youth–Boston is one example. David Rosen, Associate Executive Director, and Jean Chambers, the senior instructor, describe the program this way:

> The competency-based GED preparation curriculum combines the structure of a competency-based instructional management system with the content tested by the GED examination. It provides the distinct advantages of a competency-based format . . . [but] it does not include the life skills content often found in other competency-based adult education curricula. It is intended for programs whose students want preparation for the GED, . . . and whose teachers want the clarity, efficiency, measurability, and motivating qualities of competency-based curriculum design. The curriculum uses popular, readily available GED instructional materials from such publishers as Cambridge Book Company, Contemporary, McGraw-Hill, and Steck-Vaughn.
>
> Thirty-two "competency modules," each with specific, learner-centered objectives, activities, and pre-tests and mastery tests, are designed to teach the basic skills and knowledge needed to pass each of the five sections of the examination. . . . One module, within the writing competency area, is designed to teach paragraph composition skills, which are not directly tested by the GED examination. . . . Another special module is designed to teach test-taking skills and strategies.
>
> The curriculum guide contains competency titles and page number references for pre-tests and

mastery tests and for main and supplementary instructional activities. . . . Because the curriculum references widely used competency-based and other commercial instructional materials, it is inexpensive to adopt and well suited to a range of GED programs. . . .

Interested readers may obtain descriptions of the curriculum or copies of the curriculum guide by writing to David Rosen, Associate Executive Director, Jobs for Youth–Boston, Third Floor, 312 Stuart Street, Boston, MA 02116.

CONCLUSIONS AND RECOMMENDATIONS

The issues surrounding a program's choice of instructional methods and materials and the design of the instructional management system under which the use of these methods and materials are orchestrated for the greatest good of the students are issues that cannot be easily resolved here. The simple truth is that there are many different ways in which one might teach adults to read, write, compute, and apply skills to life-related or job-related tasks. However, for educators involved in designing instructional programs for adults, we would make the following six recommendations.

(1) **Recognize that the student population is made up of adults.** All decisions must be made with an understanding of the unique characteristics of adults as learners. Adults come to literacy programs with a reservoir of knowledge that has allowed them to function thus far, and no activities or materials should demean their status as adults. Rather, the methods and materials that are selected must reflect an adult world view and be relevant to the real-life experiences of adult learners. Because the students' obligations to families, jobs, and their communities usually precede and often assume much higher priority than their participation in an educational program, programs must be seen as enhancing the students' abilities to perform their roles outside of the classroom; education cannot be offered as an end in itself.

(2) **Supply opportunities to apply skills in adult functional contexts.** Students' motivation will be greatest when instruction is targeted to helping them learn or reinforce skills that they can apply relatively immediately to their life situations. Students should clearly see the utility of what is being taught and the efficiency of the instructional strategies that are being used to teach them; this is best accomplished by sharing the total instructional plan with students in such a way as to demonstrate how everything relates to the achievement of useful goals. At least some of the materials and instructional strategies must simulate the functional contexts (job site, home, social service center) in which the adult students are likely to use the skills being presented.

(3) **Involve students in making decisions about their educational program.** Adult students want to be active participants in identifying their own educational needs and the ways in which those needs will be addressed. Use counseling strategies, self-assessment questionnaires, and discussions of diagnostic test results to help students identify personal goals, skill strengths and weaknesses, and preferred learning styles. Programs must make every attempt to integrate students' personal goals within the curriculum.

(4) **Anticipate the multiplicity of learning goals and learning styles with a variety of educational program options.** Options for learning are critical to the success of any literacy program because the program serves a range of adult learners, each of whom brings a unique set of experiences and skills to the program.

(5) **Build a true instructional management system based on clearly stated behavioral objectives.** Good management of the instructional process begins with clearly defined learning objectives that are linked to explicit indicators of performance. In other words, students should know what they must *do* to demonstrate mastery of a particular skill or objective. Further, instructional materials and strategies must be related to learning objectives and support the students' attempts to achieve mastery of those objectives. Assessment of student achievement needs to be systematic, frequent, and related to the objectives, materials, and methods used to teach particular skills.

(6) **Build a system of documenting student progress and achievement.** The management system—the framework of the instructional process—provides the tools to document both student achievement and program effectiveness. Appropriate recordkeeping, either manual or computer-managed, must be developed to allow students and their instructors to easily determine where they are in the educational process and to provide direction for future work.

SUPPLIERS OF ADULT EDUCATION MATERIALS

The following lists of publishers of educational materials for adults are presented in alphabetical order and represent those who have been most active in the field. The inclusion or exclusion of any publisher does not indicate an endorsement or other judgment by the authors. We suggest only that interested readers obtain catalogues and evaluate for themselves the relative merits of an individual publisher's materials. For convenience, we have divided the list into two sections, publishers whose publications are primarily print materials and publishers of computer software, though many of the publishers listed offer both print and computer software materials as well as audiovisual programs.

PUBLISHERS OF PRINT MATERIALS

Arco Publishing, Inc.
215 Park Avenue South
New York, NY 10003

Barnell Loft, Ltd.
958 Church Street
Baldwin, NY 11510

Barron's Educational Series, Inc.
113 Crossways Park Drive
Woodbury, NY 11797

Cambridge, The Adult Education Company
888 Seventh Avenue
New York, NY 10106

Career Publishing, Inc.
P.O. Box 5486
Orange, CA 92667

Contemporary Books, Inc.
180 North Michigan Avenue
Chicago, IL 60601

Educators Publishing Service, Inc.
75 Moulton Street
Cambridge, MA 02238

Fearon Education/Pitman Learning
19 Davis Drive
Belmont, CA 94002

Globe Book Company
50 West 23rd Street
New York, NY 10010

Harcourt, Brace, Jovanovich
Harcourt, Brace, Jovanovich Building
Orlando, FL 32887

Jamestown Publishers
P.O. Box 6743
Providence, RI 02940

Janus Book Publishers
2501 Industrial Parkway, West
Hayward, CA 94545

Key Curriculum Project
P.O. Box 2304
Department 10
Berkeley, CA 94702

McGraw-Hill Book Company
1221 Avenue of the Americas
New York, NY 10020

Madex Associates, Inc.
90 Chenj Street
P.O. Box 519
Johnstown, PA 15901

National Textbook Company
4255 West Touhy Avenue
Lincolnwood, IL 60646

Newbury House Publishers
54 Warehouse Lane
Rowley, MA 01969

New Readers Press
1320 Jamesville Avenue
Syracuse, NY 13210

Prentice-Hall, Inc.
Englewood Cliffs, NJ 07632

Regents Publishing Company, Inc.
Two Park Avenue
New York, NY 10016

Frank E. Richard Publishing Company, Inc.
Phoenix, NY 13135

Scott, Foresman Lifelong Learning Division
1900 East Lake Avenue
Glenview, IL 60025

Steck-Vaughn Company
P.O. Box 2028
Austin, TX 78768

Sundance Publishers and Distributors, Inc.
Newton Road
Littleton, MA 01460

PUBLISHERS OF COMPUTER SOFTWARE

Conduit
P.O. Box 388
Iowa City, IA 52244

Control Data Publishing Company
80100 34th Avenue South
Bloomington, MN 55420

Designware
185 Berry Street
San Francisco, CA 94107

Education Activities, Inc.
P.O. Box 392
Freeport, NY 11520

Educational Publishing Concepts, Inc.
P.O. Box 715
St. Charles, IL 60174

MCE Incorporated
15 Kalamazoo Mall
Suite 250
Kalamazoo, MI 99007

Milliken Publishing Company
1100 Research Boulevard
St. Louis, MO 63132

Minnesota Educational Computing Consortium (MECC)
3490 Lexington Avenue North
St. Paul, MN 55112

Sunburst
Room 5
39 Washington Avenue
Pleasantville, NY 10570

BIBLIOGRAPHY

Listed below are the names and addresses of U.S. government offices, national associations, and other organizations that can be continuing resources of assistance and information. In addition to making these organizations a part of your network, we urge you to follow the advice given in Section IV of this book and develop an information-sharing network with other programs in your area. You'll find a list of the programs that were part of the NALP study in Section IV, and your state's department of education as well as the U.S. government agencies listed below can help you locate other programs in your area.

(1) The Clearinghouse on Adult Education
Division of Adult Education Services
U.S. Department of Education
Washington, DC 20202-3585

(2) The National Volunteer Network
(address as at 1 above)

(3) The Network of Adult Education Programs Serving the Disabled Person
(address as at 1 above)

(4) ERIC Clearinghouse on Adult, Career, and Vocational Education
The National Center for Research in Vocational Education
The Ohio State University
1960 Kenny Road
Columbus, OH 43210

(5) American Association of Adult and Continuing Education
1201 Sixteenth Street, N.W.
Washington, DC 20036

(6) International Reading Association
800 Barksdale Road
Newark, DE 19711

(7) The American Vocational Association, Inc.
2020 North Fourteenth Street
Arlington, VA 22210

(8) Correctional Education Association
1400 20th Street, N.W.
Washington, DC 20036

(9) National Community Education Association
1201 Sixteenth Street, N.W.
Washington, DC 20036

(10) Center for Applied Linguistics
3520 Prospect Street, N.W.
Washington, DC 20007

(11) Dissemination Network for Adult Education
1575 Old Bayshore Highway
Burlingame, CA 94010

(12) Push Literacy Action Now
(Newsletter: *The Ladder*)
2311 Eighteenth Street, N.W.
Washington, DC 20009

The following publications have been divided into two major sections, those that deal with instructional methods and materials and those that deal with adult learning theory.

Instructional Methods and Materials for Adults

Adult Literacy: Programs That Work. Washington, DC: National Diffusion Network, U.S. Department of Education, 1984.

August, Bonne T. "Teaching Writing in the Adult Literacy Program." *Journal of Adult Literacy and Basic Education*, Volume 3, Number 2, Summer 1979. (CE 509211)

Aron, Helen. "The Impact of Computers on Literacy." *Lifelong Learning: The Adult Years*, Volume 6, Number 4, 1982. (CE 512946)

Bacon, Margaret. "What Adult Literacy Teachers Need to Know about Strategies for Focusing on Comprehension." *Lifelong Learning: The Adult Years*, Volume 6, Number 6, 1983. (CE 513263)

Berg, J., and Wallace, V. A. *A Selected Bibliography of Functional Literacy Materials for Adult Learners*. Upper Montclair, NJ: Montclair State College, 1980.

Bloom, Benjamin S. "The Search for Methods of Group Instruction as Effective as One-to-One Tutoring." *Educational Leadership*, Volume 41, Number 8, 1984, pages 4–17.

Bowren, F. R., and Zintz, M. V. *Teaching Reading in Adult Basic Education*. Dubuque, IA: William C. Brown, 1977.

Campbell, A. B. "Cooperative Student Instruction (CSI): A Refreshing New Approach to Learning." *Journal of Adult Literacy and Basic Education*, Volume 3, Number 2, 1979.

Center for Applied Linguistics. *From the Classroom to the Workplace: Teaching ESL to Adults*. Washington, DC: Center for Applied Linguistics, 1983.

Cervero, R. M. "The Relationship between the GED Testing Program and Competency-Based Education. *Journal of Adult Literacy and Basic Education*, Volume 2, Number 4, 1979.

Cole, J. W., and Glass, J. C. "The Effect of Adult Student Participation in Program Planning on Achievement, Retention, and Attitude." *Adult Education*, Volume 27, Number 2, 1977.

Colvin, Ruth, and Root, Jane. *TUTOR: Techniques Used in the Teaching of Reading* (rev. ed.). Syracuse, NY: Literacy Volunteers of America, Inc., 1981.

Darling, Sharon, et. al. *Attitudes, Application, Action: Employability Skills for the Adult Literacy Student*. Louisville, KY: Jefferson County Public Schools, 1983. (ED 235322)

Dickinson, Gary, et. al. *Adult Basic Literacy Curriculum and Resource Guide*. Victoria, BC: British Columbia Department of Education, 1980. (CE 031847)

Fingeret, Arlene. "Social Network: A New Perspective on Independence and Illiterate Adults." *Adult Education Quarterly*, Volume 33, Number 3, 1983. (CE 513184)

Gall, Meredith D. *Handbook for Evaluating and Selecting Curriculum Materials*. Boston: Allyn and Bacon, 1981.

Griffith, W. S., and Cervero, R. M. "The Adult Performance Level Program: A Serious and Deliberate Examination." *Adult Education*, Volume 22, Number 4, 1977.

Gueulette, David G. (Ed.) *Microcomputers for Adult Learning: Potentials and Perils*. New York: Cambridge, The Adult Education Company, 1983.

Hays, Ann, et. al. "Adult Education Council of Greater Chicago: An Investigation of Materials and Methods for the Introductory Stage of Adult Literacy Education." Springfield: Illinois State Office of Education, 1967. (ED 014629)

Heathington, Betty S., and Koskinen, Patricia S. "Interest Inventory for Adult Beginning Readers." *Journal of Reading*, Volume 26, Number 3, 1982. (EJ 271139)

Herber, Harold L., and Nelson, Joan B. "Questioning Is Not the Answer." *Journal of Reading*, April 1975.

Ilyin, Donna, and Tragardh, Thomas (Eds.). *Classroom Practices in Adult ESL*. Washington, DC: Teachers of English to Speakers of Other Languages, 1978.

Jenkins, Janet. *Materials for Learning: How to Teach Adults at a Distance*. Boston: Routledge & Kegan Paul, 1981.

Johnson, Laura S. (Ed.). *Reading and the Adult Learner*. Neward, DE: International Reading Association, 1980.

Jones, E. V. *Reading Instruction for the Adult Illiterate*. Chicago: American Library Association, 1981.

Kennedy, K., and Roeder, S. *Using Language Experience with Adults: A Guide for Teachers*. Syracuse, NY: New Readers Press, 1975.

Klevins, Chester (Ed.). *Materials and Methods in Adult and Continuing Education*. Los Angeles: Klevens Publications, Inc., P.O. Box 143, Canoga Park, CA 91305, 1982.

Lawson, Virginia K. *Thinking Is a Basic Skill: Creating Humanities Materials for the Adult New Reader*. Syracuse, NY: Literacy Volunteers of America, 1981.

Lenz, Elinor. *The Art of Teaching Adults*. New York: Holt, Rinehart and Winston, 1982.

Longfield, D. "Teaching English as a Second Language to Adults: State of the Art." Paper presented at the National Adult Literacy Conference, Washington, DC, January 1984. (ED 240297)

McLagan, Patricia A. *Helping Others Learn: Designing Programs for Adults*. Reading, MA: Addison-Wesley Publishing Company, 1978.

Mager, Robert F. *Preparing Instructional Objectives*. Belmont, CA: Fearon Publishers, 1962.

Mattran, Kenneth J. "Breaking Through the Decoding Barrier: A Case Study in Adult Literacy." Paper presented at the Conference of the Commission on Adult Basic Education, April 1981. (CE 029244)

Meyer, Valerie. "Prime-O-Tec: A Successful Strategy for Adult Disabled Readers." *Journal of Reading*, Volume 25, Number 6, 1982. (EJ 259281)

Newman, A. P., and Parer, M. D. *Literacy Instructor Training, LIT-TV: A Handbook for Literacy Instructors*. (Accompanied by five films distributed through the Indiana University Audiovisual Department: *Language Experience Approach, Comprehension, Patterns in Language, Word Analysis Skills*, and *Talking It Over*.) Bloomington, IN: Indiana University, School of Education, 1978.

Newman, A. P. *Adult Basic Education: Reading*. Boston: Allyn & Bacon, 1980.

Nolan, S., and Hawkings, N. *The Vital Bibliography: A Basic Collection of Books and Learning Materials for an Adult Literacy Program*. Bloomington, IN: Monroe County Public Library, 1981.

O'Brien, R. L. *Books for Adult New Readers*. Cleveland: Project LEARN, 1980.

Parker, James, and Taylor, Paul (Eds.). *The CB Reader: A Guide to Understanding the Competency-Based Adult Education Movement*. Upper Montclair, NJ: National Adult Education Clearinghouse, 1980.

Shaugnessy, Mina P. *Errors & Expectations: A Guide for the Teacher of Basic Writing*. New York: Oxford University Press, 1977.

Simpson, Edwin, and Loveall, Phillip. "Preparing and Selecting Printed Educational Materials for New Adult Readers." Alexandria, VA: ERIC Clearinghouse in Career Information Series, No. 9 (CE 007631)

Smith, Edwin H. *Guide to Curricula for Disadvantaged Adult Programs*. Englewood Cliffs, NJ: Prentice-Hall, 1972.

Snyder, Robert E. *Guide to Teaching Techniques for Adult Classes*. Englewood Cliffs, NJ: Prentice-Hall, 1972.

"A Statewide Approach to Computer Application for Adult Literacy Programs." Monograph available through Lighthouse/Technology Project, Dr. Richard J. Lavin, Executive Director, Merrimack Education Center, 101 Mill Road, Chelmsford, MA 01824 or through Ms. Gale Ewer, Director, Massachusetts Department of Education, Springfield Regional Center, 88 Massasoit Avenue, West Springfield, MA 01089.

Trillin, Alice Stewart, and Associates. *Teaching Basic Skills in College: A Guide to Objectives, Skills Assessment, Course Content, Teaching Methods, Support Services, and Administration*. San Francisco: Jossey-Bass, 1980.

Vella, Jane K. *Learning to Listen: A Guide to Methods of Adult Nonformal Education*. Amherst, MA: Center for International Education, University of Massachusetts, 1979.

Adult Learning Theory

Barton, David. "Literacy and Awareness of Segmental Structure in Adult Learners." Paper presented at the Annual Meeting of the American Association of Applied Linguistics, December 1981. (ED 216510)

Block, J. H. (Ed.) *Mastery Learning: Theory and Practice*. New York: Holt, Rinehart and Winston, 1971.

Coles, Gerald S. "Can ABE Students Be Identified as Learning Disabled?" *Journal of Adult Literacy and Basic Education*, Volume 4, Number 3, Fall 1980 (CE 511538)

Cross, Kathryn Patricia. *Adults as Learners: Increasing Participation and Facilitating Learning*. San Francisco: Jossey-Bass, 1981.

Howe, Michael J. A. *Adult Learning: Psychological Research and Applications*. New York: John Wiley, 1977.

Kazemek, Francis E., and Rigg, Pat. (Comp.) *Adult Literacy: An Annotated Bibliography*. Newark, DE: International Reading Association, 1984.

Keege, D., and Meyer, V. "Adult Disabled Readers: Their Perceived Models of the Reading Process." *Journal of Adult Literacy and Basic Education*, 1980, pages 120–124.

Long, Huey B. *Adult Learning: Research and Practice*. New York: Cambridge, The Adult Education Company, 1983.

Malicky, N. A., and Norman, C. A. "Reading Strategies of Adult Illiterates." *Journal of Reading*, Volume 25, Number 8, pages 731–735, 1982. (EJ 261378)

Mezirow, Jack D. *Last Gamble on Education: Dynamics of Adult Basic Education*. Washington, DC: Adult Education Association of the USA, 1975.

Smith, Frank. *Understanding Reading: A Psycholinguistic Analysis of Reading and Learning to Read*. New York: Holt, Rinehart and Winston, 1971.

Sticht, Thomas G. *Evaluation of the "Reading Potential" Concept for Marginally Literate Adults*. Alexandria, VA: Human Resources Research Organization, 1982. (ED 217168)

Chapter 8
Follow-Up of Learners

In the preceding chapter, we noted that programs design instructional management systems to help students achieve stated goals and to document each step that students take toward those goals. Programs thus maintain information about students while they are participants, and they collect evidence indicating whether students can demonstrate mastery of objectives assumed to be essential to success in achieving long-range job or life goals. However, programs do not necessarily maintain information about students once they have left, whether the students have dropped out, "stopped out," or completed a given instructional program. To obtain such follow-up information, programs must design deliberate and systematic procedures.

Follow-up procedures directed at students who have dropped out of the program before completion may help the program regenerate the students' motivation and get them to return to the program. Such procedures might also yield information about some of the reasons students drop out of the program and thus help programs determine what logistical or programmatic changes they can make to improve their retention rates.

Follow-up procedures directed at graduates may help programs determine the long-term effects of participation. Specifically, these procedures may help them assess whether participation in the program made a difference in these former students' lives and whether the program correctly identified appropriate learning objectives. Assuming that graduates have had the opportunity to apply the academic and social skills they learned within the program, graduates may be in a good position to evaluate the true impact of their educational experience on their roles in their jobs, in their homes, and in their community as well as the impact on their performance in any further education or training they may have subsequently undertaken. If they discovered ways in which the program did not fully prepare them for their academic, vocational, or personal goals, their perspectives, suggestions, and recommendations may provide direction for modifications to the instructional program that will help future students. On the other hand, testimonials offered by students who attribute their success to participation in the program can be valuable in a program's recruitment and public relations activities.

Valuable as the information that can be gained from follow-up procedures may be, few of the programs in the NALP study reported having any great success in obtaining such information. The problem seems to lie both with the limitations on the financial and human resources of the program and with the nature of the student population. Programs, many of which operate with part-time, almost skeleton staff, may find that all available time and funds must be devoted to the students currently attending the program. And even when time and funds are available for follow-up on program dropouts and program graduates, former students may not be easy to locate.

In this chapter, we will describe some of the follow-up procedures the programs in the NALP study have used and recommend basic principles programs should follow in designing their own procedures.

FOLLOW-UP ON PROGRAM DROPOUTS

When staff members are able to contact students who have dropped out or "stopped out" and can show them that they are missed and that places are being held for their return, many of these students will return, often with renewed purpose. One teacher told us the story of a man who had stopped coming to classes because he felt the work was too difficult for him. Several phone calls to his wife were successful in relaying to him how the staff was willing to help him move at his own pace. This man completed his program and is now fulfilling his dream of studying to be a licensed vocational nurse. The follow-up phone calls from a concerned teacher made the difference between success and failure for him.

Adults may stop coming to a literacy program for many personal, family, or economic reasons. Transportation problems, a sick child, or even the weather can prevent steady attendance. Sometimes a misunderstanding about program expectations or a fleeting reminder of past failure can destroy a student's initial resolve to "start over again." A follow-up phone call from a staff member may or may not always end as happily as the story recounted above, but the staff member may be able to suggest ways of overcoming whatever problem may be keeping the student from attending. Such recommendations might include alternate forms of transportation, child care services, counseling services, or adjustments in the instructional process. One must recognize, however, that some problems cannot easily be resolved and that there are some adults who, for a number of reasons, may not be capable of undertaking an educational program at a given point in time.

What we are suggesting is that it is the caring attitude of the adult education professional that will help many students return to a program, whether that return is immediate or some time in the future. When the program can demonstrate that it is sincere in its goal of serving the individual needs of its students, the students are less likely to become discouraged and drop out.

Maintaining accurate attendance records complete with up-to-date phone numbers and addresses of the students' homes and places of employment are essential to effective follow-up procedures. Teachers need to systematically review their attendance logs and the sign-in sheets used by open-entry–open-exit students, and they need to periodically remind students to supply any change-of-address information. Spaces for phone number and address might even be included on weekly sign-in sheets or weekly activity logs to ensure that information on file is up to date. However, it is equally important to allow students to state their wish not to be called at home or on the job, as many students do not wish to reveal to anyone that they have been enrolled in an adult education program.

Some programs initiate follow-up after a student has missed two or three sessions or has not come into the drop-in learning laboratory for a period of one or two weeks. Programs that are pressed for time or that serve large numbers of students may find it necessary to resort to postcards or form letters (which are better than no contact at all), but personal phone calls have proven to be the most successful in getting students to return. Without the interaction that can take place on the phone, programs have no way of helping students overcome whatever problem may be preventing them from attending.

Anecdotal records of the reasons students have given for dropping out may also be useful. Programs might devote an in-service training session or general staff meeting to sharing data on dropouts and absentees. The meeting might be a forum in which staff members share strategies they have successfully employed to help students overcome barriers to consistent participation. If data has been kept for a long enough period of time for a reasonable analysis of trends, the discussion might be focused on aspects of the program that could be modified to enhance student retention. Such modifications might include adding new options in instructional methods, materials, or courses of study; supplementing existing counseling services, perhaps through strengthening ties with outside sources of counseling; and adding such support services as child care or program-supplied means of transportation. The data might also suggest the need for changes in recruitment strategies or orientation sessions; the program may need to clarify the range of services the program is equipped to provide and the students it is best able to serve. (This is an explosive issue that was discussed under the heading "Targeting the Recruitment Effort" in Chapter 3.) If the program finds that it is consistently losing a certain group of students because it cannot address the specific needs of that group, the program might need to make a concerted effort to locate a program to which these students can be referred.

FOLLOW-UP ON PROGRAM GRADUATES

We noted in the chapter on counseling that some programs conduct exit interviews with students graduating from the program in order to offer a few parting words of encouragement and to gather data on the students' perceptions of the effectiveness of the program. Few programs have the time or the money to go beyond this step and contact graduates after they have been out of the program for a period of years to discover what long-term benefits students feel they have derived from their participation in the program. The same problems noted in our description of follow-up procedures for recent dropouts exist for programs that wish to conduct long-term follow-ups on graduates. Indeed, programs that have used printed surveys or questionnaires have often been discouraged by a low rate of response. In some cases, no more than two to ten percent of those receiving the questionnaire actually returned it to the program.

Programs that routinely record, collate, and store information about student background and performance from program entry to program exit may compile a historical overview of the student population and their range of achievements. Such a document might give the program a useful profile of the kinds of students it has been able to reach (including such factors as age, sex, marital status, ethnic background, employment status, years of prior formal education, and place of residence) as well as the numbers of students who have enrolled in each of the types of programs that have been offered (e.g., the number of students who enrolled in the GED preparation program in each year of the past ten years of operation). This may have implications for improvements in recruitment strategies to broaden the student population to include adults who have not historically been attracted to the program, or it may suggest the nature of appropriate instructional materials. It may even suggest which of the program's services have seen declining enrollments and therefore might be discontinued or modified. (We'll have more to say about program evaluation in the next chapter.) Maintaining thorough records for a long enough period of time to be useful in a historical study and compiling the information in those records is a difficult task, even if one maintains student records on a computer; without a computer, the tabulation of the data may be out of the question given other pressing duties.

Despite the difficulties involved in conducting more in-depth long-range studies, they are not impossible to design. For example, the Lowell (MA) Adult Education Program conducted a follow-up study of the students who had graduated from its GED program from June 1979 (the date on which the program began operations) through February 1984. The primary work of the study was done by a graduate student from a local college as part of her course work in "Fundamentals of Research." This minimized the program's financial commitment and the amount of time program staff had to devote to the project. In addition to tabulating a statistical profile of the composition of the GED student population during this five-year period, the researcher conducted phone interviews with 221 former students, or fifteen percent of the total of 1,436 students who had completed the program during the period. To assess the long-term effects of program participation, the interviewer included questions to probe for the following information:

- What was the employment status of these former students at the time they enrolled in the program, and what was their current employment status?
- Did the former students continue their education? If so, in what kind of program or course of study?
- What effect did they think the program had had on their lives?
- What were their reasons for wanting to obtain a GED credential?
- Did they feel that the GED credential had helped them achieve their goals?
- What were their general likes and dislikes about the program?
- What suggestions would they offer for improving the program?
- Would they support continuation of the Lowell adult education services?

The researcher reported, among other findings, that:

Nearly three-fourths of the graduates interviewed reported that attaining the GED certificate has had as good an effect on their lives as they had expected. Many explained that, although they have received material benefits (better job, higher salary, etc.), the expectation of enhanced self-esteem has been satisfied, and is probably the most rewarding effect. The psychological and emotional benefits were repeatedly mentioned as the key reward GED applicants had hoped for and had received.

Some graduates (15%) complete the requirements with humble or limited expectations, only to find that it has affected their lives in a very positive way. These adults enthusiastically responded that the effect was better than they expected. Enhanced self-esteem, coupled with increased self-confidence, seems to be the underlying factor for the surprising turn of events in these people's lives. For many, the feeling of success associated with achieving their GED status prompted attempts at other new endeavors that have proven equally successful and satisfying.

Nearly eighty percent of those interviewed emphatically stated that their participation had helped them reach their goals. Whereas only sixty percent of these former students had been employed at the time they began the program, nearly eighty percent were currently employed. And of the thirty-four individuals who were currently unemployed, only three were unemployed because they had been unable to find employment; most of those who were unemployed were young mothers who were home by choice, retirees, or people enrolled as full-time students in junior or four-year colleges. Nearly forty-eight percent of the GED graduates did continue their education, and twenty-nine percent of those who had not yet enrolled in further education programs reported that they were planning to. Continued education ranged from attending Harvard to taking data-processing courses at a local vocational school.

Beyond this general confirmation that the Lowell program had been effective, the program uncovered a few areas that could be improved. The researcher discovered that most of those who reported being disappointed with events that had taken place after graduation were women who had hoped to go on to college or other training programs but whose financial problems or family responsibilities prevented them from pursuing such a course of action. The researcher thus suggested that the program offer counseling services targeted to helping such women. Small percentages of interviewees reported that they had found their GED program too easy, that they had felt rushed, or that the writing skills curriculum had not been helpful. Although the percentages were too small to be significant, the findings might indicate that expanded options in supplemental materials would not be unwelcome.

CONCLUSIONS AND RECOMMENDATIONS

Because of the cost and logistics of conducting follow-up studies, it is easy to understand why many programs do not establish systematic plans for follow-up. Programs might even agree with the director of one program who told us, "Adults often have important reasons to leave a literacy program, and dropping out may, in some cases, be a reasonable step for an adult learner." Yet without attempting to contact program dropouts, one has no way of knowing whether making adjustments within the program might have made a difference in retention rates. And without attempting to contact program graduates after the passage of some time, one has no way of confirming that the program was effective in helping students reach their ultimate goals.

We therefore make the following three recommendations:

(1) Maintain up-to-date files on all students. Establish a routine in which pertinent information is gathered on a systematic and frequent basis so that follow-up procedures can be implemented. Such thorough record-keeping will also assist programs in generating a historical profile of students it has served. If possible, use a software management system for maintaining student records and promoting easy access to them.

(2) Establish a policy under which teachers identify possible dropouts for follow-up contact. One cannot mandate the kind of student-teacher rapport that will lead to students' honestly sharing their reasons for dropping out. One also might not be able to ask overburdened teachers to make follow-up phone calls to students. However, one can and should maintain attendance records and other indicators of flagging motivation and interest so that someone on program staff can either call or write to let absent students know that they have been missed.

(3) Establish target dates on which the program will conduct a study of the long-term effects of the program on the lives of its students. A program may be unable to find appropriate resources to conduct in-depth telephone interviews even with advance planning, but it should attempt to gather information about the long-term effects of program participation if it is to evaluate program effectiveness. Establishing a timeline for conducting such a study and laying out a preliminary plan for developing or setting aside human and financial resources to undertake the work is critical to ensuring that a study of program effectiveness is in fact conducted.

Chapter 9
Program Evaluation

Program evaluation can be defined as the process of determining and documenting whether a program is achieving its goals. This process begins with a clear formulation of the goals of the program, whether set at the program level or at some higher level. Goals might also be formulated in direct response to a formal needs assessment survey (discussed in Chapter 3). But once goals have been set, some system of recordkeeping or documentation must be in place to monitor students' learning progress and the program's effectiveness in achieving its stated goals.

Program evaluation will involve all of the program components examined in Chapters 3 through 8. But effective programs not only seek to evaluate such program components as recruitment strategies, orientation and counseling procedures, diagnostic testing and assessment tools, instructional methods and materials, and follow-up procedures, they also seek to evaluate their evaluation procedures themselves. Sound evaluation procedures should assist a program's personnel in identifying the extent to which the program's goals are—or are not—being met. The program can then undertake to find the probable causes for these shortcoming as well as the solutions that will lead to a more successful program and more satisfied learners. The more specific and directed the evaluation procedures are, the more likely it is that the program will be able to identify the probable causes of unmet goals and the possible solutions.

However easy it may be to set forth the importance of evaluation procedures, it is clear from the NALP study that the evaluation procedures employed in the field are generally not very sophisticated. In part, this could be attributed to the fact that the kind of daily recordkeeping necessary for detailed and thoroughgoing evaluation is a difficult and time-consuming process. But, more than this, the program leaders interviewed in the study are not in agreement about what program evaluation is, how one goes about it, or even how useful it is. They are divided on whether evaluation is essentially a tabulation of data on such things as numbers of students served and number of GED and alternative diplomas awarded for the "final report" (summative evaluation) or a platform for action based on an ongoing look at program operations and results (formative evaluation). They are divided on how to document goals and outcomes, and indeed, on which goals and outcomes to document.

What this chapter seeks to do is to lay out the information you may need to decide the issues for yourself. We'll begin by reporting the reasons offered by the programs in the NALP study for using some form of evaluation procedure. We'll then look at the barriers that prevent programs from engaging in detailed and sophisticated evaluation procedures. Knowing *why* one might want to evaluate and balancing that against what constraints might be involved, we can turn to an examination of the means by which one might choose to evaluate. In three successive sections we'll examine (1) *when* and *what* programs evaluate, (2) *how* programs evaluate those things, and finally (3) *who* programs involve in the evaluation and with what role. At the end of the chapter, we'll offer our own conclusions for your consideration. We'll also offer for careful study a detailed evaluation document developed by the Division of Adult and Community Education, Indiana Department of Public Instruction. And should you wish more detailed information about evaluation procedures, we urge you to consult the references cited in the bibliography.

WHY DO PROGRAMS EVALUATE?

One reason that programs engage in some form of evaluation is that they are required to by their funding agencies. But this kind of evaluation may be limited to tabulations of various kinds of enrollment data, attendance patterns, student test scores, and numbers of graduates. Most of the staff members interviewed in the NALP study are clearly interested in other kinds of evaluation activities, specifically those that will help them understand how they can improve program operation and, especially, instruction. To that end, some programs formally monitor:

- educational achievement of students
- achievement of program goals
- effectiveness of program components
- effectiveness of teachers

At the Camp Hill Pennsylvania Correctional Facility, monitoring student achievement has an additional benefit—it helps inmates present a positive image to the parole board. The education department at this institution works closely with the parole board, who has agreed to use such factors as positive attitude and achievement in classes as important considerations in parole decisions.

The achievement of program goals, the effectiveness of such program components as counseling, and the effectiveness of the teaching staff can be difficult to monitor and document. As many staff members reported, goals are easier to measure when they are closely tied to quantifiable data. However, programs do want to evaluate the achievement of such broad goals as positive impact on the community as well as the more personal and affective goals of the students. "Many affective variables do mean something, more than how many grade levels [a person moved] up over an eighteen-month period," insists Mike Fox of Push Literacy Action Now in Washington, DC. "We need to look at [the students' goals] in terms of their own lives, and not some criteria set by someone else," he adds.

Clearly, programs evaluate themselves in order to measure their success. Success may be measured strictly by concrete and quantifiable data—the numbers required by funding agencies. Yet many programs are frustrated by the fact that success means more than such concrete data can demonstrate. Whatever the difficulties in documentation, these programs want to measure and report on the achievement of the affective goals of the program and the students. If the program is successful, some reason, the students' self-esteem and self-confidence will have increased; students will have not only basic education skills but also the courage to use those skills in job-related or life-related situations.

BARRIERS TO EVALUATION ACTIVITIES

The NALP study found five primary reasons that programs do not engage in detailed and sophisticated evaluation procedures: (1) lack of time, (2) lack of training, (3) perceived lack of relevance, (4) difficulty in quantifying data, and (5) problems inherent in evaluating education for the educationally disadvantaged. We can suggest some ways in which programs might overcome these barriers to engaging in full-scale evaluation activities.

Lack of Time.   Most staff members reported that there is not enough time to do a thorough job of recordkeeping and evaluation given all the other pressing responsibilities they must shoulder. Short-term priorities centering on the learner and on instruction take precedence over the long-term goal of collecting sufficient data for later retrospective analysis and eventual use in improving the program. After all, the students are here now, and their needs must be addressed as quickly as possible if the program is to retain them. Further, many adult educators are part-time employees of a program and their hours are limited to direct instruction-related activities; time spent in recordkeeping is time *not* spent with students. Yet this is a Catch-22. Without time spent in data collection, one has no way of evaluating the quality of the time that is spent with the students.

Lack of Training.   Program staffs are generally not trained in evaluation techniques. In the NALP site visit interviews, only two directors reported that they had taken courses in evaluation methodology. One way for programs to successfully implement more sophisticated evaluation procedures is to provide and/or mandate more pre-service or in-service training in evaluation techniques. Another is to tap expert evaluation services that may be available through a literacy resource or assistance center like those that exist in New York City and Boston. These centers, funded as part of citywide literacy initiatives, may offer staff services and assistance to those desiring to design and implement an evaluation plan appropriate for literacy or adult basic education programs.

Yet another avenue to gaining evaluation expertise is to obtain it experientially, by actually participating in a structured evaluation exercise. When separate or discrete training is not possible, the adoption and implementation of an evaluation procedure that requires staff involvement might provide staff members with the experience in using those skills necessary to making an analysis of their program's effectiveness in meeting its goals and in ensuring attainment of learners' goals. After this first experience, staff may then be equipped to suggest ways of making further or more refined analyses.

Perceived Lack of Relevance. Programs often see the evaluation requirements set forth by their funding agencies as a necessary evil, but not germane to their program goals. That is, they do not see how the evaluation procedures that they must follow actually help them learn about the weaknesses or strengths in their programs. This perception may or may not be justified as applied to the documents the programs currently generate. Often, because program personnel were not involved in the creation of the evaluation mechanism, the procedures may be more relevant to the funding agency, a situation that could be improved if both the oversight agency and the programs reporting to them forged evaluation requirements as a team. Given the time, expertise, and resources to do so, programs could implement procedures that would be relevant. And here, as in training, pre-service or in-service time must be given to demonstrating how the evaluation procedures are relevant.

Difficulty in Quantifying Data. As noted in the preceding section entitled "Why Do Programs Evaluate," some data can be more easily quantified and documented than other, perhaps equally or more desirable information. There seems to be general acceptance of records of retention and completion data as a measure of a program's effectiveness and success. Yet most programs seek to go beyond the limits of these statistics to document more long-term (albeit elusive) results. Even though this information is not easily quantified, many are convinced that there must be a better way to evaluate than to play the "numbers game." They are frustrated when funding agencies call for quantifiable data as the sole criteria of success. When that quantifiable data is a count of the numbers of students served, programs may be tempted to interpret/report as bodies those students who were only in the program for a short term simply because they need the points generated by reporting high numbers.

It may simply be a fact of life that some information can be gathered only by qualitative means and in anecdotal and hence largely subjective records. For example, many adult educators have pointed to increased self-esteem of learners as an important outcome of successful participation in an adult literacy program. Learners experiencing success and achievement, perhaps for the first time in an educational environment, generally feel better about themselves and their capabilities. Yet, gains in confidence and human dignity are not easily measured except perhaps through learners' own reports or self-assessment. Moreover, these gains are often not quantifiable. Although anecdotal and subjective records may be regarded as not very valuable by some members of the research community or by funding agencies, they may well be critical to the individual program's search for excellence.

Problems Inherent in Evaluating Education for the Educationally Disadvantaged. Keeping records and evaluating the results of educational programs for the disadvantaged have always been more difficult tasks than recordkeeping and evaluation for other kinds of educational programs. The population is, more often than not, made up of voluntary learners. They are more diverse and transient; their progress can be slower; and some outcomes can be harder to specify. As implied earlier, it is simply hard to define what "success" is to an adult literacy program. For some, success is the number of people served. To others, it is the number of GED certificates or alternative diplomas awarded or the number of people the program is able to retain. To still others, it is helping some, if not all, of their participants experience the joy of achievement.

Many practitioners judge their program's effectiveness by looking at a combination of these and still other outcomes. The important point is that most programs do not judge their success by looking at one monolithic outcome. Success is reflected in the achievement of a myriad of goals or outcomes for both the learners and the program itself. Programs want to evaluate the total range of what students can *do* with the skills they have acquired through program participation. Whatever the inherent difficulties in judging the effectiveness of programs working with this very special population, they should not prevent programs from taking all possible steps toward the development of evaluation procedures that could enable them to operate more effectively.

WHEN AND WHAT DO PROGRAMS EVALUATE?

Evaluation activities can take place at any point in the life of a program. A needs assessment survey might be conducted before a program opens its doors as well as at any point after the program has begun operation. Recordkeeping will normally be an ongoing process, but the analysis and use of the data in the records may take place only at the end of a given term of operation (as for an annual or quarterly report to a funding agency) or at regularly scheduled intervals during the term of operation. The question of when to evaluate is largely a function of the purpose for which the evaluation is being done. If the objective is to generate a report for a funding agency, the process might take place only toward the end of a program term. If the report itself is offered only as a final or definitive judgment of the program's effectiveness and as the basis on which funding decisions can be made, the program is engaged in *summative evaluation*. If the program's objective is to generate reports that represent an ongoing look at program operation in order to improve the program through adjustment or change, the program is engaged in *formative evaluation*. In such cases, evaluation activities may occur at more frequent intervals in the program's calendar. (This is a slight simplification of the definitions of summative and formative evaluation. For a thorough discussion of both types of evaluation, consult the text by Bloom, et al., in the bibliography. And these types of evaluation by no means exhaust the possibilities for program evaluation; for more information, you may wish to consult the text by Steele cited in the bibliography.)

Once you have settled the question of why you want to evaluate and thus when the evaluation should take place, you naturally arrive at the question of what is to be included in the evaluation. The range of possible answers to this question is virtually limitless; you can ask as much or as little as will suit the purpose for which evaluation is being conducted. But the more questions you ask and the more program areas you probe, the more likely you are to find solutions to problems you never suspected existed.

The lists of questions cited under the heading "Needs Assessments and Canvassing" in Chapter 3 and the list of factors we suggested programs evaluate about their instructional practices under the heading "How Can the Instructional System Be Managed?" indicated many of the aspects of a program one might seek to evaluate. To evaluate the effectiveness of an ongoing program, one might ask many more detailed and probing questions—especially if the intended result of the evaluation is to be an action plan for improvement. At the end of this chapter is just such a detailed questionnaire/document developed by the Division of Adult and Community Education, Indiana Department of Public Instruction. We offer this document not as a definitive set of questions for evaluators of all programs everywhere, but as a thought-provoking model from which one might derive some insights into what is possible.

Because this document is somewhat lengthy, we will summarize here the major sections under which questions are grouped. This list may not only stimulate you to examine the complete document but also open up the discussion that is the focus of the next section of this chapter—"How Do Programs Evaluate?"

PART ONE
A. Program Direction
   Under this heading, you are to list your goals and the results you have achieved with respect to the following four areas:
   • recruitment/public relations
   • staff development
   • student outcomes
   • interagency relations
B. Administrative Overview
   Under this heading, you are to offer a profile of enrollment data and attendance patterns and ultimately apply a "Positive Impact Formula" to your data

PART TWO
A. Cite your program's statement of philosophy, if it has one
B. Evaluate how well you attained the goals set forth in Part One, Section A
C. Evaluate the trends identified in Part One, Section B
D. Evaluate the staff of your programs, including volunteers, as well as the development activities you provide for them
E. Evaluate your program's facilities
F. Evaluate the instructional materials you use
G. Evaluate the instructional process—including orientation, placement, assessment, and follow-up as well as instructional methodologies
H. Evaluate the outcomes of your program both in terms of student progress and in terms of the exit data you collect
I. Evaluate the level of community awareness of your program, including your efforts at recruitment
J. Evaluate the financial and human resources you obtain from outside the program itself

HOW DO
PROGRAMS EVALUATE?

We began this chapter by stating that program evaluation can be defined as the process of determining and documenting whether a program and its learners are achieving their goals. The Indiana document represents one suggestion for what data might be collected and how it might be recorded to accomplish this objective. To most program directors in the NALP study, evaluation is a combination of formal recordkeeping and less formal internal monitoring of program operation.

Formal Recordkeeping

As noted earlier, most programs must collect data for the yearly or quarterly report to funding agencies. Those data include student test scores, hours of attendance for each student, completions, dropouts, number of graduates, demographics and ethnicity, and goal attainment statistics, to name a few. Under the heading "Goal Setting and Documentation" in Chapter 7, we suggested some of the documents that programs might use to record data about students' instructional achievements and attendance. But such data collection is difficult and time consuming. In large programs, data management can consume a substantial portion of the director's time.

Even small programs feel the need to manage information more efficiently. When asked what an ideal program evaluation system would be, the director of a small community-based program replied, "a microcomputer." He echoes over half of the directors interviewed in the NALP study who do *not* have computers to manage the daily, monthly, and yearly statistics they must compile to satisfy funding requirements. It is clear that computers are no longer a luxury in literacy programs. They are a necessity if programs are to be expected to monitor the growing array of statistics that formal recordkeeping demands.

Once data has been collected, however, it can be used for more than generating a report to the funding agency. It can be used for the program's and the students' purposes as well. The collection and dissemination of the data is only the first step; the next steps are analysis and application of the data. Data on individual students can be used to assess learner trends and progress, as we noted in the section on instructional management in Chapter 7. The data can also be used for program planning, troubleshooting, and monitoring trends. If, for example, the program identifies a trend of declining numbers of GED completions, the program can begin to investigate the probable causes of the trend. Is it the result of ineffective recruitment efforts to enroll potential GED candidates or the ineffectiveness of instructional material, orientation sessions, diagnostic and assessment measures, or other elements of the instructional process? Or is it merely the result of a general trend in the composition of the population in the program's service area?

A small number of programs in the NALP study do use evaluation data as a springboard for planning. Jo Ann Vorst, director of the Lafayette Adult Reading Academy, explains: "That's how we plan for the next year. We look at our final report and look at where our weaknesses have been this year and look at what we need to accomplish. . . . [and] we have a meeting where we can go over the final results of the year and how we can improve ourselves for the next year." That plan then goes into the program's handbook so that each staff member is informed and participates in meeting the program's goals.

Internal Monitoring of Program Operation

When programs seek information about their strengths and weaknesses, especially with regard to more effective goals and such seemingly indefinable aspects of program operation as teacher effectiveness, programs more often turn to less formal internal monitoring than to the formal records of hard data. Staff meetings, chance encounters in the hall, and in-service sessions all represent ways programs try to monitor the day-to-day progress of the program and the instructional process.

Informal discussions and group meetings can often lead to changes in procedures or curriculum. Observing classes and interacting with staff can provide directors with a *feel* for the relative effectiveness of the program's operation. Staff meetings can be a forum for troubleshooting or doing preventative maintenance. As a program director in an Eastern city explains, "Oftentimes, we come back [from teaching a class] feeling dissatisfied with what's been going on, so we try to change materials, or switch students around, or do whatever we think will really ameliorate that."

One program developed an informal observation guide to gauge instructional climate and strategies. The guide, shown as Exhibit 9.1, serves to focus the staff's attention on key aspects of their program.

EXHIBIT 9.1 Program Observation Guide

1. What are the range of techniques used by instructors? (e.g., lecture, individualized help, group work, "sit alone" work, peer instruction)

2. What is the primary mode of instruction?

3. How flexible is the instructor in modifying instructional strategies based on student response?

4. If instructional aides are present, what do they do?

5. Are there computers available for instructional purposes? How are they used?

6. To what extent do learners appear to interact with each other on educational matters (e.g., is there any peer tutoring)?

7. To what degree do learners appear to interact on non-educational matters (e.g., socializing)?

8. What is the condition of instructional materials:

   a. How old are the textbooks?

   b. Other than computers, are there enough materials for each student?

9. How would you sum up the instructional climate in the classroom?

Unfortunately, in many programs, internal monitoring activities are not a consistent and formalized process, and decisions for changes in operation made in informal decision-making sessions may not be followed up to determine whether the changes resulted in the desired improvement. Staff meetings might be called *during* a crisis and result in Band-Aid solutions. To be effective, internal monitoring activities need to be made as much a part of the set of evaluation procedures as formal recordkeeping of hard data.

WHO EVALUATES LITERACY PROGRAMS?

Most programs are externally monitored by state, federal, or private funding agencies. Depending on the sector in which a program operates, monitoring agencies might include the Bureau of Corrections, the General Accounting Office (for military programs), or a Private Industry Council (for some employment and training programs). Private funding agencies such as the Ford Foundation also require evaluation data.

Internal evaluation activities are usually overseen by the program director. The director's tasks may include gathering statistical data as well as surveying staff, students, and sometimes advisory boards or community agencies. Soliciting staff input may be accomplished both formally in meetings and informally through daily contact.

The NALP study found that, though evaluating agencies and personnel may differ among sectors, all programs participate in some form of both external and internal evaluation. The most common external evaluators are state funding agencies, while internally, the actual tasks of program evaluation usually fall to staff. Student input, while solicited in about a third of the programs interviewed in the NALP site visits, is considered unreliable by many staff members because students' loyalty to the program often precludes any truly critical judgment.

In the following pages, we'll examine not only who might be involved in evaluation procedures but also what roles each of those parties might play.

External Evaluators

The most common type of external evaluation is that done as a requirement of the state agency from whom the program obtains funding. Programs in all sectors studied by NALP except the military participate in this kind of evaluation. But programs also occasionally retain outside consultants to obtain an objective evaluation of the effectiveness of program operation.

State or Other Oversight Agency

As we have noted, funding agency forms typically require programs to list and to document their success in attaining program objectives. Documenting objectives involves program staff in providing enrollment, testing, completion, and retention data as well as demographic information and reasons for students' separation from the program. Frequently, the emphasis is on "numbers," although some agencies do try to address less quantifiable issues as well. In one document NALP examined, the program was invited to list "outstanding" offerings and those that "needed improvement" under such broader categories as ABE and GED.

The Lafayette Adult Reading Academy piloted the self-evaluation instrument developed by the Division of Adult and Community Education of the Indiana Department of Public Instruction reproduced at the end of this chapter. The program staff rated this instrument highly for several reasons. (1) It is specific about the components of the instructional process, the heart of most literacy programs. (2) Every viewpoint is represented under the procedures for using the document. The director fills in Part One—the statements of goals and the statistical profile of enrollment and attendance data—and distributes copies of this section along with blank copies of Part Two—the evaluative questionnaire and rating scales—to all staff members. After each staff member has rated the program individually, the results are tallied and discussed by the staff as a whole. (3) The rating scales and probing questions provide an opportunity to step back and examine each of the program's components, thus isolating each potential area of difficulty. (4) It affords an overview of the interrelationships among program components. (5) It is a very positive experience. The director reports that, rather than being discouraged by possible difficulties, staff were encouraged by the large degree to which they felt the program was meeting its own objectives.

Other program directors interviewed by NALP viewed their required evaluations in a positive light for a different reason. For example, one director saw the publicity and the unmet needs reflected in the year-end report as "an opportunity to ask for more money." In addition, the commendations his program received were used to publicize his program and attract new volunteers in his largely rural state. Another director was grateful for state involvement because: "I want quality control, so I am bringing in the state to do that, and training [the inmate tutors] on workshop techniques." For programs that report to state departments of education, the state provides valuable resources that would otherwise be unaffordable.

However, not all programs in the NALP study are pleased with the evaluation procedures they are required to use. The most common complaint is that funding agency forms do not get at the heart of what literacy programs are really about—that is, instruction and confidence building. Instead, the programs become mired in reporting what are to them less significant details. One director in an East Coast ABE program characterized the state evaluation as ". . . a silly in-depth look at everything." A director at an employment and training site in the East complained about the *standards* the state had for evaluating her program. ". . . [We're] concerned about the remediation of people's basic skills, but when you're being evaluated and the emphasis is [job] placement, that's all they see. . . ."

Independent Consultants

Mandatory state agency evaluations can provide an overall look at program operation, but sometimes an objective outside evaluation is needed to address more specific program areas. One example from the NALP study is an all-volunteer literacy program in a large urban area that commissioned an outside agency to evaluate the effectiveness of its program. The focus of the evaluation was twofold: (1) an implementation study, which monitored use of the teaching techniques presented in the volunteers' training sessions, and (2) an impact study, which examined teacher and student perceptions of program effectiveness as well as reading gain scores.

The evaluation revealed that volunteers were, in fact, not implementing the instructional procedures that they had been trained to use in the areas of reading methodology, writing instruction, and student-tutor interaction. This non-implementation may or may not have been responsible for the irregular reading gains reported for the more advanced students. But the program now had the data to examine the questions. As a result of the evaluation, the program opened up the training process to include follow-up training sessions and classroom observations. It used the results to make positive, informed changes in the program. "In a way, I wish I could hide my head in the sand and wish I never knew that the training is not enough," bemoans the director. However, she does not regret the experience. She adds with conviction: "One of the problems with volunteer programs is that people don't want to look seriously at what they are doing and use the same standards to evaluate their program as they would in any other program. . . . There is no point in running a program that is not as good as it should be!"

Identifying outside evaluation consultants or agencies whose work is applicable to the needs of adult literacy programs is often not an easy task. Most educational evaluation professionals have engaged in school-related activities; few have actually worked in adult education environments where students are voluntary participants with varying self-determined learning goals. This is problematic for adult educators who would argue that adult education centers are unique environments and that adult learners are a distinctive constituency.

Nonetheless, evaluation specialists trained in both quantitative and qualitative methodologies can adapt their techniques to the needs of adult literacy programs. Because increased national attention on literacy programs has resulted in an awareness of the lack of effectiveness data to document program and learner success, many evaluators from other educational arenas and social service sectors have responded to this need. Consequently there is a growing cadre of people able to provide programs with evaluation assistance.

Specifically, the Literacy Assistance Centers that have sprung up in some cities as adjuncts to local literacy campaigns can often refer programs to evaluators or, in some cases, can offer such expertise directly. For example, both New York City and Boston have literacy resource centers that programs in those areas can contact for both referral and direct assistance.

Generally, the criteria a program should use in selecting an outside evaluation consultant or agency are:

(1) evaluators are trained in and feel comfortable using several different evaluation methodologies
(2) evaluators have a collaborative working style; they will work with programs to determine the array of measurable outcomes that are important in the view of the individual programs
(3) evaluators are adaptable; they can adjust their methods to the unique needs of an adult education environment
(4) evaluators are experienced in working in alternative education settings, preferably adult settings

Internal Evaluators

All participants in the operation of the program have a role to play in the evaluation process. The director sets the tone and expectations and orchestrates all program management efforts. Staff, who are close to the instructional process and other program operations, can provide a wealth of ideas and information. They are especially well suited to troubleshoot and to implement any change strategies that may result from an examination of a program's strengths and weaknesses. Students, too, can be a valuable part of the evaluation process. As the ultimate consumers, they may have much to say about both the direct and the subtle effects of program participation. Within the following pages, we'll examine the roles each of these participants in program operation in closer detail.

The Role of the Director

The director is the central figure in managing and evaluating program operation. Directors must juggle, among all their other management and leadership roles, some distinct responsibilities related to the evaluation process. During the NALP site visits, directors described to us the many roles they play. They highlighted the following four responsibilities:

- The director is the *primary recordkeeper* and must manage and interpret the array of facts and figures that even small programs generate.
- The director is the *manager of a network* and, as such, must integrate the data from satellite centers and other sites. This role includes scheduling as well as evaluating staff, volunteers, and programs that may be spread over a large geographical area.
- The director is a *program manager* who must remain in constant contact with staff and students. This informal contact helps him or her keep a finger on the pulse of the program.
- The director is the *primary planner,* using evaluation data to help make program decisions ranging from expansion to curriculum modification.

In the following pages, we will elaborate on these four overlapping roles of the program director.

Recordkeeper.   Directors feel responsible for assembling and interpreting both the data required by funding agencies and the data they want for internal evaluation purposes. Some directors liken this process to "creating order out of chaos." Directors interviewed by NALP described elaborate recordkeeping systems involving enrollment, attendance, and exit cards; sign-in sheets; work folders; and test scores; to name a few of the documents they must manage. They detailed weekly collection and monthly and quarterly tallying of numbers.

A real challenge in keeping accurate records is the large turnover most programs experience. In one program in a correctional institution, there is a turnover of more than 600 people in the total resident population at any one time; inmates may only stay in the program for two or three months. "[That] means the fifty-three students I have now are not the fifty-three I had four months ago," reports the director. "It's a revolving door." A large ABE program in Maine must use daily sign-in sheets to keep abreast of attendance statistics. The director explains, "It's such a big program that we have to keep track of people as they come in and go out."

Network Manager.   The more sites a director manages, the greater the record-keeping problems. The director of a large multi-site urban tutoring program in the Midwest explains that he is trying to "tighten up the information system" to keep track of 550 volunteer-student matches, together with data on their pre-testing and post-testing activities, in addition to all the other data he must record. "The key is being able to generate those lists by site easily because the information that you have on file has to be retrievable any number of ways—by student, by tutor, by site, by who was contacted this month. . . ." An ABE director from the East explains that, in ten years, his original program has grown to twelve programs that serve about 4,000 people in his community. That places heavy demands on his skills as a data manager. As it becomes more common for programs to establish satellite centers in businesses and in outlying areas, the demand for directors with data management expertise will certainly grow.

Program Manager. The director's role as program manager means going beyond recordkeeping and data collection. It includes personal contact with staff and students and a participation in program activities. The role of program manager requires directors to leave their offices and mingle. Some directors have an ease that allows them to use informal contacts and observations as measuring sticks of progress. They systematically collect and analyze their observations and use this informal data as a starting point for evaluation and problem solving. One director on the East Coast feels strongly that he needs to be "visible." The information he gathers by visiting classes, talking to students, listening to "what they are saying on the street," is part of his information-gathering process. Other directors observe classes, and many teach. They think that this is the only way to be truly in touch with instruction and student progress.

Planner. Evaluation and planning are closely related activities in some programs. Information gathered during the evaluation process can serve as the basis for several types of planning decisions. For example, the data might suggest the need for expansion. "Whoever is running the program needs to have the foresight [to see] that it's got to grow and . . . look . . . [for] the best place to grow," explains one East Coast director. Census data and needs assessment surveys help directors pinpoint locations where existing programs need to be expanded and where new programs need to be started. Evaluation data may also suggest that a program needs to be refocused because one or more of its present offerings have ceased to meet the needs of its learners. When the data that indicates a need for any of these planning decisions is carefully recorded and documented, it can then be used to convince planning boards or executive councils of the need for the decision. As one ABE director in Massachusetts said, "You must understand that the school department didn't understand a lot about what adult education should be doing, so every year I go back to the board, data in hand, evidence for starting new programs. . . ."

The Role of Program Staff

It is uncommon for a director to conduct an evaluation without the input of program staff, and this input is most often sought in staff meetings. Although the meetings are usually chaired by the director or program administrator, internal evaluation meetings appear to be a very democratic, non-threatening process in most programs. Staff are eager for information about effective procedures, methods, and materials. And when program evaluation is clearly seen as distinct from staff evaluation, staff feel free to critique program procedures without feeling that it is a direct reflection on themselves. One Midwestern teacher interviewed by NALP calls her colleagues "a very questioning bunch. . . . [We] sit down and look hard at ourselves, at what we are doing and how we can work as a team better."

Some programs design periodic meetings to look at specific problems and solutions; others discuss issues informally on an ongoing basis. The inmate president of a corrections literacy council uses a "task force" to monitor the progress of the tutoring program. Every other week, they "take a topic, and review it, and try to come up with ways of improving it." He adds that troubleshooting is easy in his program. Problems rise to the surface: "If something isn't going right, our students or tutors will tell us."

In-house evaluation sessions are also occasionally used as a platform for planning or establishing goals for the year ahead. Some staff members interviewed by NALP felt very positive about their impact on planning, as the teacher in an ABE program in the East who commented, "I feel we have a lot of opportunity to affect the course of the program." One director of a volunteer program affirmed this influential role of staff, saying: "In our staff meetings, we do a lot of looking at our program, and trying to make changes based on that. . . . We improve a lot in informal ways." And, to plan for each year, the director of a community-based program takes one day each spring to meet with her administrative staff to review the evaluation forms that were completed by students and staff.

Unfortunately, not all programs have tried to establish a planning component within the in-house evaluation procedure. Some staff meetings focus only on immediate problems and do not focus on the overall effectiveness of the program's strategies. Yet staff can play a vital role in planning because they are often the first to see problems and can suggest important areas for investigation and possible change. Programs that set goals and focus on them in in-house evaluation sessions with staff express the greatest degree of satisfaction with their evaluation procedures.

The Role of Students

Students most frequently participate in program evaluation through questionnaires and surveys administered at the end of the term. As mentioned earlier, it can be difficult to collect reliable data from students. Jobs for Youth–Boston has addressed this problem by making the student evaluation form very specific. Instead of limiting the students to giving yes and no responses to general questions, the questionnaire is targeted to each of the program's objectives. Objectives measured include (among others) achievement, appropriateness of work, learning style, relationship with teacher, and even reasons for absence. Sample questions from this evaluation form appear in Exhibit 9.2.

EXHIBIT 9.2 Excerpts from Jobs for Youth–Boston Student Evaluation Form

---

Is the work your teacher puts in your folder helpful?

    Always   Most of the time   Sometimes   Never

**EXHIBIT 9.2 Excerpts from Jobs for Youth–Boston
Student Evaluation Form (*continued*)**

Is the work in this program at the right level of difficulty?

    Too hard   Just right   Too easy

Most of the time, how does the classroom feel to you?

    Too noisy   Just right   Too quiet

    Too hot   Just right   Too cold

Does your teacher explain things well most of the time?

    Always   Sometimes   Never

How could she or he improve?

When you don't come to class, why not? (Circle all that apply.)

    Sickness   Bad weather   No money for transportation

    No child care   Too tired   Working at a job

    Feeling depressed   Doesn't seem worth it

CONCLUSIONS AND RECOMMENDATIONS

In this chapter, we have examined what program evaluation means to programs and the methods they use to record and evaluate the success of their programs in meeting their goals. Literacy educators spend a great deal of time in recordkeeping and evaluation activities, and they have a sincere interest in improving the quality of their instructional programs. What many programs lack, however, is a well-developed management plan for collecting, analyzing, and using program and student evaluation data for program improvement and for proof of program effectiveness. Few directors in the NALP study could describe their methods or standards for judging program effectiveness, and many equated evaluation procedures with those used in filling out the required reports to their funding agencies. Evaluation efforts tended to be *pro forma* (submitting the required reports) or sporadic (staff meetings that address a multitude of problems, but set no long-term plan to implement and follow up on changes in program strategies).

Lack of time, lack of expertise, and the difficulty of defining success for the literacy population are indeed obstacles to making sophisticated evaluation procedures a part of the management plan. Yet some programs have addressed these issues by carefully defining the goals of each of the components of their programs and devising instruments that will help them measure their achievement of those goals. When evaluation procedures focus on all program components in relationship to staff, students, and the community, they can form the basis for planning efforts that will help programs continue to meet the challenge of effectively serving the needs of adult students.

The authors make the following four recommendations to programs that desire to build a solid program evaluation component.

(1) **Develop evaluation expertise.** Read, take courses, or consult with local evaluation experts to formulate a plan for an effective program evaluation component with detailed evaluation procedures matched to the unique features of your program.

(2) **Define program goals and objectives.** Enlist the participation of students, staff, and community members in setting program goals. Set goals that are concrete enough to be measurable and specific enough to address the discrete goals of learners and program staff. Consider doing a needs assessment survey.

(3) **Design both summative and formative evaluation instruments to measure program goals.** Included in this process should be (a) an efficient information management system—ideally, a computer—for recording student data; (b) instruments to collect student, staff, and community input; and (c) instruments to measure the effect of instruction in functional ways. With respect to the latter, programs should be able to assess what learners can do differently as a result of their participation in the program.

(4) **Create and implement a unified system for collecting, analyzing, and using data for making changes in program components.** The system should be an integral part of the routine operation of the program. It should specify responsibilities, procedures, and timelines for evaluation tasks and should embrace all program components.

The document on the following pages (Exhibit 9.3) was developed by the Division of Adult and Community Education, Indiana Department of Public Instruction (Harold H. Negley, Superintendent). An overview of this document can be found on pages 171 and 172 of this chapter, and comments from the staff of one program that has used it can be found on pages 180 and 181.

Exhibit 9.3 contains the following:

I   Self-Evaluation for Adult Basic Education Programs, Part One

   1)   Program Direction

   2)   Administrative Overview

      a)   Number of Program Sites

      b)   Reason for Separation

      c)   Positive Impact Formula

II Self-Evaluation for Adult Basic Education Programs, Part Two

   1)   Program Direction

   2)   Administrative Overview

   3)   Staffing

   4)   Facilities

   5)   Instructional Materials

   6)   Instructional Processes

   7)   Outcomes

   8)   Community Awareness

   9)   Resources

EXHIBIT 9.3 Indiana State Program Evaluation Form

**SELF-EVALUATION
FOR
ADULT BASIC EDUCATION PROGRAMS
PART ONE**

Part One is to be completed by the program administrator, duplicated, and distributed to program staff along with Part Two. The program administrator will complete as many of the questions as possible.

Program _____ Date _____

I. PROGRAM DIRECTION

Program Plan

To complete, list the goals for each section and summarize the results of each. If you have a federally funded program, take the list of goals from your 1982–83 federal proposal.

1. Please list and number the Recruitment/Public Relations Goals:

    Summarize Results:

2. Please list and number the Staff Development Goals:

    Summarize Results:

3. Please list and number the Student Outcome Goals:

    Summarize Results:

4. Please list and number the Interagency Relations Goals:

    Summarize Results:

Each "box" represents (check one):

_____ 10 students (small programs)

_____ 100 students (medium programs)

_____ 1000 students (large programs)

Annual Enrollment

| FY'79 | FY'80 | FY'81 | FY'82 | FY'83 |

II. ADMINISTRATIVE OVERVIEW

Program Sites

To complete the program site chart, count each separate building or satellite center operating.

NUMBER OF PROGRAM SITES

FY '79	FY '80	FY '81	FY '82	FY '83

Program Impact

To calculate the Positive Impact Rate, complete the Reasons for Separation chart citing the number of students reported on the Annual Statistical Report. Programs not receiving federal adult education funds may not have this information.

REASONS FOR SEPARATION

A. Positive termination, e.g., got job, accomplished goal   ____
B. Encountered obstacles, e.g., child care, personal problems, transportation   ____
C. Program did not meet needs/lack of interest   ____
D. Class terminated   ____
E. Student released from institution   ____
F. Unknown reasons   ____

            G. Total Separations   ____

POSITIVE IMPACT FORMULA

From the Reasons for Separation Chart determine the adjusted total. Subtract D (Class Terminated) and E (Released from Inst.) from G (Total Separations):

$$G \;\underline{\hspace{3cm}}$$

$$D \;\underline{\hspace{1.5cm}} \; + \; E \;\underline{\hspace{1.5cm}} \; = \; - \;\underline{\hspace{3cm}}$$

_____ Adjusted Total

Divide A (Positive Terminations) by Adjusted Total to determine Positive Impact Rate:

A ____ ÷ Adjusted Total __ = __ % Positive Impact Rate

SELF-EVALUATION
FOR
ADULT BASIC EDUCATION PROGRAMS
PART TWO

Part Two is to be completed individually by program staff members. A copy of Part One of the self-evaluation instrument, once it has been completed by the program administrator, will be needed when completing Part Two. Each staff member will complete as many of the questions as possible. The self-evaluation is to be returned to the program administrator.

Program _____

Job Title _____ Date _____

I. PROGRAM DIRECTION

Philosophy

1. Does your program have a statement of philosophy?   _____ Yes
                                                         _____ No
                                                         _____ Don't Know

2. If yes, please summarize below.

Goals

1. To what extent are you satisfied with the goals listed in Part One of this self-evaluation. Put a check at the selected point along the line.

Very				Somewhat				Not at all
9	8	7	6	5	4	3	2	1

2. To what extent do you feel last year's Recruitment/Public Relations goals were met? Put the number of each goal at the selected point along the line.

Very				Somewhat				Not at all
9	8	7	6	5	4	3	2	1

I. PROGRAM DIRECTION

3. To what extent do you feel the Staff Development goals have been met? Put the number of each goal at the selected point along the line.

Very				Somewhat				Not at all
9	8	7	6	5	4	3	2	1

4. To what extent do you feel the Student Outcome goals have been met? Put the number of each goal at the selected point along the line.

Very				Somewhat				Not at all
9	8	7	6	5	4	3	2	1

5. To what extent do you feel the Interagency Relations goals have been met? Put the number of each goal at the selected point along the line.

Very				Somewhat				Not at all
9	8	7	6	5	4	3	2	1

6. Have program goals been re-prioritized since 1980?

    _____ Yes
    _____ No
    _____ Don't Know

7. To what degree have your problem goals changed since 1980?

Very				Somewhat				Not at all
9	8	7	6	5	4	3	2	1

8. If program goals have changed at least to some extent, who participated in the decision to change the goals (check all you know)?

    _____ Program administrators/coordinators
    _____ Teachers
    _____ Paraprofessionals/aides
    _____ Counselors
    _____ Students
    _____ School district personnel
    _____ State staff member
    _____ Local advisory council
    _____ Other (please specify) _____

_____

    _____ Don't know who participated

II. ADMINISTRATIVE OVERVIEW

1. Based on the Five Year Enrollment Trend Chart from Part One of this evaluation, what is your program's overall enrollment trend?

2. What explanations might there be for major enrollment trends?

3. Based on the Contact Hour Per Program Quarter Chart, are there seasonal attendance patterns apparent over the three years?

4. What explanations might there be for such patterns?

5. Based on the Number of Program Sites Chart, what changes has your program had in the number of sites?

6. What might be reasons for these changes?

7. To what extent are you satisfied with your program's positive impact rate? Put a check at the selected point along the line.

Very				Somewhat				Not at all
9	8	7	6	5	4	3	2	1

III. STAFFING

Staffing Activities

1. Do you have a clear understanding of your job responsibilities?

_____ Yes
_____ No

2. Do you understand the "chain of command" in your program?

_____ Yes
_____ No
_____ Don't Know

III. STAFFING

3. Using the job titles listed in Part One of this evaluation, list those who are responsible for the following tasks:

publicity _____

recruitment _____

selecting instructional materials _____

orientation of students _____

staff development _____

student assessment _____

program and staff evaluation _____

counseling _____

classroom attendance records _____

program-wide recordkeeping _____

interagency contracts _____

4. Are there any responsibilities which are not clearly assigned to any staff member? If yes, please specify.
   - _____ Yes
   - _____ No
   - _____ Don't Know

5. Is there a formal staff orientation for new staff members? If yes, briefly describe.
   - _____ Yes
   - _____ No
   - _____ Don't Know

6. Are the staff development needs of your program staff assessed? If yes, describe how and by whom.
   - _____ Yes
   - _____ No
   - _____ Don't Know

7. Are there enough staff development opportunites available to your staff?
   - _____ Yes
   - _____ No
   - _____ Don't Know

8. Are there periodic evaluations of program staff members? If yes, briefly describe how often and what techniques are used.

Instructional	_____ Yes _____ No	_____
	_____ Don't Know	_____
Counseling	_____ Yes _____ No	_____
	_____ Don't Know	_____
Administrative	_____ Yes _____ No	_____
	_____ Don't Know	_____
Support Staff	_____ Yes _____ No	_____
	_____ Don't Know	_____

9. If you have no formal evaluation, do you feel such procedures would benefit your program?

____ Yes
____ No
____ Don't Know

10. To what extent are you satisfied with your program's staffing activities? Put a check at the selected point along the line.

Very				Somewhat				Not at all
9	8	7	6	5	4	3	2	1

Volunteers

1. Does your program utilize volunteers?

____ Yes
____ No
____ Don't Know

2. If yes, where do these volunteers come from (specify sources)?

3. If yes on question 1, how are your volunteers utilized?

4. To what extent are you satisfied with your program's use of volunteers? Put a check on the selected point along the line.

Very				Somewhat				Not at all
9	8	7	6	5	4	3	2	1

5. If your program is not currently using volunteers, do you feel your program would benefit from the use of volunteers?

____ Yes
____ No
____ Don't Know

IV. FACILITIES

1. Do you have classes located near the following:

mass transportation	____ yes	____ no	____ Don't know
minority neighborhoods	____ yes	____ no	____ Don't know
ethnic neighborhoods	____ yes	____ no	____ Don't know
senior citizens	____ yes	____ no	____ Don't know
the main entrance of the building	____ yes	____ no	____ Don't know

2. Are your current facilities accessible to handicapped students and senior citizens?

____ Yes
____ No
____ Don't Know

IV. FACILITIES

3. Related to the following factors, do you feel that your facilities are adequate (refer to the office or classroom in which you work)?

	Offices		Classrooms	
size	___ yes ___ no		___ yes ___ no	
lighting	___ yes ___ no		___ yes ___ no	
ventilation	___ yes ___ no		___ yes ___ no	
flexibility/adaptability	___ yes ___ no		___ yes ___ no	
safety	___ yes ___ no		___ yes ___ no	
furniture	___ yes ___ no		___ yes ___ no	
bulletin boards/ chalkboards	___ yes ___ no		___ yes ___ no	
access to restroom	___ yes ___ no		___ yes ___ no	
access to informal areas	___ yes ___ no		___ yes ___ no	

4. If there are other offices or classrooms which are inadequate, please describe:

5. To what extent are you satisfied with your program's facilities? Put a check at the selected point along the line.

Very				Somewhat				Not at all
9	8	7	6	5	4	3	2	1

V. INSTRUCTIONAL MATERIALS

1. Indicate those materials which are used in your program:

Level 1–4	___ Reading	___ Math	___ ESL
Level 4–5	___ Reading	___ Math	___ ESL
Level 5–9	___ Reading	___ Math	___ ESL
Level 9–12	___ Reading	___ Math	___ ESL

___ GED preparation
___ living skills
___ ESL
___ consumable workbooks and worksheets
___ non-consumable workbooks and worksheets
___ non-consumable hardback books
___ non-consumable kits
___ pamphlets ___ magazines ___ newspapers
___ instructional equipment
other (please specify): _____

I am not familiar with the instructional materials.

2. Are supplemental materials available in all above areas?   ___ Yes
                                                               ___ No
                                                               ___ Don't Know

If no, which areas have only basic materials? _____

_____

3. How often are materials other than the basic materials assigned to students?

_____ All the Time _____ Often _____ Seldom _____ Never
_____ Don't know

4. Are materials readily available to all classes?   _____ Yes
                                                            _____ No
                                                            _____ Don't Know

5. To what extent are you satisfied with the materials available in your program? Put
   a check at the selected point along the line.

Very				Somewhat				Not at all
9	8	7	6	5	4	3	2	1

VI: INSTRUCTIONAL PROCESSES

Orientation of Students

1. Is there a planned procedure for orienting students into   _____ Yes
   the program?   _____ No
                                                                _____ Don't Know

2. If yes, does the orientation include what the program   _____ Yes
   can or cannot do?   _____ No
                                                                _____ Don't Know

3. To what extent are you satisfied with your program's orientation procedures? Put
   a check at the selected point along the line.

Very				Somewhat				Not at all
9	8	7	6	5	4	3	2	1

4. If you have no planned orientation, do you feel it would   _____ Yes
   benefit students to have one developed?   _____ No
                                                                _____ Don't Know

5. If an orientation is developed, who should be responsible for implementing it?

(Job Title) _____

VI. INSTRUCTIONAL PROCESSES

Assessment

1. Do you use a formal system for assessing levels of performance in the following areas?

    If yes, what instrument is used?

    Reading   ____ Yes ____ No   _____
                   ____ Don't Know

    Math   ____ Yes ____ No   _____
                   ____ Don't Know

    Coping Skills   ____ Yes ____ No   _____
                   ____ Don't Know

    ESL   ____ Yes ____ No   _____
                   ____ Don't Know

2. Do you use informal ways of assessing levels of   ____ Yes
    performance?   ____ No

    Topical Area   Description of Assessment

    _____   _____

    _____   _____

    _____   _____

3. Are personal goals of students explored and recorded?   ____ Yes
                                                         ____ No
                                                         ____ Don't Know

    If yes, which of the following areas are included in students' personal goals?

    ____ driver's license
    ____ law and government/citizenship
    ____ community resources
    ____ health/safety
    ____ occupations/career education
    ____ interpersonal relations
    ____ others (please specify) _____

    _____

    ____ Don't know

4. To what extent are you satisfied with your program's assessment procedures? Put a check at the selected point along the line.

Very				Somewhat				Not at all
9	8	7	6	5	4	3	2	1

Placement

1. Which of the following are taken into consideration when a student is placed in a learning setting?

    _____ level(s) of performance
    _____ academic goals
    _____ personal goals
    _____ psychological and/or social needs
    _____ preferred learning styles
    _____ other (please specify) _____
    _____ Don't know

2. Are learning experiences provided which specifically   _____ Yes
    address students' personal goals?   _____ No
                                                             _____ Don't Know

3. If your program cannot serve an individual, is the   _____ Yes
    student referred to another more appropriate setting?   _____ No
                                                             _____ Don't Know

4. To what extent are you satisfied with your program's procedures for placement? Put a check at the selected point along the line.

Very				Somewhat				Not at all
9	8	7	6	5	4	3	2	1

Follow-up Procedures

1. Is the initial placement of the student checked to ensure   _____ Yes
    that the students are at the right level?   _____ No
                                                                _____ Don't Know

    If so, please describe:

2. Is there a procedure for determining early success or   _____ Yes
    failure of each student?   _____ No
                                                                _____ Don't Know

    If so, please describe:

VI. INSTRUCTIONAL PROCESSES

3. Is there a procedure to check on students who are absent for short periods of time?

_____ Yes
_____ No
_____ Don't Know

If so, please describe:

4. Are student goals, which were identified upon entry to the program, referred to throughout the time the student attends?

_____ Yes
_____ No
_____ Don't Know

5. Are there other procedures employed by your program to follow-up on the decisions made when a student enters your program?

_____ Yes
_____ No
_____ Don't Know

If so, please describe:

6. If you do not have any follow-up procedures (items 1–5), do you feel your students might benefit from such procedures?

_____ Yes
_____ No

7. Do students receive regular reports on their progress? If so, please describe how progress is reported and how often.

_____ Yes
_____ No
_____ Don't Know

8. If students receive no progress reports, do you feel such reports would benefit students?

_____ Yes
_____ No
_____ Don't Know

9. To what extent are you satisfied with your program's follow-through procedures? Put a check at the selected point along the line.

Very				Somewhat				Not at all
9	8	7	6	5	4	3	2	1

Instructional Methods

1. Rank the instructional methods used in your classroom (0 = not used, 1 = most frequently used, 2 = second most used, etc.)?

_____ students working individually
_____ instructional staff working one-on-one with students
_____ higher level students tutoring lower level students
_____ community resource people working with students
_____ small groups of students working together
_____ instructional staff lecturing or demonstrating to large group of students
_____ I am not familiar with methods used

VI. INSTRUCTIONAL PROCESSES

2. Do students spend much time waiting for instructional help?

____ Yes
____ No
____ Don't Know

3. Are different instructional methods used in different classrooms or with students with different needs?

____ Yes
____ No
____ Don't Know

4. To what extent are you satisfied with the instructional methods used in your program? Put a check at the selected point along the line.

Very				Somewhat				Not at all
9	8	7	6	5	4	3	2	1

VII. OUTCOMES

Student Progress

1. Does your program collect and record academic progress of students?

____ Yes
____ No
____ Don't Know

2. Does your program gather data concerning students' personal goals, other than academic, such as coping or life skills?

____ Yes
____ No
____ Don't Know

3. Does your program have a procedure for gathering information about changes in students as a direct or indirect result of participation in your program?

____ Yes
____ No
____ Don't Know

4. If yes, how is this information gathered?

____ interviews with students
____ information volunteered by students
____ fellow students
____ surveying counselors and/or teachers
____ other, please specify: _____

_____

5. Do you feel this information is worth collecting to indicate your program's "true" impact?

____ Yes
____ No
____ Don't Know

VII. OUTCOMES

6. Do you maintain an on-going file of personal success
stories for PR purposes?

_____ Yes
_____ No
_____ Don't Know

7. To what extent are you satisfied with your program's recording of student progress
data? Put a check at the selected point along the line.

Very				Somewhat				Not at all
9	8	7	6	5	4	3	2	1

Exit Data

1. Does your program know <u>why</u> students leave the program?

_____ Yes
_____ No
_____ Don't Know

2. If yes, how are these reasons determined?

_____ exit interview
_____ follow-up phone call
_____ follow-up letter
_____ information received from other students
_____ information received from other agencies
_____ other, please specify: _____

_____

3. Is this information valuable to your program for:

_____ making changes in schedules
_____ making changes in curricula or techniques
_____ funding
_____ evaluating teacher effectiveness
_____ awareness and support
_____ informing other community agencies
_____ preparing press releases and articles
_____ don't know

4. To what extent are you satisfied with your program's current follow-up procedures?
Put a check at the selected point along the line.

Very				Somewhat				Not at all
9	8	7	6	5	4	3	2	1

5. How might your program's follow-up be improved?

VIII. COMMUNITY AWARENESS

1. By which means do you inform the community of your program: For recruitment?

   To promote community support?   Indicate how often:

   Newspaper
   _____ _____ press releases—class schedules   _____
   _____ _____ press releases—feature articles   _____
   _____ _____ columns, editorials   _____
   _____ _____ space filler logos   _____
   _____ _____ letters to the editor   _____

   Radio
   _____ _____ news releases—class schedules   _____
   _____ _____ news announcements   _____
   _____ _____ public service announcements   _____
   _____ _____ community calendar/talk shows   _____

   Television
   _____ _____ news releases—class schedules   _____
   _____ _____ news announcements   _____
   _____ _____ community calendar/talk shows   _____
   _____ _____ requests for film coverage   _____

   Public Speaking
   _____ _____ service clubs   _____
   _____ _____ community groups   _____
   _____ _____ professional associations   _____

   Printed Materials
   _____ _____ pamphlets/flyers   _____
   _____ _____ posters   _____
   _____ _____ newsletters/articles   _____

   Personal Contacts
   _____ _____ past and/or current students   _____
   _____ _____ community agencies   _____
   _____ _____ social organizations   _____
   _____ _____ business/industry   _____

   Other (please specify)

   _____ _____ _____   _____

          _____

   _____   I am not familiar with these efforts.

VIII. COMMUNITY AWARENESS

2. To what extent are you satisfied with the current level of community <u>awareness</u> of your program? Put a check at the selected point along the line.

Very				Somewhat				Not at all
9	8	7	6	5	4	3	2	1

3. To what extent are you satisfied with the current level of community <u>acceptance</u> <u>and support</u> of your program?

Very				Somewhat				Not at all
9	8	7	6	5	4	3	2	1

IX. RESOURCES

Funding

1. Does your program have multiple funding sources?   _____ Yes
   _____ No
   _____ Don't Know

2. If yes, please specify such sources as JTPA, Businesses, Community Agencies, and so forth.

3. If no, have you explored sources of multiple funding?   _____ Yes
   _____ No
   _____ Don't Know

   If no, why not?

4. To what extent are you satisfied with your program's funding?

Very				Somewhat				Not at all
9	8	7	6	5	4	3	2	1

School Corporation/Agency Resources

1. Check those resources of your school corporation/agency to which you have easy access and which have been utilized by your program.
   _____ _____ reading specialists
   _____ _____ math specialists
   _____ _____ art specialists
   _____ _____ science specialists
   _____ _____ special education professionals
   _____ _____ audio/visual equipment

_____ _____ diagnostic services
_____ _____ health services
_____ _____ recreation services
_____ _____ professional inservice (relating to adult education role)
_____ _____ Other (please specify) _____

IX. RESOURCES

2. Check the things your school corporation/agency does in support of your program:

_____ student transporation
_____ visits to your program site(s)
_____ child care
_____ expediting funding procedures
_____ expediting reporting procedures
_____ publicity/PR
_____ released time for professional development
_____ travel support for professional development
_____ other direct financial support
_____ other types of support (please specify) _____

3. To what extent are you satisfied with the support of your school corporation/agency?

Very				Somewhat				Not at all
9	8	7	6	5	4	3	2	1

Other Resources

1. Has your program established a relationship with outside agencies, institutions, or individuals?

_____ Yes
_____ No
_____ Don't Know

If yes, which ones?

_____ community agencies
_____ service agencies
_____ social clubs
_____ governmental agencies
_____ business and industry
_____ advisory council or committee
_____ key individuals
_____ other (please specify) _____

2. List those agencies and institutions which share resources with your program:

personnel _____

volunteers _____

materials _____

supplies _____

equipment _____

referrals _____

publicity/PR _____

counseling _____

services such as eye examinations, hearing tests, etc. _____

_____

other (please specify resource and agency) _____

IX. RESOURCES

3. To what extent are you satisfied with your program's use of other resources?

Very				Somewhat				Not at all
9	8	7	6	5	4	3	2	1

4. Do you feel your program would benefit from a greater _____ Yes
   sharing of resources? _____ No
   _____ Don't Know

5. Would your agency support the exploration and establish- _____ Yes
   ment of such arrangements? _____ No
   _____ Don't Know

6. Whose responsibility should it be to explore and establish such arrangements?
   (Job Title) _____

BIBLIOGRAPHY

Anderson, S. B., and Ball, S. *The Profession and Practice of Program Evaluation.* San Francisco: Jossey-Bass, 1978.

An Evaluation Guide for Adult Basic Education Programs: Step-by-Step Instructions, Including the Questionnaires and Other Forms Needed for Evaluation. New York: Columbia University, Teachers College, Center for Adult Education, 1974.

Bloom, Benjamin S., Hastings, J. T., and Madaus, G. F. *Handbook on Formative and Summative Evaluation of Student Learning.* New York: McGraw-Hill, 1971.

Darkenwald, Gordon G. *Problems of Dissemination and Use of Innovations in Adult Basic Education.* New York: Columbia University, Teachers College, Center for Adult Education, 1974. (ERIC ED 101 187)

Grotelueschen, Arden D. *Evaluation in Adult Basic Education: How and Why.* Urbana, Illinois: University of Illinois at Urbana-Champaign, Office for the Study of Continuing Professional Education, 1976.

Stalford, Charles B. (ed.) *An Evaluation Look at Nontraditional Postsecondary Education.* Washington, D.C.: National Institute of Education, 1979.

Steele, S. M. *Contemporary Approaches to Program Evaluation.* Washington, D.C.: Capitol Publications, 1977.

Wolf, R. M. *Evaluation in Education.* New York: Praeger, 1979.

Worthen, B., and Sanders, J. *Educational Evaluation: Theory and Practice.* Worthington, OH: C. A. Jones, 1973.

SECTION III

Conclusions
for Practitioners

Chapter 10
Managing the Program

If the practices we have described in this text are to be successfully implemented and result in effective adult literacy programs, there is a need for the kind of managerial leadership Natasha Josefowitz defines in her book *Path to Power* (Addison-Wesley, 1980, page 199). She defines a leader as a person who has "(1) the authority to decide what should happen and who should do it, (2) the responsibility to make it happen, [and] (3) the accountability for what does actually happen." Up to this point, we have concerned ourselves largely with the first and third parts of this definition. Within the seven chapters of Section II, we explored the decisions program leaders must make about what should happen and who should be involved, though some of the decisions made at the program level may be dependent on decisions made by leaders on levels higher than the on-site program director, manager, or coordinator. And in our discussion of program evaluation in Chapter 9, as well as in our discussion of managing the instructional system in Chapter 7, we addressed the issue of accountability. As we have suggested, accountability factors may be limited to such indicators of program success as the numbers of students served or the numbers of program participants receiving GED or alternative high school diplomas. However, the definitions of success implicit in such evaluation yardsticks may have far-reaching consequences for every aspect of program operation, including whom programs target for recruitment as well as how programs structure their curriculum designs.

What concerns us now is how one shoulders the responsibility to "make it happen"; that is, how program leaders obtain and manage the financial, physical, and human resources necessary for effective program operation and how they communicate the tasks program personnel are expected to perform. Obtaining the necessary resources is by far the greatest challenge program leaders must face, and many are disheartened by the compromises inadequate resources force them to make regarding the extent or quality of the services their programs can offer. Few of the programs in the NALP study reported that they enjoy the luxury of sufficient levels of funding; well-equipped, comfortable, affordable, and conveniently located facilities; and a large enough staff of highly trained teachers, counselors, and support persons to serve all those who apply to the program for help.

In describing how they have attempted to cope with such situations, many of the program directors we interviewed confided that they occasionally felt inadequate, uncertain, or helpless, both because of the other demands on their time and because of the very real problems in locating sources of adequate funding. With a few notable exceptions, government funding is woefully inadequate to serve as the sole financial base for effective program operation. Problems in finding adequate funding will also mean problems in finding qualified staff who are willing to work within possibly ill-equipped or even unsafe facilities, with larger-than-manageable numbers of students, and with a level of compensation below what they might command outside the field of adult education. One must recognize that program directors can become overwhelmed by a host of unpredictable crises in the day-to-day management of program operations— a breakdown in the building's heating system, the resignation of a valued staff member to accept a better paying position, rumors of severe cutbacks in funding, and personal problems of both staff and students—and time spent in resolving such day-to-day crises does diminish the time available for activities designed to help the program achieve more long-term objectives.

We cannot suggest within this chapter that there are easy solutions to the problems faced by program directors, and we cannot suggest that such problems as the lack of adequate funding will ever disappear. However, within separate sections of this chapter, we will explore the problems program leaders face relative to obtaining and managing financial, physical, and human resources and describe some of the ways they have coped with limited resources. We will preface this discussion with a description of the qualities of leadership vital not only to the immediate operation of programs but also to the future of adult literacy education. Although it is not within the scope of this text to provide detailed management information on such topics as budgeting procedures for non-profit organizations or successful grant proposal writing (interested readers should consult the texts cited in the bibliography), we will describe the skills the program director should possess and suggest the activities in which the director should be regularly involved.

THE LEADERSHIP ROLE

Implicit in the concept of leadership is the notion that program directors possess a clear notion of program philosophy (whether or not they are the architects of that philosophy) and the ability to communicate it not only to program staff but also to funding agencies, community leaders, and legislators. That is, leaders embody a set of principles that others are willing to follow. The program philosophy will be reflected in the program's plans for recruitment, orientation, counseling, diagnostic testing, student assessment, and instructional methods and materials. To the extent that staff members understand the underlying philosophy—that is, the extent to which they understand why they are doing what they are expected to do—directors can reduce the frequency of direct involvement in many day-to-day operations. Effective human resource management (discussed in greater detail later in this chapter) thus depends in large degree on how clearly the program's leaders set objectives for program staff and how consistent those objectives are with overall program philosophy.

The director's success will also depend on the credibility of the program philosophy, and it is important that both the program staff and the larger community believe in what the program is doing. The director cannot hope to be a successful leader by taking a position tantamount to saying: "Trust me. I know what's best for the students even if neither you nor they do." When the development of the program philosophy and the mix of program services is based on a community needs assessment (see

Chapter 3) the communication of program philosophy to the larger public should result in greater public support. And program staff are not only more likely to support such a service-oriented philosophy but are also more likely to be able to contribute to the kind of problem solving involved in addressing the needs of the community. One director of a community-based program referred to needs assessments as the first prerequisite to effective program management:

First of all, you've got to see a need for [your] program. You must do a community needs assessment. . . . You've got to work very hard laying the foundation before you think about [any of the program components]. [Once you have matched program components to your community needs assessment], you yourself have to believe in what you're doing. Once you do this, once you have a plan, it comes naturally. . . . [You can then] tell people what you feel and what you can do. . . .

The leadership role that program directors play thus extends beyond the walls of the program; in a very real sense, the program director is the chief representative, spokesperson, or advocate for the program. As an advocate, the director must be in equal parts a networker, a politician, and a public relations agent. The networks directors build enable them to keep track of new funding opportunities, new or different instructional strategies or other trends in the field, and opportunities for collaborations with other relevant agencies. A strong network of others committed to the field is also critical to the role of political advocacy.

Political advocacy remains a priority despite the recent media attention given to the problems of illiteracy and the programs that attempt to address the issue and despite the expressions of concern and verbal support from politicians. Programs are far from winning the battle for the level of financial support that attention and concern should engender. Yet, overwhelmed as they are by the problems of day-to-day operation, few directors have the time for such direct political action as lobbying efforts or giving testimony in front of federal or state legislative committees. Involvement in the political action committees of such national organizations as the American Association for Adult and Continuing Education (AAACE's address is cited in the bibliography to Chapter 7 along with those of other relevant national organizations) and active support of state and local adult education organizations and literacy networks can be an effective means to the same end. Program directors have an obligation to be aware of pending legislation that will affect them and to actively support initiatives to secure the best possible deal for the field of adult education.

Another kind of political acumen directors should possess is that required to argue a program's case to current and potential sources of funding. A program's survival or ability to operate to the full extent of its potential will depend in part on how persuasively the director can write grant proposals and how effectively the director can identify and work with the power structure of the program's oversight or funding agency. However, as will become clear in the section on managing financial resources, political savvy alone may do little in the face of the current funding climate.

Advocacy for the program extends beyond the obvious political arenas; it is also implicit in all the program's public relations activities. In our discussion of the goals of public relations activities in Chapter 3, we noted two primary goals: (1) eliciting community support, which may or may not include overtly soliciting direct donations of money, space, equipment, person-time, or in-kind services, and (2) building a service network to extend the range of services available to program participants. It is important to underscore here that, although the program can earn the community's support through a one-time demonstration of how effectively it is fulfilling genuine community needs, the program cannot assume that that support will continue indefinitely. With so many social issues vying for public attention, literacy programs must consistently remind the community what the program is doing and how much it is in need of ongoing support. It is important to share program success stories, but literacy programs need not be shy about letting the community know when they are being hurt by funding cuts and how the cuts will ultimately hurt the community. Program directors should thus build a calendar detailing when and how they will use the media and public speaking engagements to get the public involved in the fight for the best possible adult literacy program.

The kind of leadership we have just described is not easy to provide. One program director described the advocacy role as "probably the hardest, most frustrating, pain-in-the-ass aspect of the whole job. . . . [yet] the incredible key thing." It is made all the more difficult in view of the time required to perform the other management roles we will discuss in the following pages.

MANAGING FINANCIAL RESOURCES

Perhaps no activity consumes as much of the director's time and energy as attempting to secure the level of funding necessary for the survival of the program. Given the deep cuts in federal and state expenditures in all human service areas, many budgets are being drastically reduced. This has taken its toll in terms of the services that can be offered: course offerings are being reduced, staff are being laid off, and in many instances, learners must be turned away or put on waiting lists.

These financial problems are not unique to any one kind of program. We heard much the same dilemma expressed by all directors, whether they were directors of federally-funded or state-funded ABE programs, community-based programs, employment and training programs, or programs within the military, correctional institutions, or postsecondary education institutions. Given the fact that federal appropriations have been restricted under the Adult Education Act and the Jobs Training Partnership Act, those who depend exclusively on government funding have been hit especially hard. The lack of increases in federal appropriations year after year has meant that programs cannot fulfill their potential. California, for example, served 600,000 adults in 1983 and estimates that at this level at least 1,000 undereducated adults have to be turned away *every week*—and this is true despite the fact that California's level of state funding was one of the highest per capita in the United States (indeed, in 1984, the California state budget was larger than the entire federal budget under the Adult Education Act).

Programs operating on federal ABE funds complain not only about the cuts but about the administrative headaches caused by the complexity of the required funding formula. Others complain about the general bureaucracy that inhibits the ability of the program to respond quickly to the demands of the community or to the needs of its staff and students. For example, the director of one program in the Northeast finds that her hands are tied even when it comes to covering trivial expenses: "Well, I see other programs that are smaller, and they have their own checkbooks; they just write their own checks. We can't do that. *Everything* has to be a purchase order. It takes four to six weeks for those kinds of things to be processed. It's bureaucratic." Yet she seemed to accept that this is a condition she must learn to accommodate when she added, "We are the largest program in the state, so I guess you have to expect that."

Programs have found themselves scrambling to locate new sources of funding to offset cutbacks. The director of a community-based system in the East reported that he and his colleagues came very close to closing their doors permanently:

The funding stopped at the end of our two-year fiscal plan. Although we saw the disaster coming, we had no idea how bad things would get. We had to scrounge desperately. I mean our budget went down $100,000! It's incredible! We did not know how we were supposed to continue. We cancelled the entire GED program and put many students into large classes for basic skills work.

Correctional programs also depend largely if not exclusively on government funding, and one director of a correctional program in the Midwest reported: "Money is tighter here in the last couple of years than ever before. . . . We have to turn down everything." She seemed almost resigned to her problem when she added, "When you are dealing with federal funds, you have to expect that."

The director of a military program in the South pointed out that changes in general budgetary priorities in the federal government have meant changes in the funding for education within the military just as they have for civilian ABE programs:

Unfortunately, the Congress and the President started fighting over defense spending, and things that go first are not the missiles, or the tanks, or the guns. It's educational services. They and the quality-of-life programs in the armed services are hit the hardest, and hit first. We are underfunded now, and I am seriously concerned for the coming years.

The most frustrating aspect of the financial calamity, as many directors pointed out, is that they must watch their programs deteriorate rather than improve despite making financial sacrifices (including voluntary cuts in their own salaries) and increasing the amount of time they commit to their jobs. "There have been cutbacks, we are all overworked now," said a director of an ABE program in the Southeast. "Just to keep funding, we have to constantly write proposals, at least one every week, just to keep ourselves together. Every place we apply to has had cutbacks. We get less each year." The director of a postsecondary program in the Midwest illustrated one unfortunate consequence of the situation by noting: "People need to have the security of making money, of having a job. The ongoing uncertainty and loss of revenue certainly is exhausting for teachers and administrators, and it's taking its toll. We are losing our best people!"

Those program directors who have stayed to wage the fight have found it necessary to develop financial management expertise both in balancing budgets at current levels of funding and in raising funds from new and probably nontraditional sources.

To balance their budgets, directors must look for ways to reduce program expenditures and make the most of every available dollar. Ultimately, this may mean making the difficult decision to reduce or eliminate services. In the past, programs whose enrollments were predominantly in GED preparation courses, for example, could also feature a basic literacy program and a life skills component. These programs may now have to make a choice regarding the program's emphasis; they may need to direct their resources more narrowly to those they are best able to serve. Unfortunately, this amounts not only to a reduction of literacy services but also to a loss of the diversity of literacy services. It may be that a strong referral network of programs, each of which has chosen to reduce services to those they do best, can form a consortium under which the aggregate services available to the community will not be so radically reduced.

As directors work with more sources of funding, they will need considerably greater ability in managing the separate financial statements each funder may require. Even such new sources of funding as the Job Training Partnership Act (JTPA) require greater skill than ever in managing complex budgets. As the director of an employment and training program in the East explained, such new budgeting procedures may not give the program the freedom to allocate resources in the manner it finds most judicious:

> The new law came out for JTPA saying that 70% of your funds must now be spent on training. That leaves 30%. 15% is for administrative cost, and another 15% is for everything else including support services. Under CETA, 69% of the funds were for stipends, going directly to the student, and 20% for administrative cost. They have identified and narrowed the definition of budget items, and a lot of what once was called "service" has been squeezed out. The real losers are the students, no doubt about it. In addition, JTPA is a far smaller program that CETA.

The transition from CETA to JTPA money has necessitated other management skills, not the least of which is understanding the more rigorous state audits for what is essentially a much smaller amount of funding. "The system is just getting into place," said the director of an employment and training program in the West, ". . . and by 1985 there will be an extensive state-by-state evaluation of all programs. They have incentive awards for those who do well; if you're not doing well, you stand a good chance of losing state support."

The current climate requires a rethinking of the role of the program director. Program directors who used to see themselves primarily as administrators now have to be prepared to become grant writers, project developers, and public relations specialists. One director of a community-based program in the East told us: "When you're limiting your staff because you have to limit your money, you have to . . . be out there hustling for the next dollar . . . [even though you may believe] . . . your time could be used more profitably for direct services." Programs that are managed by people who can handle this professional conflict appear to have a distinct advantage.

As competition increases for federal ABE dollars or other funds for literacy initiatives, fundraising and grantsmanship skills become more critical. Some, such as the director of one ABE program believe they are prepared: "The competition in writing proposals will continue to be stiff, but I am confident because I have developed good skills in writing proposals. There is a lot of competition for that ABE money!" Others, such as the director of a correctional program in the Midwest, are not so confident: "Grant writing training is what I need. Nobody here has the knowledge to write a grant, and there is no money for training."

Coupled with skill in writing proposals is the skill in locating sources of funding to which one can submit a proposal. The director of a Midwestern postsecondary program stated that she needed $420,000 in foundation support but that she wasn't at all sure where that money would come from. Her preliminary inquiries established that she will have to compete with fundraisers from institutions such as Harvard University that have trained developers/writers on their staffs. (Interested readers will find several texts on fundraising, sources of funding, and grant writing listed in the bibliography at the end of the chapter.)

As we suggested earlier in this chapter, one must go beyond finding ways of merely coping with things as they are; one must become an advocate for adult education and attempt to gather public and political support for improved funding. At this writing, it is still too early to tell the impact of the National Literacy Initiative of President Reagan and former Secretary of Education Terrell Bell on legislation or private sector commitments, but many hope that it is a signal of better things to come.

MANAGING PHYSICAL RESOURCES

The physical resources of the program include the building or buildings that house offices and classroom facilities together with the buildings' systems of lighting, plumbing, heating, and cooling, as well as all the equipment from telephones to desks to library shelves to program-supplied materials necessary to operate the program. Directors may or may not be responsible for acquiring all of these physical resources, but they do bear the responsibility for monitoring expenses for them. Directors must also invest time and energy to maintain or improve the program's physical plant, and some are occasionally pressed into service as unpaid electricians, carpenters, or plumbers.

The first priority for programs is finding a sufficient amount of space in which to operate the program, though not all programs find this a difficult problem. For example, all of the military facilities we visited were generally adequate and reasonably comfortable, and those employment and training programs that operate in space donated by private industries also have few problems related to the physical plant itself. Many of the public adult education programs located within existing public school buildings and those programs located within postsecondary institutions are less likely to encounter space problems than programs within correctional institutions or community-based programs.

The problem for correctional institutions is particularly acute, given the general overcrowding in almost all state and federal institutions. The director of a program in a correctional facility in the East spends a great deal of time drumming up classroom or tutoring space:

> Well, you want me to run a literacy program? I need more room. Where am I going to put these guys; we can't sit on the ceiling. At this point, the new superintendent walks in and complains, ordering us out of the chapel where we had been holding a class. See, space is the big thing here, second only to security.

This director, like many we talked to, had to find a creative solution. The classes are now held outdoors in the prison's courtyard in an area adjacent to the basketball court.

Community-based programs face a space problem for a different reason. Many are so perilously underfunded that they cannot afford to pay for the space they need. As the director of one program on the West Coast commented: "At the beginning of last year, the question was to find a locale for the program, since our old space is now occupied by a business that can afford the constant increases in rent. There was no space in the schools; we tried that. We also tried the storefronts, but that again is a question of finances."

Frequently, the lack of affordable facilities forces programs either to condense offices and classrooms to fit the available space or to split up parts of their operation that they'd prefer to have together (the latter situation is not the same as having satellite sites of a central program). The director of a program in the Midwest described a not atypical problem: "We need better facilities so that the administrative office could be in a separate room from the classroom, and it would be helpful to have the library adjacent to the classrooms, not two miles uptown." Some programs, such as one affiliated with a postsecondary institution, have found ways of splitting parts of their operation without affecting services: "The college is our sponsor, and our offices are at the junior high school, a public school just around the corner. We are all in the same vicinity, all within walking distance—and it's costing us absolutely nothing."

Lack of space may also mean making compromises in the way the program delivers some services. For example, the director of a community-based program in the West stated: "I would like to improve our orientation, but there is this space problem. We have no large room to do orientations for each of the new classes. What we really need is an auditorium."

Programs operating in large urban areas have discovered yet another problem in finding suitable space. Many such programs need to ensure that their facilities are accessible to their students by public transportation, and many attempt to solve the accessibility problem by locating the program directly within the neighborhoods in which the students live. This, in turn, may create the situation described by the director of a community-based program in a large Midwestern city:

> In many neighborhoods where we have teaching sites, there is a large amount of change occurring. We've had students who have been shot; we've had a tutor who has been murdered. . . . And that is not unusual for the areas we are typically working in. So, we are really concerned about space and the specific location of space. I think that given the fact that 70% of our students live in poverty, you are going to find that students will come to class a lot more often if they can get to a place that is accessible; I feel that accessibility is more important than safety, but given our experiences, that seems almost silly to say.

In many cases, literacy programs have to compete for space that can be leased more profitably to commercial users. When underfunded programs have difficulty in keeping up with their rent, landlords may become impatient and force the program to move on. Programs recognize that they will have difficulty establishing themselves without a fixed and well-equipped facility, and they fear that periodic relocations will result in the loss of many students.

Space that is affordable and conveniently located may, however, have other problems that make the facility less than desirable. The director of an employment and training program in the West described her facility this way: "We found one major problem—heat! The storm windows are bad, and there is only one thermostat in the whole building. We have to use space heaters. Our landlord spends the winters in Greece. On the coldest days, the students don't come because they know they will be cold."

Directors must be resourceful in finding solutions to the problems of space. The director of a postsecondary program in the Northeast had to find a solution to the fact that the program's students are spread over a wide geographical area. "They are thirty-five miles from here, some of them sixty. . . . The tutors tell me if they have four or five people ready for the GED. I take the test out there, and I use the community room or the local bank. In this one town, the community room is a little wooden house. I have to get there at 8:00 to heat the place first. While they take the test, I babysit all their children."

The solution to the space problem often hinges on the director's creativity in utilizing community resources or in arranging partnerships with various types of sponsoring agencies. In the last decade, the private sector has become more receptive to the notion of providing resources to literacy programs. The director of an employment and training program illustrates this change:

> The company gives us a large, heated space with all the equipment we can possibly use. They are very good about lending us other facilities for special programs. The space is there. It is available for us; we just have to request it.

The space problem, like the funding problems we described earlier in the chapter, are not likely to go away without a major commitment on the part of the government and the widespread support of the general public.

MANAGING HUMAN RESOURCES

A program's human resources are its most vital resource. With appropriate guidance and ongoing support, the staff can become a cohesive and dedicated team that can overcome many of the problems we have discussed in this chapter. Program directors who directly or indirectly provide such guidance and support can do much to help staff members extend their creative abilities and grow as professional members of the team. Unfortunately, lack of time or funds for planning and implementing full-scale in-service training programs and problems in assembling large numbers of part-time staff members have prevented many directors from offering the kinds of staff development opportunities they might like. What we will discuss in the following pages are the ways in which program directors in the NALP study have addressed such problems and set a climate under which staff members have been challenged to perform to the fullest extent of their potential.

In our discussion of leadership qualities, we noted that those directors who communicate program philosophy and program objectives clearly to staff can expect that staff will understand why they are doing what they are expected to do. Staff can thus be held accountable for meeting certain measurable objectives and, possibly more importantly, will be able to contribute to the kinds of decision making and problem solving that will be necessary if the program is to remain flexible enough to serve the diverse and changing needs of its students and its community effectively. Providing adequate guidelines becomes especially important in view of the fact that credentialed instructors and counselors may have training in early childhood, secondary, or higher education rather than adult education, and noncredentialed staff (especially volunteer tutors) may have no prior training in education.

Exactly what should be included in guidelines provided to staff is the matter of some debate. Indeed, under the heading "How Can the Instructional System Be Managed?" in Chapter 7, we discussed at some length what might be involved in the development and dissemination of curriculum guidelines. We noted that not all adult educators share the view that program directors should be involved in matters of curriculum and instruction or, for that matter, the view that curriculum guidelines are desirable given the diversity of learning needs, learning styles, and goals of adults. Directors in many programs do not believe that they have sufficient expertise in areas beyond program administration and thus delegate decisions about instructional objectives, methods, and materials to a curriculum supervisor or lead teacher. However those responsible decide the matter of setting specific curriculum objectives, it is important for staff to know the larger underlying educational and methodological assumptions of the program. Within those guidelines, a director or curriculum supervisor is free to encourage staff to experiment and be creative. Without guidelines, however, the director is risking an "anything goes" approach, and staff often flounder. "When you don't have a director who takes charge in any way of the teachers as a whole, you're going to have a lot of teachers who really aren't teaching people . . . ," asserted the director of a large multi-service, community-based program.

Directors bear the ultimate responsibility for setting the direction for professional growth and development and thus continued improvement in the program's delivery of services by providing staff with necessary leadership and resources in curriculum and methodology, by creating opportunities for staff to reflect on what they are doing in the classroom, and by assisting staff in setting and achieving personal goals. One director in the East accomplishes this by asking staff to specify program areas that they would like to study—e.g., computer-assisted instruction, curriculum design, outreach, testing—as a complement to their regular teaching assignments. By involving staff in setting their own objectives, this director finds that staff are more eager to take responsibility for their own self-development and are less likely to resent being held accountable for achievement of their goals come staff evaluation time. Other directors encourage staff involvement in helping to improve the overall program by using staff meetings for group discussions and problem-solving sessions on such topics as program sequence, training needs, and teaching techniques, while still others arrange for staff to observe exemplary programs.

Leaving aside the larger issues of staff development and staff evaluation for a moment, one must first address the issue of building the environment in which such activities can take place. The fact that many staff work different shifts or work at different program sites, while providing for the flexibility students may need, tends to promote a feeling of isolation from the program as a whole. Even though literacy instructors are able to interact with their adult students, they need to be able to talk over their successes and failures, their doubts, and their questions with others who share like concerns.

Directors often provide the opportunity for staff members to share experiences with another professional by visiting classes regularly or by making it a policy for all staff to attend staff meetings. Such classroom observations or staff meetings yield the best results when staff do not perceive these activities as the director's attempts to check up on them or to enforce certain imposed standards or methodologies. Directors get better performance from staff members by addressing them as professionals and demonstrating that the director's role is to facilitate the resolution of any problems or the acquisition of teaching skills. Even with inexperienced staff, directors can accomplish much more by patiently explaining and modeling appropriate behaviors than by dictating strict adherence to prescribed procedures. When it is not possible to give such inexperienced personnel direct support to the extent they may require, the director might pair the inexperienced teacher with a more experienced teacher for some team teaching or for a special project.

It is not easy to build a staff that sees itself as a team with all members offering mutual support, advice, and encouragement. The difficulty lies in providing opportunities to assemble large numbers of part-time staff members who may also be spread over a number of satellite centers. Yet the director can easily defeat the goals of the program if part-time staff members are not made a part of the team. "I see this as a whole staff, not full-timers and part-timers. I don't like that separation. It is almost like being elitist," stated the director of a large ABE program in Maine who regularly brings all staff together. One program director in the Midwest believes firmly that, even though some staff members are part-time, they must have a "full-time attitude." To her, attendance at monthly meetings symbolizes part of that commitment.

Program directors have found a number of ways to overcome some of the problems of bringing staff together. They may alternate staff meetings between days and nights or hold separate meetings for day and night staff. They may resort to convening small-group committee meetings to provide teachers and counselors opportunities to share concerns and engage in group problem-solving experiences. Whatever the strategy, one must structure an atmosphere for professional growth and development much as one structures the atmosphere for the educational growth and development of the program's students.

Staff Development

As we have just suggested, helping staff members to acquire or improve their skills is not unlike helping any adult learner. One needs to diagnose which skills should be the target of training and then build a set of learning experiences designed to help staff acquire the target skills and apply them within their daily routines. The logistics and time problems we have already noted certainly interfere with the program's ability to design such a training program, and a lack of funding may make planning extensive in-service or pre-service programs that much more difficult, if not impossible.

Staff development activities may extend to arranging for staff to attend local, state, or even national adult education conferences. Such conferences do provide an opportunity to compare notes with other programs, and many offer excellent workshops on selected topics. However, they do not provide the opportunity to discuss how skills might be applied within the context of the program or to engage in the kind of group problem solving that might benefit the program as a whole. Attendance at conferences or out-based training sessions can be a useful *part* of a program's overall plan for staff development, but staff will need more than such activities if the program is to derive the full benefit of training.

What we will suggest is a four-part model for developing and implementing an effective staff development plan.

Step 1—Conduct a Needs Assessment. One must begin by defining the competencies that staff must be expected to have to serve the students within the program. Within the chapters of Section II, we suggested a number of areas that might be the target of in-service training: characteristics and counseling needs of adults; testing strategies, both for diagnosis/placement and for assessment; use of behavioral objectives and competency statements; teaching methodologies and instructional management techniques; and self-evaluation procedures. Program directors can determine which of these competencies staff may need to develop or improve both by examining the files on staff and by openly soliciting staff opinion through self-assessment questionnaires. Staff may well wish to focus all available in-service time on instructional techniques rather than such larger issues as curriculum planning or construction of appropriate diagnostic and assessment measures. The director may need to supply the balanced view of staff capabilities and skill needs. Indeed, less experienced teachers may not be able to anticipate what skills they will need.

Step 2—Design the Overall Staff Development Plan. Once a "laundry list" of staff training needs has been compiled, the director must establish priorities. Any educational staff will have a wide variety of common and individual needs, and not all of them can be accommodated within the limits of in-service time and budgets. Directors will need to choose those skills that are of greatest importance to the delivery of quality educational services. Directors must also recognize that it takes time to develop the kinds of sophisticated skills we have suggested, and he/she must therefore develop limited training goals. It is better to have a staff thoroughly grounded in writing measurable behavioral goals and objectives, for example, than to have a staff that has merely been exposed to a wide variety of topics. Especially for part-time staff, there may be little time outside the training sessions to do further investigation or reading; thus, goals should be achievable within the context of the training sessions.

Step 3—Implement Training Activities. How one designs the actual activities from which staff will be expected to reach the desired objectives is not very different from designing student learning activities. Literacy educators know that their students do not acquire skills by merely talking about them briefly. Mastery of skills takes careful demonstration, as well as opportunities for practice and application within the real-life contexts that require the skills. These same principles of adult education apply to staff training. Traditional workshop or lecture formats may serve to inform or create awareness of new approaches and ideas, but they will rarely help staff to acquire new behaviors. Training sessions should thus be long enough and frequent enough to introduce, explain, practice, and apply the target skills.

Experienced members of the staff are usually quite willing to attend training sessions aimed at areas in which they already consider themselves to be expert. Directors can make use of such staff members as resource people within the training session; often, by having to teach someone else the what, why, and how-to of a skill, the teacher develops new insights into the uses and possible modifications of the skill. And, by using staff members who have regularly worked with the program's student population, all training can be provided solidly within the context of the program.

Outside resources may be brought in to do part or all of the training. Consultants from the state department of education or the state university's department of adult education are certainly the most affordable resources and are usually the most accessible to programs. When such outside resources are employed, however, they must be thoroughly briefed on program operation and the expected outcomes of training.

Step 4—Build In Follow-Up Activities.   Research indicates that most innovations fail not in the initial implementation, but in the follow up. Skills once acquired will not necessarily be consistently employed without periodic reinforcement. As staff attempt to implement the skills from training sessions in their classrooms or tutoring sessions, they may well need to discuss the results with someone. Directors may accomplish this by informally asking, "How is Skill X working for you?" or by holding follow-up staff discussion sessions. Directors might circulate memos or journal articles on the topic of the training session to promote continuing discussion and awareness of the topic.

Staff Evaluation

Closely related to staff development and training is the issue of staff evaluation, yet for many staff members, the concept of evaluation holds strong negative connotations. In the kind of atmosphere we have described in this chapter, staff evaluation should become merely a term for activities aimed at helping staff members discover what will make them the most effective members of the team, that is, what skills they possess or need to improve to achieve their individual goals as well as the goals of the program.

When staff know the goals of the program and have had a hand in setting objectives for their performance, they are unlikely to resent evaluation activities. If they do not clearly understand what is expected of them and do not get consistent feedback on their performance, they will be quite surprised and rightfully indignant should a director suggest that their performance is unacceptable. Staff evaluation should therefore be an ongoing activity aimed at promoting professional growth.

Some directors build full-scale performance appraisal systems and regularly set aside time for both formal and informal discussions of performance. Under such a system, the director may share with staff a concrete list of objective performance standards complete with a description of how these standards should be demonstrated. Such a document is not unlike a job description, except that it is much more specific about tasks and measures of performance. When staff have the opportunity to review and discuss this list of standards with the director or curriculum supervisor before the first class sessions and can accept the standards as reasonable, it is a small step to holding staff accountable for meeting minimum performance standards.

Managing Volunteer Staff

While some directors we interviewed declared that volunteers are "more trouble than they are worth," many directors have built successful literacy programs using an all-volunteer staff. Volunteers are potentially a rich talent pool for underfunded and struggling programs. They may be especially attractive for any of the following reasons:

- the use of unpaid personnel can ease budget problems
- potentially, a sufficient number of volunteers can be recruited to help the program reduce long waiting lists
- one-to-one tutoring means personal attention to individual needs, interests, and learning styles of the learners (though, as suggested under the heading "Group Versus Individualized Instruction" in Chapter 7, not all educators look favorably on the social isolation of learners)
- by providing instruction in the students' homes, volunteers can help programs serve the hardest to reach

Many volunteers do possess innate talents and strong "people skills," and certainly they are dedicated to the concept of helping illiterate adults. Yet the use of volunteers as the primary instructional staff means making adjustments in the kinds of staff development and training activities the program provides. The equivalent of three days' training, no matter how well designed, cannot provide a volunteer tutor with the arsenal of techniques necessary to teach this most challenging of learners. The director of a community-based program noted: "Tutors need to be better trained. They need a background in reading theory and process. And they need exposure to as many different methods as possible."

If tutors have been poorly trained in a rapid-fire orientation and are then sent out into the field with only sporadic supervision, both the tutors and the students will suffer. Unfortunately, in too many programs, a consistent plan for supervision either has not been developed or is extremely difficult to carry out. Often, the tutor and the student move along not knowing how to cope with problems or how to search for alternatives. Tutors may become discouraged and cut short their commitment because they have had no chance to share their problems or seek solutions to persistent questions.

In designing a plan for using volunteer staff, we recommend the following three steps:

(1) **Match tutors and students.** Develop a questionnaire or checklist to determine both the tutor's and the student's attitudes toward crucial variables in the instructional process. Student variables, such as personal

goals, learning style, and preferences for certain materials, should match the tutor's philosophy. Tutor variables, such as flexibility, willingness to change, and commitment to further their training, are important in building a reliable and competent tutoring staff. Beyond the easily stated variables, directors will need to recognize the importance of personality and philosophy of life on making a suitable match.

(2) **Provide supervision.** Tutors need to be valued and supported in exactly the same way that one values and supports a paid teaching staff. As members of the team, their input should be considered in designing a system for supervision. Although it may be physically impossible for the program director to supervise each tutor, programs have successfully used trained volunteer supervisors or peer supervisors to enhance the quality of instruction volunteer tutors offer.

(3) **Make volunteer staff development a goal.** Target staff development activities for each year, and follow up with chances for volunteer staff to share and compare the results. Keep goals focused so that supervisors can concentrate on attainable and simple objectives.

CONCLUSIONS

Managerial leadership, as we have described it in this chapter, will be reflected in the ways in which program directors obtain and manage the program's financial, physical, and human resources and in the ways in which they perform the role of program advocate. To help their programs realize their fullest potential, directors must:

- clearly communicate overall program philosophy both to program staff and to the community
- develop detailed plans for each program component complete with clearly stated objectives that reflect overall program philosophy
- design and monitor recordkeeping systems that will help program staff evaluate the relative effectiveness of planned staff and student activities in meeting the stated objectives
- implement procedures for regularly reviewing program effectiveness data and systematically refining statements of objectives, methodologies aimed at achieving objectives, and evaluation criteria or procedures
- maintain communications with a network of other adult education professionals and social service providers to stay abreast of funding opportunities, trends and possible improvements in all aspects of program operation and delivery of services, and potential collaborative efforts
- maintain communications with the community both to ensure that the program is continuing to serve community needs (through needs assessments) and to ensure ongoing community support (through public relations activities)
- develop sufficient expertise in grantsmanship and political savvy to tap new sources of funding

- employ sound financial management and budgeting procedures to manage operations on tight budgets
- creatively solve problems in finding adequate facilities
- provide opportunities for the continuing professional growth and development of the program staff
- create an atmosphere in which all staff members (including noncredentialed volunteers and part-time staff) see themselves as legitimate professionals working as a team to achieve the stated objectives of the program

The foregoing eleven activities must be balanced against other day-to-day demands on the director's time. Directors who face the challenge of engaging in all these activities can, however, expect to reap the benefits of being able to document program effectiveness and more successfully wage the battle for the kind of public and government support that adult literacy programs need and deserve.

BIBLIOGRAPHY

Association for Community Based Education. *Directory of Foundation Funding Sources*. Washington, DC: 1984.

Bitterman, J. E. "Management Perspectives in Federally Funded Adult Basic Education in New York City." Ed.D. Thesis, Teachers College, Columbia University.

Brown, A. (Ed.). *Handbook for Organizing and Managing a Literacy Program*. Washington, DC: U.S. Government Printing Office, 1979.

Conners, T., and Callaghan, C. T. *Financial Management for Nonprofit Organizations*. New York: American Management Institute, 1982.

Crozier, M. *The Bureaucratic Phenomenon*. Chicago: University of Chicago Press, 1964.

Darkenwald, G. *Project F.I.S.T. (Functional In-Service Training)*. New Brunswick, NJ: Rutgers University Press, 1983.

Delalic, E. "Pre-Service Training for Teachers of Adult Basic Education." Jasper, IN: Vincennes University, 1981. (ERIC ED 210481)

Donaldson, L., and Scannell, E. *Human Resource Development: The New Trainer's Guide*. Reading, MA: Addison-Wesley, 1978.

Drezner, S. M., and McGurdy, W. B. *A Planning Guide for Voluntary Human Service Delivery Agencies*. New York: Family Service Association of America, 1979.

Drucker, P. *Management Tasks, Responsibilities, Practices*. New York: Harper and Row, 1974.

Finch, R. E. *Building a Successful Adult Basic Education Program: The Director's Role*. Columbus, OH: State of Ohio Department of Education, 1973.

The Foundation Grants Index. Irvington, NY: Columbia University Press. Published annually.

Gaby, P. V., and Gaby, D. *Nonprofit Organization Handbook: A Guide to Fund Raising, Grants, Lobbying, and Membership Building*. Englewood Cliffs, NJ: Prentice-Hall, 1979.

Grantsmanship Center News. Los Angeles: Grantsmanship Center. Bimonthly journal.

Haase, A. "Law and Policy in Educating Undereducated Adults." Paper presented at the Annual Meeting of the International Reading Association, April 1981. (ERIC ED 205943)

Halperin, S. *A Guide for the Powerless—And Those Who Don't Know Their Own Power.* Washington, DC: Institute for Educational Leadership, 1981.

Ilsley, P. J., and Niemi, J. A. *Recruiting and Training Volunteers.* New York: McGraw-Hill, 1981.

Laubach Literacy Action. *Organization Handbook: How to Organize and Sustain a Volunteer Literacy Program.* Syracuse, NY: New Readers Press, 1983. *Public Relations and Fund Development Handbook.* Syracuse, NY: New Readers Press, 1976.

Literacy Volunteers of America, Inc. *Management Handbook for Volunteer Programs.* Syracuse, NY: 1984.

Mager, R., and Pipe, P. *Analyzing Performance Problems, or You Really Oughta Wanna.* Belmont, CA: Fearon Pitman, 1970.

Miller, J. M. *ABE/ESL Volunteer Program Organizational Handbook.* Seattle: Washington State Office of the Superintendent of Public Instruction, 1983.

Mintzberg, H. *The Nature of Managerial Work.* New York: Harper and Row, 1973.

Mitiguy, N. *The Rich Get Richer and the Poor Write Proposals.* Amherst, MA: Citizen Involvement Training Project, 1978.

Nadler, L. *Developing Human Resources.* Houston: Gulf Publishing Company, 1970.

Orem, R. A. "Teacher Background and Its Effects on ABE Classroom Practice." *Journal of Adult Literacy and Basic Education*, Volume 3, Number 4, pages 271–279.

Public Management Institute. *Managing Staff for Results.* San Francisco: 1980.

Richards, A. *Managing Volunteers for Results.* San Francisco: Public Management Institute, 1979.

Whaples, G. C., and Waugaman, D. "Lobby Is Not a Four-Letter Word." *Lifelong Learning: The Adult Years,* Volume 5, Number 8, April 1982.

Wilson, M. *The Effective Management of Volunteer Programs.* Boulder, CO: Volunteer Management Associates, 1976. Higher education.

Chapter 11
Conclusions from the NALP
Promising Practices Search

As we stand back and survey our findings, we recognize the unique opportunity we have had to observe and report on the current state of adult literacy instruction and practice. Our central mission was to describe program instruction and operation, and we have painted that picture in rich detail. What emerges from the description is that "what works"—or the most effective literacy practices—results from a systems approach to program design and implementation. Successful programs have been designed as total educational systems under which there is a balanced emphasis on (1) clearly stated learning objectives, (2) assessment of learner needs and progress, (3) instructional processes, (4) guidance and counseling, and (5) program management and evaluation.

Specifically, successful programs have the following characteristics:

- They are clear about their overall goals and their philosophy of instruction.
- They develop measurable goals for every component of the program (e.g., recruitment, orientation, counseling) so that they can monitor their success in meeting these goals.
- They assist potential learners in determining if the program is well suited to the learners' goals and expectations.
- They are explicit about intended learning outcomes for participants and their standards for judging success in achieving outcomes, and this information is shared with program participants.
- They carefully diagnose each learner's educational needs and strengths and develop an individually tailored learning plan for each participant.
- They tie learning objectives to instructional methods and materials and to assessment strategies.
- They provide frequent feedback to learners on their progress in mastering their learning objectives, and they carefully document that progress.
- They frequently evaluate their program's effectiveness in meeting its goals in each of the component areas, and they use this evaluation data to improve their literacy program.

The greatest strength of such educational systems is that they produce observable results for participants and yield management information for staff, thus enabling programs to measure and document their success. Key to this determination of effectiveness, however, is the explicitness of program and learner goals and the systematic and thorough documentation of progress in meeting those goals.

229

It is on this key point that we discovered one of the greatest problems facing the field of adult education. Our conversations with literacy educators underscore the fact that they generally share no common criteria for evaluating their performance. Standards of success range from such limited though concrete definitions as the numbers of students served to such broad and vague definitions as making fundamental changes in people's lives. The problem is exacerbated by the fact that adult educators are often not trained in evaluation methods. In fact, as we have pointed out, adult educators are often not trained in their profession at all. In addition, the demands of developing instructional strategies and tailoring materials to provide services to learners consumes so much of the staff's energy that little time is allocated to the kinds of evaluation activities that would result in improved practice.

Nonetheless, most of the literacy practitioners we interviewed stated that they both want to and need to document their program's success. In the current competitive funding arena in which resources are scarce and the demands on those resources are numerous, the lack of documented effectiveness data severely reduces opportunities for programs to develop a stable and secure funding base. Further, the lack of evidence about the results of practice lends credence to the view that adult literacy educators are less than "professional" or "creditable."

Despite the need to implement improved evaluation procedures and generate more substantial effectiveness data, there is much that we do know about what works, and we *have* identified successful practices and programs. One characteristic successful programs have in common is the clarity of their statements about program purpose, learning objectives, and the means of measuring learners' mastery of those objectives. A second characteristic these programs have in common is the use of a structured management system that integrates the program components so that all are focused on the learners' achievement of the stated objectives. We believe that programs that adopt these characteristics within a systems approach will be able to produce the effectiveness data they need to substantiate their claims for scarce resources and to allow their staff to feel secure about their competence as literacy service providers.

However, there is still a great deal to be done to package and widely distribute "best of breed" curricular materials, promising practices, and complete educational systems. Also, to reach more people more effectively, there is a need for more wholesale development efforts that incorporate new technologies for instruction and management.

If we are to disseminate such knowledge and if we are to achieve the goal of extending opportunity to those who may be currently disenfranchised, there is a need for large investments in the literacy and adult education infrastructure and longer term investments in the education of individuals. We know that there is no quick and simple means of providing functionally illiterate adults with the skills they need to compete effectively. Short-term interventions that do not have sequential activities and follow-up support to reinforce instruction, to apply skills in real-life contexts, and to expand the opportunities open to the learners are by themselves not effective in producing lasting achievement for program participants.

Consequently, the development of a pyramid of opportunities and services for educationally disadvantaged adults is critical to the success of large investments in adult education. We must maximize what existing programs do well and avoid stretching them beyond their capabilities to provide effective services; rather, we must capitalize on the natural system of service providers who serve distinct constituencies by developing brokering or referral services among programs and looking to a broader and more collaborative alignment of interested parties. Also critical to the success of such a system is investment both in the validation and packaging of model programs and in the creation of a technical assistance system to help programs adapt model systems to local needs and preferences.

We should not be discouraged. The NALP Promising Practices Search suggests that past investment in basic skills, work/education opportunities, and remediation efforts for adults have had substantial payoffs for society. With more effective systems design, increased human and financial resources, and the possibility of more reasoned implementation and better management of educational systems, the rate of return on the money, time, energy, and commitment should be increased. In our view, there can be few more profitable investments for the future of America.

SECTION IV
Networking

Chapter 12
Building a Resource Network

Many of the literacy practitioners we interviewed were concerned that they had little time to meet with peers and few resources to spend on staff development or technical assistance to improve or modify their practice. The sense of being isolated from others who face the same issues, constraints, and opportunities was a consistent theme in many of our discussions.

One response to the need to bring literacy educators together both to share concerns and to share information on instructional strategies and materials is the formation of peer technical assistance, information, or advocacy networks and coalitions. Two examples of such networks are the Coalition of Adult Education Providers in New York City and the Boston (MA) Network for Alternative and Adult Education.

The Coalition for Adult Education Providers is composed of representatives from community-based organizations and community colleges that offer literacy services. The coalition's primary purpose is to bring literacy educators together to share information, to assist each other in adopting innovative practices, and to advocate for more attention and resources for literacy programs.

Similarly, the Boston Network is made up of individuals and organizations who provide adult education and training services. Monthly meetings are planned to address specific methodological and curricular issues. Also, opportunities are provided for peer technical assistance, with programs helping each other modify or improve instructional program design.

Both networks draw members from a variety of settings, though they do restrict membership to programs that actually provide educational services. Other networks have been created to serve certain special interests such as the type of service provided (e.g., ESL) or the institutional base out of which the program operates (e.g., employment and training programs).

We believe that networking is one way to overcome the constraints literacy educators face in obtaining state-of-the-art information and peer support, and we encourage you to consider strategies for linking educational service providers in your area. To that end, the remainder of this chapter lists the programs that responded to the NALP mail survey. The programs are listed alphabetically by state and then alphabetically by city within the state. Following the program's name, we have indicated in brackets whether the program is a state or local public education program [state/local], an employment and training program [E & T], a community-based organization [CBO], or operating within a postsecondary institution [postsecondary], a correctional institution [corrections], or the military [military]. To the extent that programs provided data on their survey questionnaires, we have detailed the services they provide.

These program profiles may help you locate other literacy providers in your area who target the same constituency or offer similar services to those you currently provide or would like to provide in the future. We hope you will find this information useful as you attempt to create your own network, extend your circle of colleagues, and gather information on effective literacy practice.

General Bibliography

At the end of specific chapters in this text, we have included bibliographies of those resources that might prove helpful in a further investigation of the topic of a given chapter. The following bibliography does not duplicate the earlier bibliographies; rather, we present here a list of texts and articles of a more general or global nature. We have also included materials that address constituency-specific or other special-interest issues that may have been inappropriate for inclusion in earlier bibliographies but are nonetheless of interest to many readers.

GENERAL REFERENCES

Adult Performance Level Project. *Final Report: The Adult Performance Level Study.* Austin: University of Texas, 1977.

Alamprese, J. *New York State External High School Diploma Program.* Syracuse, NY: Syracuse Research Corporation, 1979.

Anderson, R., and Darkenwald, G. *Participation and Persistence in American Adult Education.* New York: College Entrance Examination Board, 1979.

Baumann, J. F. "Coping with Reading Disability: Portrait of an Adult Disabled Reader." *Journal of Reading,* Volume 27, Number 6, pages 530–535, 1984. (EJ 294819)

Boggs, D. L. "Teacher Aides in Ohio ABE Programs: Their Characteristics, Functions, Learning Needs, and Relationships with Teachers." *Journal of Adult Literacy and Basic Education,* Volume 1, Number 2, pages 51–61, 1977.

Boraks, N. "Research and Adult Literacy Programs." *Journal of Adult Literacy and Basic Education,* Volume 5, Number 1, pages 5–11, 1981.

Boshier, R. "Educational Participation and Dropout: A Theoretical Model." *Adult Education,* Volume 20, Number 4, pages 255–282, 1973.

Boyd, R., and Martin, L. "A Methodology for the Analysis of the Psychosocial Profiles of Low Literate Adults." *Adult Education Quarterly,* Volume 34, Number 2, pages 85–96, 1984. (EJ 289246)

Bright, J. P., et. al. *An ESL Literacy Resource Guide: A Handbook for ESL/Adult Educators in Illinois.* Arlington Heights: Illinois Statewide English as a Second Language/Adult Education Service Center, 1982. (ED 223871)

Brooke, W. M. (Ed.). *Adult Basic Education.* Toronto: New Press, 1972.

Carroll, J. B., and Chall, J. S. (Eds.). *Toward a Literate Society: A Report from the National Academy of Education.* New York: McGraw-Hill, 1975.

Chall, J. "New Views on Developing Basic Skills with Adults." Paper presented at the National Adult Literacy Conference, Washington, DC, January 1984. (ED 240299)

Courtenay, B., et. al. "Functional Literacy among the Elderly: Where We Are(n't)." *Educational Gerontology*, Volume 8, Number 4, pages 339–352, 1982. (EJ 270858)

Cross, K. P. *Adults as Learners*. San Francisco: Jossey-Bass, 1981.

Darkenwald, G. C., and Larson, G. A. (Eds.). *New Directions for Continuing Education: Reaching Hard-to-Reach Adults*. San Francisco: Jossey-Bass, 1980.

Darling, S. *Jefferson County Adult Reading Project: Final Report*. Louisville, KY: Jefferson County Board of Education, 1981. (ED 204600)

Darling, S., et. al. *Organizing a Successful Adult Literacy Program*. Louisville, KY: Jefferson County Public Schools, 1983. (ED 235320)

Development Associates. "An Assessment of the State-Administered Program of the Adult Education Act: Final Report." Arlington, VA: 1980. (ED 195700)

Dickinson, G., and Clark, K. M. "Learning Orientations and Participation in Self-Education and Continuing Education." *Adult Education*, Volume 26, Number 1, pages 3–15, 1975.

Eberle, A., and Robinson, S. *The Adult Illiterate Speaks Out: Personal Perspectives on Learning to Read and Write*. Washington, DC: National Institute of Education, 1980.

Eyster, G. *Different Strokes for Different Folks*. Morehead, KY: Morehead State University, Appalachian Adult Education Center, 1982.

Fingeret, A. "Through the Looking Glass: Literacy as Perceived by Illiterate Adults." Paper presented at the Adult Education Research Association Annual Meeting, New York City, March 1982. (ED 222698)

Fitzgerald, G. "Can the Hard-to-Reach Adults Become Literate?" *Lifelong Learning: The Adult Years*, Volume 7, Number 5, pages 4–5, 1984. (EJ 294399)

Fogoros, A. W. *Project WE CARE (Workers' Education and Community Awareness of Resources for Education)*. Pittsburgh, PA: Information and Volunteer Services of Allegheny County, 1981. (ED 217146)

Gambrelle, L., and Heathington, B. "Adult Disabled Readers' Metacognitive Awareness about Reading Tasks and Strategies." *Journal of Reading Behavior*, Volume 13, Number 3, pages 215–222, 1981.

Gold, P. C., and Horn, P. L. "Achievement in Reading, Verbal Language, Listening Comprehension and Locus of Control of Adult Illiterates in a Volunteer Tutorial Project." *Perception and Motor Skills*, Volume 54, pages 1243–1250, 1982.

Gold, P. C., and Johnson, J. A. "Entry Level Achievement Characteristics of Youth and Adults Reading Below Fifth Grade Equivalent: A Preliminary Profile and Analysis." *Psychological Reports*. Volume 50, pages 1011–1019, 1982.

Goodman, D., and Peppers, J. "Comparative Functional Literacy of APL Graduates and Wichita East High School Graduating Seniors." *Journal of Adult Literacy and Basic Education*, Volume 2, Number 3, pages 158–164, 1978.

Guthrie, J. T. "Research: Literacy for Science and Technology." *Journal of Reading*, Volume 27, Number 5, pages 478–480, 1984.

Heisel, M., and Larson, G. "Literacy and Social Milieu: Reading Behavior of the Black Elderly." *Adult Education Quarterly,* Volume 34, Number 2, pages 63–70, 1984. (EJ 289244)

Howe, M. J. A. (Ed.). *Adult Learning: Psychological Research and Applications.* New York: John Wiley, 1977.

Hunter, C., and Harman, D. *Adult Illiteracy in the United States.* New York: McGraw-Hill, 1979.

Irish, G. "Reflections on Ends and Means in Adult Basic Education." *Adult Education,* Volume 25, Number 2, pages 125–130, 1975.

Karnes, F. A., Ginn, C. N., and Maddox, B. B. (Eds.). *Issues and Trends in Adult Basic Education: Focus on Reading.* Jackson: University Press of Mississippi, 1980.

Kasom, C. "The Illiterate Elderly." Paper presented at the White House Conference on Aging, Washington, DC, December 1981. (ED 215282)

Kirschner Associates. *An Analysis of Selected Issues in Adult Education.* Washington, DC: U.S. Office of Education, 1976.

Knowles, M. *The Modern Practice of Adult Education.* New York: Cambridge, The Adult Education Company, 1980.

Lamorella, R., et. al. "Teaching the Functionally Illiterate Adult: A Primer." *Reading Horizons,* Volume 23, Number 2, pages 89–94, 1983. (EJ 274147)

Levine, K. "Functional Literacy: Fond Illusions and False Economies." *Harvard Educational Review,* Volume 52, Number 3, pages 249–266, 1982. (EJ 267893)

Lindsey, J., and Jarman, L. "Adult Basic Education: Six Years after Kavale and Lindsey's Literature Review." *Journal of Reading,* Volume 27, Number 7, pages 609–613, 1984. (EJ 296611)

Long, H. *Adult Learning: Research and Practice.* New York: Cambridge, The Adult Education Company, 1983.

Longfield, D. "Teaching English as a Second Language to Adults: State-of-the-Art." Paper presented at the National Adult Literacy Conference, Washington, DC, January 1984. (ED 240297)

Mangum, G. "Adult Literacy in Utah: Even a Leader Has Unmet Needs." Paper presented at the National Adult Literacy Conference, Washington, DC, January 1984. (ED 240287)

Mercier, L. Y. (Ed.). *Outlook for the 80's: Adult Literacy.* Washington, DC: Dingle Associates, 1981. (ED 211701)

Mezirow, J., Darkenwald, G., and Knox, A. *Last Gamble on Education: Dynamics of Adult Basic Education.* Washington, DC: Adult Education Association of the USA, 1975.

Michigan State University, East Lansing, Non-Formal Education Information Center. *Literacy and Basic Education: A Selected, Annotated Bibliography. Bibliography #3.* East Lansing: Michigan State University, 1981. (ED 232824)

Newsom, R., and Foxworth, L. "Locus of Control and Class Completion among ABE Clients." *Journal of Adult Literacy and Basic Education,* Volume 4, Number 1, pages 41–49, 1980.

Polley, B. "Project ALMS (Adult Literacy Mission Support): An Adult Basic Reading Project." Edinboro (PA) State College, 1981. (ED 209424)

Rigg, P., and Kasemek, F. "Adult Illiteracy in the USA: Problem and Solutions." *Convergence: An International Journal of Adult Education*, Volume 16, Number 4, pages 24–31, 1983. (EJ 294318)

Robinson, J. "Educational Broadcasting and Socially Deprived Groups in the Adult Community." *Adult Education*, Volume 51, Number 6, pages 337–344, 1979.

Rosenblum, S., and Darkenwald, G. "Effects of Adult Learner Participation in Course Planning on Achievement and Satisfaction." *Adult Education Quarterly*, Volume 33, Number 3, pages 147–153, 1983.

Rossman, M., Fisk, E., and Roehl, J. *Teaching and Learning Basic Skills: A Guide for Adult Basic Education and Developmental Education Programs*. New York: Columbia University, Teachers College Press, 1984.

Samuels, F., and Gierach, L. "The Design and Implementation of an Urban Adult Basic Education Program." Paper presented at the National Adult Education Conference, Philadelphia, PA, December 1983. (ED 237657)

Sticht, T. *Literacy and Human Resources Development at Work: Investing in the Education of Adults to Improve the Educability of Children*. Alexandria, VA: Human Resources Research Organization, 1983.

———. "Strategies for Adult Literacy Development." Paper presented at the National Adult Literacy Conference, Washington, DC, January 1984. (ED 240300)

Travis, T. "Selected Factors Contributing to Reading and Mathematics Achievement of Adult Learners." *Journal of Adult Literacy and Basic Education*, Volume 5, Number 1, pages 12–24, 1984.

Waite, P. A. "The Role of Volunteers in Adult Literacy Programs." Paper presented at the National Adult Literacy Conference, Washington, DC, January 1984. (ED 240294)

Wallerstein, N. "Literacy and Minority Language Groups: Community Literacy as Method and Goal." Paper presented at the National Adult Literacy Conference, Washington, DC, January 1984. (ED 240298)

Whaples, G., and Rivera, W. *Lifelong Learning Research Conference Proceedings*. College Park, MD: University of Maryland, 1983.

Wolf, E., and Kavanagh, C. "Adult Illiteracy: A Public Library Responds." *Catholic Library World*, Volume 55, Number 3, pages 125–128, 1983. (EJ 288541)

Yin, R., Granai, S., and Alamprese, J. *To Find an Education: New Options for Adult Basic Education Programs*. Washington, DC: National Center for the Study of Professions, 1982.

COMMUNITY-BASED EDUCATION

Association for Community-Based Education. *Adult Literacy: Study of Community-Based Literacy Programs*. Washington, DC, 1983.

Eggert, J. D. "Concerns in Establishing and Maintaining a Community-Based Adult Literacy Project." Paper presented at the National Adult Literacy Conference, Washington, DC, January 1984. (ED 240295)

Harris, J. E. "The Design and Administrative Management of Literacy Training Programs in South Carolina." Paper presented at the National Adult Literacy Conference, Washington, DC, January 1984. (ED 240293)

EMPLOYMENT AND TRAINING PROGRAMS

Jacob, E., and Crandall, J. A. "Job-Related Literacy: A Look at Current and Needed Research." (ED 178903)

Lauterborn, R. F. "Reading: Why Industry Cares and What One Company Is Doing about It." Paper presented at the Annual Meeting of the International Reading Association, New Orleans, LA, April 1981. (ED 205910)

Mikulecky, L., and Diehl, N. *Job Literacy: Reading Research Center Technical Report*. Bloomington, IN: Indiana University, 1980.

Mikulecky, L., and Strange, R. "Effective Literacy Training Programs for Adults in Business and Municipal Employment." In Orasanu, J. (ed.) *A Decade of Reading Research: Implications*. Hillsdale, NJ: Lawrence Erlbaum Associates, in press.

Munns, K. L. "Why Can't Johnny's Parents Read?" *Reading Improvement*, Volume 19, Number 2, pages 144–148, 1982. (EJ 266961)

Sticht, T. *Literacy and Vocational Competence*. Columbus, OH: National Center for Research in Vocational Education, 1978.

Taylor, J., and Fox, W. "Differential Approaches to Training." Professional Paper Number 47–67. Alexandria, VA: Human Resources Research Organization, 1967.

Tenopyr, M. L. "Realities of Adult Literacy in Work Settings." Paper presented at the National Adult Literacy Conference, Washington, DC, January 1984. (ED 240290)

MILITARY PROGRAMS

Begland, R. R. "A Multi-Faceted Approach to the Development of the Army's Functional Basic Skills Education Program (BSEP)." Paper presented at the Adult Education Research Association Annual Meeting, Los Angeles, 1981.

Duffy, T. "Literacy Instruction in the Military," Paper presented at the National Adult Literacy Conference, Washington, DC, January 1984.

Fox, W., Taylor, J., and Caylor, J. "Aptitude Level and the Acquisition of Skills and Knowledge in a Variety of Military Training Tasks." H.U.M.R.R.O. Technical Report 69–6. Alexandria, VA: Human Resources Research Organization, 1969.

Huff, K., Sticht, T., Joyner, J., Groff, S., and Burkett, J. "A Job-Oriented Reading Program for the Air Force: Development of Field Evaluation." HumRRO, FR-WD-CA-77-3. Alexandria, VA: Human Resources Research Organization, 1977.

Sachar, J., and Duffy, T. "Reading Skill and Military Effectiveness." Paper presented at the Adult Education Research Association Annual Meeting, 1977.

CORRECTIONAL PROGRAMS

Gold, P. C. "Literacy Training in Penal Institutions." Paper presented at the National Adult Literacy Conference, Washington, DC, January 1984. (ED 240292)

Gold, P. C., and Horn, P. L. "Intelligence and Achievement of Adult Illiterates in a Tutorial Project: A Preliminary Analysis." *Journal of Clinical Psychology*, Volume 39, Number 1, pages 107–113, 1983. (EJ 275941)

Gold, P. C., and Johnson, J. A. "Prediction of Achievement in Reading, Self-Esteem, Auding and Verbal Language by Adult Illiterates in a Psychoeducational Tutoring Program." Unpublished paper. Johns Hopkins University, 101 Whitehead Hall, Baltimore, MD 21218.

Gold, P. C., and Steurer, S. J. "Graduate Training of Correctional Education Staff Working with Adult Illiterates: A Model Program." *Journal of Correctional Education*, Volume 34, Number 2, 1983.

Linden, R., and Perry, L. "Effectiveness of Prison Education Programs." *Journal of Offender Counseling Services and Rehabilitation*, Volume 6, Number 4, pages 43–57, 1982.

McCollum, S. G. "Some New Directions in Correctional Education." U.S. Bureau of Prisons. Paper presented at the Correctional Education Association Conference, Baltimore, MD, 1982.

McCollum, S. G. "New Incentives for Education Programs." U.S. Bureau of Prisons. Paper presented at the Correctional Education Association Conference, Houston, TX, 1983.

Sherk, J. "Diagnosis of Reading Difficulties in a Correctional Institution." Unpublished research. Kansas City: University of Missouri, Department of Reading, 1969.

Author unknown. "Education—A Weapon against Crime: A Forum on Prisoner Education." Summary proceedings, U.S. Department of Education, Office of Vocational and Adult Education/Corrections Program, Washington, DC, 1981. (ED 208218)

Author unknown. "Adult Basic Education (4901)—Curriculum Performance Standard." Washington, DC: U.S. Department of Justice, Federal Prison System, 1982.

POSTSECONDARY EDUCATION PROGRAMS

Cosby, J. P. *Remedial Education—Is It Worth It?* Educational Resources Information Center. Fort Lauderdale, FL: Nova University, 1975. (ED 099067)

Cross, K. P. *Accent on Learning: Improving Instruction and Reshaping the Curriculum.* San Francisco: Jossey-Bass, 1976.

Fadale, L. M. *Developmental Studies for Occupational Students: Postsecondary Programs.* Ithaca, NY: Cornell Institute for Research and Development in Occupational and Continuing Education, 1977.

Grede, J., and Friedlander, J. "Adult Basic Education in Community Colleges." *Junior College Research Review*, August 1981.

Maxwell, M. *Improving Student Learning Skills: A Comprehensive Guide to Successful Practices and Programs for Increasing the Performance of Underprepared Students*. San Francisco: Jossey-Bass, 1979.

Memering, D. "Forward to the Basics." *College English*, Volume 39, Number 5, pages 553–561, 1978.

Rizzo, B. "Peer Teaching in English I." *College Composition and Communication*, Volume 26, pages 394–396, 1975.

Roueche, J. E. (Ed.). *A New Look at Successful Programs*. San Francisco: Jossey-Bass, 1983.

Roueche, J. E., and Kirk, R. *Catching Up: Remedial Education*. San Francisco: Jossey-Bass, 1973.

Roueche, J. E., and Mink, O. *Holistic Literacy in College Teaching*. San Francisco: Jossey-Bass, 1980.

Roueche, J. E., and Snow, J. J. *Overcoming Learning Problems: A Guide to Developmental Education in College*. San Francisco: Jossey-Bass, 1977.

Roueche, S. D., and Comstock, V. N. "A Report on Theory and Method for the Study of Literacy Development in Community Colleges." Austin: Programs in Community College Education, University of Texas, 1981.

Richardson, R. C., et. al. *A Report on Literacy Development in Community Colleges: Technical Report*. Tempe: Arizona State University, Department of Higher and Adult Education, 1982. (ED 217925)

Trillin, A. S., and Associates. *Teaching Basic Skills in College: A Guide to Objectives, Skills Assessment, Course Content, Teaching Methods, Support Services, and Administration*. San Francisco: Jossey-Bass, 1980.

Wood, N. V. *College Reading and Study Skills*. New York: Holt, Rinehart & Winston, 1978.

Yarrington, R., et. al. "Literacy in Community Colleges: Junior College Resource Review." Los Angeles: ERIC Clearinghouse for Junior Colleges, 1982. (ED 217946)

Mini-Profiles

The following is a listing, by state, of Adult Education Programs that were used in the NALP study, and their services offered.

ALABAMA

Adult Basic Education Program [state/local]
309 Twenty-Third Street, North
Birmingham, Alabama 35203
205/251-1157

SERVICES OFFERED

- English as a second language
- basic skills education
- GED preparation
- parent's basic skills
- Adult Performance Level activities
- job survival training & career development

Adult Learning Center [state/local]
515 South Union Street
Montgomery, Alabama 36197
205/269-3774 or 3775

SERVICES OFFERED

- English as a second language
- basic skills education
- GED preparation
- remediation and coping skills program

Adult Education [postsecondary]
Wallace State Community College
Post Office Drawer 1049
Selma, Alabama 36701
205/875-2634

SERVICES OFFERED

- English as a second language
- basic skills education
- GED preparation
- job training in coordination with JTPA

Tuscaloosa County Adult Education Program
[state/local]
2314 Ninth Street
Tuscaloosa, Alabama 35403
205/758-0411

SERVICES OFFERED

- English as a second language
- basic skills education
- GED preparation
- career counseling
- GED merit scholarship program
- mental health component
- remediation for technical college learners

Programmed Learning for Adult Continuing
Education (The PLACE) [state/local]
310 East Tallassee Street
Wetumpka, Alabama 36092
205/567-5358

SERVICES OFFERED

- English as a second language
- basic skills education
- GED preparation

ALASKA

SERRC Adult Education Programs, Southeast
Alaska [state/local]
538 Willoughby Avenue
Juneau, Alaska 99801
907/586-6860

SERVICES OFFERED

- English as a second language
- basic skills education
- GED preparation
- life skills in job seeking, health education, consumerism, job training, government & law, and community resources
- Literacy Volunteers of America (volunteer tutor program for adults in reading and beginning level ESL)

ARIZONA

Refugee Link Program [CBO]
525 North Seventh Street
Tempe, Arizona 85006
602/257-2900

SERVICES OFFERED

- English as a second language for refugees

CALIFORNIA

Project CLASS [state/local]
Clovis Adult School
914 Fourth Street
Clovis, California 93612

SERVICES OFFERED

- English as a second language
- basic skills education
- Project CLASS is a series of competency-based instructional materials designed for teaching life skills topics to adult students enrolled in ABE and ESL programs.

Language Learning Centers [CBO]
7400 E. Imperial Highway
Downey, California 90232-3375
213/922-7801

SERVICES OFFERED

- English as a second language
- basic skills education
- GED preparation
- one-to-one tutoring in literacy

South Coast Literacy Council [CBO]
505 Dartmoor Street
Laguna Beach, California 92651
717/494-1982

SERVICES OFFERED

- English as a second language

La Puente Valley Adult Schools [state/local]
1110 Fickewirth Avenue
La Puente, California 91744
818/330-7896

SERVICES OFFERED

- English as a second language
- basic skills education
- GED preparation
- vocational
- job training
- programs for handicapped adults
- programs in correctional facilities for incarcerated adults

Adult Basic Education Program [state/local]
Los Angeles Unified School District
1320 West Third Street, Room 900
Los Angeles, California 90017
213/625-6471

SERVICES OFFERED

- English as a second language
- basic skills education

Neighborhood Centers Adult Education Program [state/local]
Oakland Unified School District
1025 Second Avenue, Administration Annex #308
Oakland, California 94606
415/452-1612

SERVICES OFFERED

- English as a second language
- basic skills education
- VESL (vocational English as a second language), in concert with community agencies

Literacy Volunteers of America—Placentia Affiliate
411 East Chapman Avenue
Placentia, California 92670
714/528-1906

SERVICES OFFERED

- English as a second language
- basic skills education

Sequoia District Adult School [state/local]
Broadway and Brewster
Redwood City, California 94063
415/369-6809

SERVICES OFFERED

- English as a second language
- basic skills education
- GED preparation
- vocational (limited)
- high school diploma program

Vocational Education Special Projects
[E & T]
San Mateo County Office of Education
333 Main Street
Redwood City, California 94063
415/363-5439

SERVICES OFFERED

- basic skills education
- vocational
- job training

Salinas Adult School, ESL Program [state/local]
431 West Alisal
Salinas, California 93901
408/757-3931

SERVICES OFFERED

- English as a second language

Academic Remedial Training (ART)
[military]
Recruit Training Command ART Code 2441
San Diego, California 92133
619/225-3436

SERVICES OFFERED

- English as a second language
- basic skills education
- preparation for academic requirements of basic training at RTC

Continuing Education Centers
[postsecondary]
San Diego Community College
5350 University Avenue
San Diego, California 92105
618/230-2144

SERVICES OFFERED

- English as a second language
- basic skills education
- vocationally oriented ESL and basic skills

Job-Oriented Basic Skills (JOBS) School
[military]
Service School Command (3330)
San Diego, California 92133
619/225-4544/4545/4554

SERVICES OFFERED

- basic skills education
- vocational
- job training
- general military training, close order drill, inspections, watch standing, and physical training

ATLAS (Academy for Teaching Literacy to
Adult Students) [CBO]
1054 Carson Drive
Sunnyvale, California 94806
408/735-1212 or 732-4355

SERVICES OFFERED

- English as a second language
- basic skills education
- GED Preparation
- vocational basic skills in conjunction with electronics and job readiness
- job training for underemployed and unemployed youth, adults, and seniors

COLORADO

H. C. Tinsley School [corrections]
Buena Vista Correctional Facility
Box R
Buena Vista, Colorado 81211
303/395-2418

SERVICES OFFERED

- English as a second language
- basic skills education
- GED preparation
- social education classes including marriage and family, psychology, and life skills

ABE/GED Program [corrections]
Centennial Correctional Facility
Post Office Box 600
Canon City, Colorado 81212
303/275-4721

SERVICES OFFERED

- English as a second language
- basic skills education
- GED preparation

Academic Education Program [corrections]
Colorado Women's Correctional Facility
Box 500
Cannon City, Colorado 81212
303/275-4181, ext. 411

SERVICES OFFERED

- basic skills education
- GED preparation

Adult Education Center [state/local]
917 East Moreno
Colorado Springs, CO 80903
303/635-6750

SERVICES OFFERED

- English as a second language
- basic skills education
- GED preparation

Adult Education Tutorial Program
[state/local]
1615 Ogden Street
Denver, Colorado 80218
303/831-9556

SERVICES OFFERED

- English as a second language
- basic skills education
- GED preparation
- job training

Area Vocational Program [E & T]
602 East Sixty-Fourth Street
Denver, Colorado 80229
303/289-5931

SERVICES OFFERED

- English as a second language
- basic skills education
- GED preparation
- vocational
- job training

Mi Casa Resource Center for Women [CBO]
571 Galapago
Denver, Colorado 80210
303/573-1302

SERVICES OFFERED

- basic skills education
- GED preparation
- job training
- Saber Es Poder Educational Program/ Adult Educational Program (Knowledge is Power)
- Mi Carrera/Obrera Youth Program
- nontraditional job vocational training
- training-career awareness, assertiveness, sex-role stereotyping
- cultural awareness
- Esperanza (Hope)
- displaced homemakers program—job preparation

Right to Read of Weld County, Inc.
[state/local]
1211 A Street
Greeley, Colorado 80631
303/352-9477

SERVICES OFFERED

- English as a second language
- basic skills education
- driver's education
- citizenship education

Jefferson County Adult Education
[state/local]
10801 West 44th Avenue
Wheat Ridge, Colorado 80033
303/422-2387

SERVICES OFFERED

- English as a second language

CONNECTICUT

Adult Basic Education [E & T]
Aetna Institute for Corporate Education
151 Farmington Avenue
Hartford, Connecticut 06156
203/727-4322

SERVICES OFFERED

- English as a second language
- basic skills education
- GED preparation

Literacy Volunteers of Connecticut, Inc.
[CBO]
576 Farmington Avenue
Hartford, Connecticut 06105
203/236-55466

SERVICES OFFERED

- English as a second language
- basic skills education

Community Action for Greater Middletown
[CBO]
CAGM Adult Learning Center
93 Broad Street
Middletown, Connecticut 06457
203/347-4465, ext. 49 or 27

SERVICES OFFERED

- English as a second language
- basic skills education
- GED preparation

Literacy Volunteers of Greater Norwalk
[CBO]
South Norwalk Branch Library
10 Washington Street
South Norwalk, Connecticut 06854
203/853-7437

SERVICES OFFERED

- English as a second language
- basic skills education
- pre-job training

Literacy Volunteers of Stamford [CBO]
c/o The Ferguson Library
96 Broad Street
Stamford, Connecticut 06901
203/964-1000

SERVICES OFFERED

- English as a second language
- basic skills education

Literacy Volunteers of Greater Hartford
[CBO]
60 Hamlin Drive
West Hartford, Connecticut 06116
203/523-5841

SERVICES OFFERED

- English as a second language
- basic skills education

DELAWARE

Adult Basic Education (ABE) Program
[state/local]
Christina School District
83 East Main Street
Newark, Delaware 19711
302/454-2251

SERVICES OFFERED

- English as a second language
- basic skills education
- GED preparation

DISTRICT OF COLUMBIA

Community Adult Learning Laboratory
(Project CALL) [state/local]
First and P Street, N.W.
Washington, DC 20001
202/673-7365

SERVICES OFFERED

- basic skills education
- GED preparation

Push Literacy Action Now (PLAN, Inc.)
[CBO]
2311 18th Street, N.W.
Washington, DC 20009
202/387-7775

SERVICES OFFERED

- basic skills education
- GED preparation (industry based)
- testing, information referral, advocacy

70,001 Ltd. [E & T]
600 Maryland Avenue, S.W.
West Wing, Suite 300
Washington, DC 20024
202/484-1013

SERVICES OFFERED

- basic skills education
- GED preparation
- job training
- work-readiness training and motivational
  activities
- private sector job placement

FLORIDA

"Community Volunteerism" [state/local]
School Board of Levy County
Post Office Box 129
Bronson, Florida 32621
904/486-2169

SERVICES OFFERED

- basic skills education

Adult Education [state/local]
Flagler County School Board
P.O. Box 755
Bunnell, Florida 32010
904/445-3550

SERVICES OFFERED

- English as a second language
- basic skills education
- GED preparation
- vocational

Adult Basic Education/High School
Completion/Community Education
[postsecondary]
Brevard Community College, Cocoa Campus
1519 Clearlake Road
Cocoa, Florida 32926
305/632-1111, ext. 3180

SERVICES OFFERED

- English as a second language
- basic skills education
- GED preparation
- alternative high school credentialing program
- vocational
- job training
- community education
- continuing education

Adult Basic Education [state/local]
701 South Andrews Avenue
Fort Lauderale, Florida 33316
305/524-8006

SERVICES OFFERED

- English as a second language
- basic skills education
- adult basic education/elderly
- exceptional adult basic education

Learn to Read, Inc. [CBO]
118 East Monroe Street
Jacksonville, FL 32202
904/353-0288

SERVICES OFFERED

- Free reading and writing lessons to adult illiterates

Academic Remedial Training [military]
Recruit Training Command
Orlando, Florida 32813
305/646-5871, 646-4358

SERVICES OFFERED

- English as a second language
- basic skills education
- remedial reading class for recruits deficient in reading skills

Adult General Education [state/local]
Orange County Public Schools
434 North Tampa Avenue
Orlando, Florida 32809
305/442/3200, ext. 518

SERVICES OFFERED

- English as a second language
- basic skills education
- GED Preparation
- Alternative high school credentialing program

Adult Literacy League [state/local]
P.O. Box 90
Orlando, Florida 32803
305/299-500, ext. 3265 (Mon., Tues., Wed.)

SERVICES OFFERED

- basic skills education

Adult Refugee ESL/VESL Project [CBO]
8434 Avenue C, Building 126
Orlando, Florida 32812
305/857-2553

SERVICES OFFERED

- English as a second language
- ESL survival skills and pre-vocational program

Sarasota County Adult Basic Education
Program [state/local]
4748 Bentua Road
Sarasota, Florida 33583
813/924-1365

SERVICES OFFERED

- English as a second language
- basic skills education
- GED preparation
- job training
- exceptional adult education

HAWAII

Adult Basic Education Program at Aiea
Community School [state/local]
98-1278 Ulune Street
Aiea, Hawaii 96701
808/487-3657

SERVICES OFFERED

- English as a second language
- basic skills education
- GED preparation

Hawaii Adult Basic Education Program
[state/local]
595 Pepeekeo Street, H-2
Honolulu, Hawaii 96852
808/395-9451

SERVICES OFFERED

- English as a second language
- basic skills education

General Education Mastery Program
[state/local]
Waipahu Community School for Adults
94-1211 Farrington Highway
Waipahu, Hawaii 96797
808/671-7176

SERVICES OFFERED

- basic skills education
- alternative high school credentialing
  program

ILLINOIS

Alternate Schools Network [CBO]
1105 W. Lawrence #210
Chicago, Illinois 60640
312/728-4030

SERVICES OFFERED

- English as a second language
- basic skills education
- GED preparation
- alternative high school·credentialing
  program
- vocational
- job training

Literacy Volunteers of Chicago [CBO]
207 S. Wabash Avenue, Eighth Floor
Chicago, Illinois 60604
312/663-0543

SERVICES OFFERED

- English as a second language
- basic skills education

English as a Second Language (ESL)
Program [CBO]
Elgin YWCA
220 East Chicago Street
Elgin, Illinois 60120
312/742-7930

SERVICES OFFERED

- English as a second language

Adult Education: Grant Funded
[postsecondary]
College of Lake County
19351 West Washington Street
Grayslake, Illinois 60030
312/223-6601, ext. 402

SERVICES OFFERED

- English as a second language
- basic skills education
- GED preparation
- vocational

Lawrence Adult Center [state/local]
101 East Laurel
Springfield, Illinois 62704
217/525-3144

SERVICES OFFERED

- English as a second language
- basic skills education
- GED preparation
- alternative high school credentialing program
- vocational
- job training
- on-site clerical training in local businesses
- academic training in drug rehabilitation center and Goodwill Industries
- Indochinese refugee consortium

Adult Basic Education [postsecondary]
Waubonsee Community College
Illinois Route 47 at Harter Road
Sugar Grove, Illinois 60554
312/466-4811

SERVICES OFFERED

- English as a second language
- basic skills education
- GED preparation
- vocational
- job training

Literacy Volunteers of Central DuPage
County [CBO]
208 N. Williston Street
Wheaton, Illinois 60187
312/665-2629

SERVICES OFFERED

- English as a second language
- basic skills education

INDIANA

Monroe County Community School
Corporation Adult Education Program
[state/local]
315 North Drive
Bloomington, Indiana 47401
812/339-3481

SERVICES OFFERED

- English as a second language
- basic skills education
- GED preparation
- alternative high school credentialing program
- vocational
- job training
- continuing community education program

VITAL (Volunteers in Tutoring Adult
Learners) [CBO]
Monroe County Public Library
303 E. Kirkwood
Bloomington, Indiana 47401
812/339-2271

SERVICES OFFERED

- English as a second language
- basic skills education
- GED preparation

Ft. Wayne Literacy Council, Inc., Laubach
Affiliate [CBO]
910 Broadway
Ft. Wayne, Indiana 46802
219/422-5141

SERVICES OFFERED

- English as a second language
- basic skills education

Hammond Adult Basic Education [E & T]
Area Career Center
5727 Sohl Avenue
Hammond, Indiana 46320
219/932-0504

SERVICES OFFERED

- English as a second language
- basic skills education
- GED preparation
- Career planning/job skill training
- Career Search—TEDS Microcomputer Evaluation and Assessment Center (MESA), TEDS/GIS, and Entrance Standards Assessment

Shiloh Temple Adult Basic Education [CBO]
P.O. Box 61
Harrodsburg, Indiana 47434
812/824-9317

SERVICES OFFERED

- GED preparation

Baker Adult Basic Education Center
[state/local]
West Central Joint Services
8650 West Washington Street
Indianapolis, Indiana 46231
317/248-8616

SERVICES OFFERED

- English as a second language
- basic skills education
- GED preparation
- competency-based instruction for everyday life skills

Lafayette Adult Reading Academy [CBO]
Lafayette School Corporation
604 N. Seventh Street
Lafayette, Indiana 47901
317/742-1595 or 742-0075

SERVICES OFFERED

- English as a second language
- basic skills education
- GED preparation
- alternative high school credentialing program (private agreement with local schools)
- survival and job literacy skills

Indiana Vocational Technical College
[E & T]
310 North Meridian
Lebanon, Indiana 46052
317/482-6906

SERVICES OFFERED

- basic skills education
- GED preparation

Adult Basic Education Program
[postsecondary]
Vincennes University
CSC-32
Vincennes, Indiana 47591
812/885-4263

SERVICES OFFERED

- basic skills education
- GED preparation

KANSAS

Adult Learning Center [postsecondary]
Dodge City Community College
1201 First Avenue
Dodge City, Kansas 67801
316/225-0186

SERVICES OFFERED

- English as a second language
- basic skills education
- GED preparation

FREE
Community Resource Center [CBO]
215 S. Gordy
El Dorado, Kansas 67042
316/321-4030

SERVICES OFFERED

- English as a second language
- basic skills education
- GED preparation
- alternative high school credentialing program

KENTUCKY

Adult Literacy Council [state/local]
Ashland Public Schools
1420 Central Avenue
Ashland, Kentucky 41101
606/329-9777

SERVICES OFFERED

- Reading program for functionally illiterate

Operation Read [CBO]
1737 Russell Cave Road
Lexington, Kentucky 40505
606/293-1588

SERVICES OFFERED

- adult literacy tutoring

Jefferson County Adult Reading Program
[state/local]
4409 Preston Highway
Louisville, Kentucky 40213
502/456-3400

SERVICES OFFERED

- basic skills education

Appalachian Adult Learning Center [CBO]
Corner of Second and Tippett
Morehead, Kentucky 40351
606/783-2871

SERVICES OFFERED

- basic skills education
- GED preparation
- outreach staff or paraprofessionals who work with students in their homes
- volunteer teacher program to work with target population of illiterate adults in the community
- "Sentence to Read" program serves young adults referred by court system

Adult Learning Center [postsecondary]
Murray State University
Room 206, Stewart Stadium
Murray, Kentucky 42701
505/762-6971 or 6972

SERVICES OFFERED

- English as a second language
- basic skills education
- GED Preparation
- Volunteer Adult Reading Programs (VARPS) upon demand in nine counties in the West Kentucky Adult Education Network (WEAEN)

Owensboro Adult Learning Center [CBO]
1716 Frederica Street
Owensboro, Kentucky 42301
202/926-3569

SERVICES OFFERED

- English as a second language
- basic skills education
- GED preparation
- alternative high school credentialing program
- literacy

LOUISIANA

Plantation Education Program, Inc. [CBO]
808 Jefferson Terrace #25D
New Iberia, Louisiana 70560
318/364-8716

SERVICES OFFERED

- basic skills education
- GED preparation

Adult Literacy Project [postsecondary]
Department of Curriculum and Instruction
University of New Orleans
New Orleans, Louisiana 70148
504/286-6533

SERVICES OFFERED

- adult basic education (Microcomputer Software Development Project to Promote Functional Literacy—two series of software lessons have been developed and piloted)

Operation Mainstream [CBO]
936 St. Charles Avenue
New Orleans, Louisiana 70130
504/568-9622, Ext. 228

SERVICES OFFERED

- English as a second language
- basic skills education
- GED preparation
- alternative high school credentialing program
- vocational
- job referral

MAINE

SAD #9 Franklin County Adult Basic Education
[state/local]
Tutorial Program
P.O. Box 643
15 Middle Street
Farmington, Maine 04938
207/778-3460

SERVICES OFFERED

- English as a second language
- basic skills education
- GED preparation

Lewiston Adult Education [state/local]
156 East Avenue
Lewiston, Maine 04240
207/784-8990

SERVICES OFFERED

- English as a second language
- basic skills education
- GED preparation
- offer basic skills training to area business and industry

Portland Adult Community Education (PACE) [state/local]
Intown Learning Center
68 High Street
Portland, ME 04103
207/780-4215

SERVICES OFFERED

- English as a second language
- basic skills education
- GED preparation

Sprague Electric Company Educational Sponsorship Program [E & T]
Sprague Electric Company
Sanford, Maine 04073
207/324-4140

SERVICES OFFERED

- English as a second language
- GED preparation
- vocational
- job training

MSAD 24 Adult Education [state/local]
29 Poplar Street
Van Buren, Maine 04785
207/868-5793

SERVICES OFFERED

- English as a second language
- basic skills education
- GED preparation
- vocational
- high school diploma program

MARYLAND

Harbor City Learning Center [E & T]
4801 Liberty Heights Avenue
Baltimore, Maryland 21207
301/396-0093

SERVICES OFFERED

- GED preparation
- alternative high school credentialing program
- vocational
- job training

Reading Laboratory, Adult Institutions
[corrections]
Maryland State Department of Education
200 West Baltimore Street
Baltimore, Maryland 21201
301/659-2055

SERVICES OFFERED

- basic skills education

Catonville Occupational Training Center
[E & T]
5621 Old Frederick Road
Catonville, Maryland 21228
301/788-5611

SERVICES OFFERED

- basic skills education
- GED preparation
- vocational
- job training

Literacy Council of Montgomery County,
Maryland, Inc. [CBO]
401 Fleet Street
Rockville, Maryland 20850
301/762-6800

SERVICES OFFERED

- English as a second language
- basic skills education

MASSACHUSETTS

Adult Basic Education Program [corrections]
Massachusetts Department of Correction
100 Cambridge Street
Boston, Massachusetts 02202
617/727-8682

SERVICES OFFERED

- English as a second language
- basic skills education
- GED preparation
- vocational
- job training

Jobs for Youth–Boston, Inc. [E & T]
312 Stuart Street
Boston, Massachusetts 02116
617/338-0815

SERVICES OFFERED

- basic skills education
- GED preparation
- job readiness instruction and counseling
- job placement and follow-up

Quincy School Community Council Adult
ESL [state/local]
885 Washington Street
Boston, Massachusetts 02111
617/426-0628

SERVICES OFFERED

- English as a second language (bilingual)

Community Learning Center [CBO]
614 Massachusetts Avenue
Cambridge, Massachusetts 02139
617/547-1589

SERVICES OFFERED

- English as a second language
- basic skills education
- GED preparation
- alternative high school credentialing program
- vocational
- job training and pre-training

Adult Basic Program [state/local]
76 Congress Avenue
Chelsea, Massachusetts 02150
617/884-2758

SERVICES OFFERED

- English as a second language
- basic skills education
- GED preparation

Directions in Adult Learning [CBO]
Education Center, Building 1728
Hanscom Air Force Base, Massachusetts
01731
617/861-2026

SERVICES OFFERED

- English as a second language
- basic skills education
- GED preparation

Lowell Adult Education Program [state/local]
Kirk Street Entrance, Lowell High School
Lowell, Massachusetts 01852
617/458-9007

SERVICES OFFERED

- English as a second language
- basic skills education
- GED preparation
- Lowell Adult Competency-Based Instruction Program

Somerville Center for Adult Learning
Experience (SCALE) [state/local] .

99 Dover Street
Somerville, Massachusetts 02144
617/625-1335

SERVICES OFFERED

- English as a second language
- basic skills education
- GED preparation
- alternative high school credentialing program
- vocational
- job training
- home-based tutoring for ABE/GED

Hamden County Jail Education Program
[corrections]
79 York Street
Springfield, Massachusetts 01105
413/781-1560

SERVICES OFFERED

- English as a second language
- basic skills education
- GED preparation
- vocational
- special education: Chapter I

MICHIGAN

Literacy Council of Washtenaw County
[CBO]
c/o Ann Arbor Public Library
343 South Fifth Avenue
Ann Arbor, Michigan 48104
313/482-5715

SERVICES OFFERED

- basic literacy (1–4)

Offender Aid and Restoration/Learning
Center [corrections]
201 North Perry
Pontiac, Michigan 48058
313/334-4330

SERVICES OFFERED

- basic skills education
- GED preparation
- vocational
- job training
- computer technology

MINNESOTA

Metro-North AB/CE (Anoka-Hennepin
District #11) [state/local]
11289 Hanson Boulevard, NW
Coon Rapids, Minnesota 55433
612/755-8220, ext. 237

SERVICES OFFERED

- English as a second language
- basic skills education
- GED preparation
- alternative high school credentialing
  program

Industrial Fair Break [E & T]
Magnetic Peripherals, Inc.
Control Data Corporation
6740 Shady Oak Road
Eden Prairie, Minnesota 55344
612/828-7474

SERVICES OFFERED

- basic skills education
- GED preparation

Five School District AB/CE Consortium
[postsecondary]
Itasca Community College
1851 Highway 169 East
Grand Rapids, Minnesota 55744
218/327-1774

SERVICES OFFERED

- English as a second language
- basic skills education
- GED preparation

- alternative high school credentialing
  program

ESL Ten-Week Program [E & T]
Minnesota Mutual Life Insurance Company
400 North Robert Street
St. Paul, Minnesota 55101
612/298-7812

SERVICES OFFERED

- English as a second language

Minnesota Literacy Council [CBO]
1524 West County Road, C2
St. Paul, Minnesota 55113
612/636-3499

SERVICES OFFERED

- English as a second language
- basic skills education

St. Paul Literacy Project [CBO]
270 North Kent
St. Paul, Minnesota 55102
612/224-4601

SERVICES OFFERED

- English as a second language
- volunteer tutoring of adults in reading and
  writing skills

Pre-College Program [postsecondary]
Meridian Junior College
5500 Highway 19 North
Meridan, Mississippi 39305
601/483-8241

SERVICES OFFERED

- English as a second language
- basic skills education
- GED preparation
- alternative high school credentialing
  program

MISSISSIPPI

Adult Basic Education [postsecondary]
Itawamba Junior College
653 Eaton Boulevard
Tupelo, Mississippi 38801
601/842-5621

SERVICES OFFERED

* basic skills education
* GED preparation

MISSOURI

Adult Basic Education (ABE/GED)
[state/local]
Department of Elementary and Secondary
Education
P.O. Box 480
Jefferson City, Missouri 65102
314/751-3504

SERVICES OFFERED

* English as a second language
* basic skills education
* GED preparation
* job readiness skills and life coping (APL)
  skills

Prescriptive Learning System for Corrections
Institutions [corrections]
Missouri Department of Corrections
2729 Plaza Drive
Jefferson City, Missouri 65102
314/751-2389, Ext. 312

SERVICES OFFERED

* basic skills education
* GED preparation
* job training

MONTANA

Helena Adult Learning Center [state/local]
529 North Warren Street
Helena, Montana 59601
406/442-2671

SERVICES OFFERED

* English as a second language
* basic skills education
* GED preparation
* alternative high school credentialing
  program
* vocational
* job training

Adult Basic Education [E & T]
Missoula Vocational Technical Center
909 South Avenue West
Missoula, Montana 59801
406/721-1330

SERVICES OFFERED

* English as a second language
* basic skills education
* GED preparation
* alternative high school credentialing
  program

NEBRASKA

Adult Learning Center [state/local]
Alliance City Schools
1450 Box Butte
Alliance, Nebraska 69301
308/762-1580

SERVICES OFFERED

* English as a second language
* basic skills education
* GED preparation

Adult Guided Studies (ABE) [postsecondary]
Southeast Community College
8800 O Street
Lincoln, Nebraska 68520
402/471-3333, ext. 263

SERVICES OFFERED

* English as a second language
* basic skills education
* GED preparation

Adult Basic Education [postsecondary]
Northeast Technical Community College
801 E. Benjamin Avenue
Post Office Box 469
Norfolk, Nebraska 68701
402/371-2020, ext. 270

SERVICES OFFERED

* English as a second language
* basic skills education
* GED preparation
* life skills improvement

Adult Basic Education [postsecondary]
Independent Learning Center
Nebraska Western College
Scottsbluff, Nebraska 69361
308/635-3606

SERVICES OFFERED

* English as a second language (at centers off campus)
* basic skills education
* GED preparation
* college developmental courses

Nebraska Center for Women, Adult Basic
Education [corrections]
Route 1, Box 33

York, Nebraska 68467
402/362-3317

SERVICES OFFERED

* basic skills education
* GED preparation
* vocational
* college preparatory

NEW HAMPSHIRE

Project Second Start [CBO]
17 South Fruit Street
Concord, New Hampshire 03301
603/228-1341

SERVICES OFFERED

* English as a second language
* basic skills education
* GED preparation
* alternative high school credentialing program
* job training (secretarial)
* career education and counseling
* alternative high school for adolescents

Adult Learning Center [CBO]
4 Lake Street
Nashua, New Hampshire 03062
603/882-9080

SERVICES OFFERED

* English as a second language
* basic skills education
* GED preparation
* alternative high school credentialing program
* vocational
* job training

NEW JERSEY

Project FIST (Functional In-Service Training)
[postsecondary]
Middlesex County College
Division of Community Education CN-61
Edison, New Jersey 08818
201/249-7987

SERVICES OFFERED

- basic skills education
- volunteer literacy program

Union County Regional Adult Learning
Center [state/local]
David Brearley Regional High School
Monroe Avenue
Kenilworth, New Jersey 07033
201/272-4480

SERVICES OFFERED

- English as a second language
- basic skills education
- GED preparation
- alternative high school credentialing
  program

Focus on Literacy, Inc. [CBO]
P.O. Box 504
Laurel Spring, New Jersey 08021
609/784-1113

SERVICES OFFERED

- basic skills education
- literacy program for adults

Skills Enhancement for Writing [E & T]
Mutual Benefit Life Insurance Company
520 Broad Street
Newark, New Jersey 07101
201/481-7019 or 7098

SERVICES OFFERED

- skills enhancement for writing

Clerk Typist Training Program at Prudential
Insurance Company of America [E & T]
Newark Private Industry Council, Inc.
32 Green Street, Room 213
Newark, New Jersey 07102
201/624-7990

SERVICES OFFERED

- job training

Literacy Volunteers of the Somerville Area
[CBO]
17 East Spring Street
Somerville, New Jersey 08876
201/725-5076

SERVICES OFFERED

- basic skills education

Literacy Volunteers of America, Ocean
County, New Jersey [CBO]
21 Pine Street
Toms River, New Jersey 08753
201/349-5323

SERVICES OFFERED

- basic skills education

NEW YORK

Bronx Educational Services [CBO]
3422 Bailey Place
Bronx, New York 10463
212/884-9797

SERVICES OFFERED

- literacy education for 0–3.9 and 4.0–5.9
  learners

Adult Learning Centers/Great Neck Public
Schools [state/local]
105 Clover Drive
Great Neck, New York 11021
516/482-8650, ext. 616

SERVICES OFFERED

- English as a second language
- basic skills education
- GED preparation
- alternative high school credentialing program
- vocational
- job training
- consumer education

Project GRASP [state/local]
Southern Adirondack Educational Center, BOCES
Dix Avenue
Hudson, Falls, New York 12839
518/793-7721, ext. 212 or 224

SERVICES OFFERED

- basic skills education
- GED preparation

Bank Street Basic Skills Academy [CBO]
610 West 112th Street
New York, New York 10025
212/663-7200, ext. 427

SERVICES OFFERED

- basic skills education
- GED preparation
- job training

The Fortune Society Tutoring Program [corrections]
39 West 19th Street, Seventh Floor
New York, New York 10011
212/206-7070

SERVICES OFFERED

- basic skills education
- GED preparation

Literacy Volunteers of New York City, Inc. [CBO]
200 West 70th Street
New York, New York 10023
212/873-4462

SERVICES OFFERED

- basic skills education

Riverside Adult Learning Center [CBO]
490 Riverside Drive
New York, New York 10027
212/222-5900

SERVICES OFFERED

- English as a second language

"New Horizons" [state/local]
Oceanside Community Education
School #4, Community Activities Building
Oceanside Road
Oceanside, New York 11572
516/678-6572

SERVICES OFFERED

- English as a second language
- basic skills education
- GED preparation

Literacy Volunteers [corrections]
Sing Sing Correctional Facility
354 Hunter Street
Ossining, New York 10562
914/941-0108, 365

SERVICES OFFERED

- English as a second language
- basic skills education

Literacy Volunteers of Rochester, Inc. [CBO]
75 College Avenue
Rochester, New York 14607
716/473-7197

SERVICES OFFERED

- English as a second language
- basic skills education

Literacy Volunteers of Schenectady [CBO]
153 Nott Terrace
Schenectady, New York 12308

SERVICES OFFERED

- English as a second language
- literacy tutoring

White Plains Literacy Program [state/local]
Rochambeau School
228 Fisher Avenue
White Plains, New York 10606
914/997-2344

SERVICES OFFERED

- English as a second language
- basic skills education
- GED preparation

NORTH CAROLINA

ABLE (Adult Basic Literacy Education)
[postsecondary]
Central Piedmont Community College
Post Office Box 35009
Charlotte, North Carolina 28235
704/373-6911

SERVICES OFFERED

- basic skills education

Basic Skills Education Program (BSEP)
[military]
Army Education Division
Building 2-1127
Fort Bragg, North Carolina 28307
919/396-6982

SERVICES OFFERED

- English as a second language
- basic skills education

Caldwell Community College and Technical
Institute [postsecondary]
Post Office Box 600
Lenoir, North Carolina 28645
704/728-4323

SERVICES OFFERED

- English as a second language
- basic skills education

Cuban/Haitian Entrant Program and
Farmworkers English Language School
[CBO]
Box 33315, Migrant and Seasonal
Farmworkers Association
Raleigh, North Carolina 27606
919/851-7611

SERVICES OFFERED

- English as a second language
- basic skills education
- job training

NORTH DAKOTA

State Adult Education Programs [state/local]
Department of Public Instruction
Bismark, North Dakota 58505
701/224-2393

SERVICES OFFERED

- English as a second language
- basic skills education
- GED preparation
- job training

Adult Learning Center [state/local]
Bismark Public Schools
1107 South Seventh Street
Bismark, North Dakota 58501
701/255-3550

SERVICES OFFERED

- English as a second language
- basic skills education
- GED preparation
- job training
- displaced homemakers
- career search

OHIO

Project LEARN [CBO]
2238 Euclide Avenue
Cleveland, Ohio 44115
216/621-9483

SERVICES OFFERED

- English as a second language
- basic skills education

Elyria City Schools Adult Basic Education
Program [state/local]
Maplewood Administration Center
2206 West River Road
Elyria, Ohio 44035
216/324-7500, ext. 340

SERVICES OFFERED

- basic skills education
- GED preparation
- job training

Adult Basic Education, Southwestern City
Schools [state/local]
2975 Kingston Avenue
Grove City, Ohio 43123
614/877-2318

SERVICES OFFERED

- English as a second language
- basic skills education
- GED preparation
- volunteer tutor reading component

London Adult Basic Education [state/local]
60 S. Walnut Street
London, Ohio 43140
614/852-5700 or 852-9843

SERVICES OFFERED

- basic skills education
- GED preparation
- basic skills and GED preparation for
  Workfare clients for county welfare
  department

Marion City Schools, ABE [state/local]
910 East Church Street
Marion, Ohio 43302
614/387-3300

SERVICES OFFERED

- English as a second language
- basic skills education

Scioto Valley-Southeastern Ohio ABE
Program [state/local]
P.O. Box 600
Piketon, Ohio 45661
614/289-4033

SERVICES OFFERED

- English as a second language
- basic skills education
- GED preparation
- program services a nine-county region in
  southern and southeastern Ohio—21
  centers

Adult Basic Education/GED [E & T]
Upper Valley Junior Vocational School
8811 Career Drive
Piqua, Ohio 45356
513/778-1980, ext. 238

SERVICES OFFERED

- English as a second language
- basic skills education
- GED preparation

OKLAHOMA

Altus Adult Learning Center [state/local]
Box 558
611 West Pecan
Altus, Oklahoma 73521
405/482-0367

SERVICES OFFERED

- English as a second language
- basic skills education
- GED preparation

Adult Basic Education [state/local]
Lawton Public Schools
Post Office Box 1009
Lawton, Oklahoma 73501
405/355-7727

SERVICES OFFERED

- English as a second language
- basic skills education
- GED preparation

Adult Basic Education [state/local]
Central State Hospital
P.O. Box 1007
Norman, Oklahoma 73070
405/329-7970, ext. 226

SERVICES OFFERED

- basic skills education
- GED preparation

Paul's Valley Adult Basic Education
[state/local]
301 North Chickasaw
Paul's Valley, Oklahoma 73075
405/238-3596

SERVICES OFFERED

- basic skills education

Pryor Adult Basic Education Program
[state/local]
Box 548
Pryor, Oklahoma 74361
918/825-3509

SERVICES OFFERED

- basic skills education

Adult Basic Education [state/local]
Tulsa Public School
P.O. Box 45208
Tulsa, Oklahoma 74147
918/743-3381, ext. 286

SERVICES OFFERED

- English as a second language
- basic skills education
- GED preparation

OREGON

Adult Basic Education [postsecondary]
Central Oregon Community College
Bend, Oregon 97701
503/382-6112

SERVICES OFFERED

- English as a second language
- basic skills education
- alternative high school credentialing program
- Indian education

Adult Basic Education [postsecondary]
Treaty Oak Community College
300 East Fourth Street
The Dalles, Oregon 97058
403/296-5444

SERVICES OFFERED

- English as a second language
- basic skills education
- GED preparation
- alternative high school credentialing program

Volunteer Tutoring Program [postsecondary]
Portland Community College
12000 S.W. Forty-Ninth Avenue
Portland, Oregon 97219
503/244-6111

SERVICES OFFERED

- English as a second language
- basic skills education
- GED preparation
- citizenship

Developmental Learning [postsecondary]
Chemeketa Community College
4000 Lancaster Drive, NE
Salem, Oregon 97309
503/399-5093

SERVICES OFFERED

- English as a second language
- basic skills education
- GED preparation
- alternative high school credentialing

program
- pre-vocational

PENNSYLVANIA

Correctional Education Program [corrections]
State Correctional Institution at Camp Hill
Box 200
Camp Hill, Pennsylvania 17011
717/737-4531

SERVICES OFFERED

- basic skills education
- GED preparation
- alternative high school credentialing program
- vocational

Chester County Library Literacy Program
[CBO]
Chester County Library
400 Exton Square Parkway
Exton, Pennsylvania 19341
215/363-0884

SERVICES OFFERED

- basic skills education

Adult Literacy Project of Beaver County
Federated Library System [CBO]
1260 North Brodhead Road
Monaca, Pennsylvania 15061
412/728-5588

SERVICES OFFERED

- English as a second language
- basic skills education—literacy and math
- citizenship preparation
- mental health/mental retardation (tutoring at mental health/mental retardation sites in county)
- jail-based literacy classes
- employment skills seminars and classes
- pathfinders (awareness packets for parents who have trouble with basic reading and writing to help prevent second- and third-generation illiteracy)
- industrial literacy (awareness of basic literacy needs of employees in cooperation with Beaver County industries)

The Center for Literacy, Inc. [CBO]
3723 Chestnut Street
Philadelphia, Pennsylvania 19104
215/382-3700

SERVICES OFFERED

- English as a second language
- basic skills education

Functional Skills Program [military]
Philadelphia Naval Yard
Philadelphia, PA

SERVICES OFFERED

- basic skills education

Reader Development Program [CBO]
Logan Square
Philadelphia, Pennsylvania 19103
215/686-5346

SERVICES OFFERED

- library program (provides books to agencies in the city that work with adults with low reading skills. Served 99 agencies in 1983—ESL, literacy, vocational, etc.)

Lutheran Settlement House Women's Program [CBO]
10 East Oxford Avenue
Philadelphia, Pennsylvania 19125
215/426-8610

SERVICES OFFERED

- basic skills education
- GED preparation

PUERTO RICO

Summer Literacy Project [state/local]
Education Extension Area
Department of Education
Hato Rey, Puerto Rico 00919
809/754-9211

SERVICES OFFERED

- basic skills education

Project One Teach One [state/local]
Department of Education, Box 759
Urb. Industrial Tres Monjitas
Hato Rey, Puerto Rico 00919
809/754-1145

SERVICES OFFERED

- basic skills education

SOUTH CAROLINA

Adult Education Program [state/local]
School District of Aiken County
Post Office Box 1137
Aiken, South Carolina 29802
803/648-1311, ext. 236

SERVICES OFFERED

- English as a second language
- basic skills education
- GED preparation
- alternative high school credentialing program
- adult literacy

South Carolina Adult Education Program [state/local]
Office of Adult Education
1429 Senate Street, Room 209-A
Columbia, South Carolina 29201
803/758-3217

SERVICES OFFERED

- English as a second language
- basic skills education
- GED preparation
- state high school diploma

South Carolina Literacy Association [CBO]
815 Elmwood Avenue
Columbia, South Carolina 29202
803/256-0550

SERVICES OFFERED

- English as a second language
- basic skills education
- local council development and management

South Carolina State Board for Technical & Comprehensive Education [postsecondary]
111 Executive Center Drive
Columbia, South Carolina 29210
803/758-6933

SERVICES OFFERED

- basic skills education
- GED preparation
- 16-college system—developmental studies to upgrade students to succeed in technical college curricula

School District of Greenville County, Adult Education [state/local]
206 Wilkins Street
Greenville, South Carolina 29605
803/232-2429

SERVICES OFFERED

- English as a second language
- basic skills education
- GED preparation
- alternative high school credentialing program

Institute for Community Education and Training [CBO]
Post Office Box 1937
Hilton Head, South Carolina 29910
803/681-5095 or 681-2031

SERVICES OFFERED

- basic skills education
- job training

SOUTH DAKOTA

Adult Basic Education [military]
Douglas School System
One Patriot Drive
Ellsworth Air Force Base, South Dakota 57706
605/923-1106

SERVICES OFFERED

- English as a second language
- basic skills education
- GED preparation

Dakota Plains Institute of Training
[state/local]
Box 128
Marty, South Dakota 57361
605/384-5403

SERVICES OFFERED

- basic skills education
- GED preparation
- training Indian adults as volunteer ABE/
  GED instructors

Community Education and Adult Education
[state/local]
Dakota Junior High Vocational Building
6th and Columbus
Rapid City, South Dakota 57701
605/394-4043

SERVICES OFFERED

- English as a second language
- basic skills education
- GED preparation
- vocational
- job training
- life enrichment classes

Coolidge High School [corrections]
South Dakota State Penitentiary
1600 North Drive, Box 911
Sioux Falls, South Dakota 57117-0911
603/339-6769

SERVICES OFFERED

- basic skills education
- GED preparation
- high school diploma program

TENNESSEE

Adult Reading Program [state/local]
Montgomery County Schools
Post Office Box 867
Clarksville, Tennessee 37040
615/647-5681

SERVICES OFFERED

- basic skills education

Adult Reading Program [state/local]
Carter County Superintendent's Office
Academy Street
Elizabethton, Tennessee 37643
615/542-6256

SERVICES OFFERED

- basic skills education
- job training

Memphis Literacy Council [CBO]
703 South Greer at Spottswood
Memphis, Tennessee 38111
901/327-6000 or 6001

SERVICES OFFERED

- volunteer tutorial program for adults
  reading below fifth grade level

TEXAS

Collin County Adult Literacy Council
[state/local]
Allen Independent School District
Box 13
Allen, Texas 75002
214/423-9401

SERVICES OFFERED

- basic skills education

Adult Basic Education [postsecondary]
Austin Community College
Post Office Box 2285
Austin, Texas 78768
512/495-7532

SERVICES OFFERED

- English as a second language
- basic skills education
- GED preparation
- alternative high school credentialing program

Nueces County A.C.E. Cooperative
[state/local]
3902 Morgan
Corpus Christi, Texas 78405
512/888-8285

SERVICES OFFERED

- English as a second language
- basic skills education
- GED preparation
- bilingual instruction for Spanish-speaking adults

Education Planning for Pre-Release Inmates
Program [corrections]
Dallas Independent School District
3400 Garden Lane
Dallas, Texas 75215
214/421-1051

SERVICES OFFERED

- English as a second language
- basic skills education
- GED preparation

Ex-offender Program for Parolees
[corrections]
3400 Garden Lane
Dallas, Texas 75215
214/421-1051

SERVICES OFFERED

- English as a second language
- basic skills education
- GED preparation

Houston Community College System Adult
Co-Op [postsecondary]
Adult and Continuing Education Center
3333 Fannin, Suite 112
Houston, Texas 77004
713/630-7283 or 630-7266

SERVICES OFFERED

- English as a second language
- basic skills education
- GED preparation
- alternative high school credentialing program
- vocational
- job training
- life skills

State-wide Implementation of Educational
Planning for Ex-offenders [corrections]
Region VI Education Service Center
3332 Montgomery Road
Huntsville, Texas 77340
409/295-9161
(This is a statewide project, not a single program.)

SERVICES OFFERED

- basic skills education
- GED preparation
- alternative high school credentialing program (competency-based high school diploma project)
- basic coping skills

Windham School System [corrections]
Post Office Box 40
Huntsville, Texas 77340
409/291-5171

SERVICES OFFERED

- English as a second language
- basic skills education
- GED preparation
- alternative high school credentialing program
- vocational
- job training

American Preparatory Institute [military]
Central Texas College
Post Office Box 786
Killeen, Texas 76541
817/526-1312

SERVICES OFFERED

- English as a second language
- basic skills education
- GED preparation
- alternative high school credentialing program
- job training—military specialties

East Texas Adult Education Cooperative
[state/local]
Rusk Independent School District
204 East Third Street
Rusk, Texas 75784
214/683-5623

SERVICES OFFERED

- English as a second language
- basic skills education
- GED preparation

Adult Learning Center [state/local]
3201 Lincoln
Texarkana, Texas 75501
214/792-9341

SERVICES OFFERED

- English as a second language
- basic skills education
- GED preparation
- alternative high school credentialing program

- vocational
- job training

Heart of Texas Community Education Co-op
[CBO]
805 South Eighth Street
Waco, Texas 76706
817/753-1546

SERVICES OFFERED

- English as a second language
- basic skills education
- GED preparation
- alternative high school credentialing program
- job training
- U.S. citizenship

Wichita Adult Literacy Council, Inc.
[state/local]
301 Loop 11
Wichita Falls, Texas 76305
817/322-6928, ext. 260

SERVICES OFFERED

- basic skills education

UTAH

Adult/Community Education Coordinator
[CBO]
65 East 400 North
Price, Utah 84501
801/637-1732

SERVICES OFFERED

- basic skills education
- GED preparation

Provo Adult High School [state/local]
1125 North University Avenue
Provo, Utah 84604
801/373-6550, ext. 274

SERVICES OFFERED

- English as a second language
- basic skills education
- GED preparation
- alternative high school credentialing program

Adult Basic Education [E & T]
Salt Lake Skills Center
4315 South 6th East
Salt Lake City, Utah 84105
801/531-9310, ext. 343

SERVICES OFFERED

- basic skills education
- vocational-related reading in auto mechanics

Sperry/Community Educational High School
Completion [state/local]
233 West 200 North
Salt Lake City, Utah 84103
801/363-4476

SERVICES OFFERED

- basic skills education
- GED preparation
- adult high school completion
- technical writing

Adult Learning Center [postsecondary]
Dixie College
225 South 700 East
St. George, Utah 84770
801/673-4811, ext. 261

SERVICES OFFERED

- English as a second language
- basic skills education
- GED preparation
- alternative high school credentialing program
- vocational
- job training

VERMONT

Vermont Institute for Self-Reliance [CBO]
Box 66
East Calais, Vermont 05650
802/456-8837

SERVICES OFFERED

- basic skills education
- GED preparation
- alternative high school credentialing program
- a correspondence course dealing with the programs listed above
- a newspaper course dealing with GED preparation

VIRGINIA

Fairfax County's External Diploma Program
[state/local]
Annandale Adult Center
4700 Medford Drive
Annandale, Virginia 22003
703/750-2693

SERVICES OFFERED

- alternative high school credentialing program

Literacy Council of Northern Virginia, Inc.
[CBO]
John Calvin Presbyterian Church
6531 Columbia Pike
Annandale, Virginia 22003
301/256-3444

SERVICES OFFERED

- English as a second language
- basic skills education

Refugee Education and Employment Program
[E & T]
1601 Wilson Boulevard
Arlington, Virginia 22209
703/276-8145

SERVICES OFFERED

- English as a second language
- job placement and counseling services

Northern Virginia Reading Clinic, Inc.
[CBO]
7927 Jones Branch Drive
McLean, Virginia 22102
703/556-9180

SERVICES OFFERED

- basic skills education
- GED preparation
- individual evaluation and remediation of
  reading and learning disabilities

Literacy Volunteers of Virginia Institutes
[corrections]
P.O. Box 3500
Staunton, Virginia 24401
703/885-1141

SERVICES OFFERED

- basic skills education

Operations Specialist "A" School Remedial
Reading [military]
Fleet Combat Training Center, Atlantic
Dam Neck
Virginia Beach, Virginia 23461
804/425-4480

SERVICES OFFERED

- vocational
- remedial reading provided to first-term
  enlistees of USN who fail reading criteria
  prerequisite for entrance into first
  technical radar training.

VIRGIN ISLANDS

Day Adult Education [state/local]
Box 6640
Charlotte Amalie, St. Thomas
Virgin Islands 00801
809/774-6899

SERVICES OFFERED

- basic skills education
- GED preparation

WASHINGTON

Whatcom Literacy Council [CBO]
P.O. Box 1292
Bellingham, Washington 98227-1292
206/676-2104

SERVICES OFFERED

- English as a second language
- basic skills education

Basic Skills Education Program [military]
Army Education Center
AFZH-PAE
Fort Lewis, Washington 98407
206/967-4988

SERVICES OFFERED

- English as a second language
- basic skills education

Developmental Education [postsecondary]
Edmonds Community College
20000 68th Avenue West
Lynnwood, Washington 98306
206/771-1522

SERVICES OFFERED

- English as a second language
- basic skills education
- GED preparation
- alternative high school credentialing
  program

Washington Literacy [CBO]
107 Cherry Street, Suite 205
Seattle, Washington 98104
206/447-3623

SERVICES OFFERED

- English as a second language
- basic skills education
- volunteer basic and ESL tutor training

The Women and Family Refugee Project
[CBO]
South 121 Arthur
Spokane, Washington 99202
509/536-1303 or 1245

SERVICES OFFERED

- English as a second language

WEST VIRGINIA

Literacy Volunteers of the Eastern Panhandle
[CBO]
Martinsburg Public Library
Martinsburg, West Virginia 25401
304/267-8933

SERVICES OFFERED

- English as a second language
- basic skills education

Literacy Program of the Mary H. Weir Public
Library [CBO]
3442 Main Street
Weirton, West Virginia 26062
304/748-7396

SERVICES OFFERED

- English as a second language
- basic skills education
- GED preparation

WISCONSIN

GOAL/English As A Second Language
[E & T]
Fox Valley Technical Institute
1825 North Bluemound Drive
Appleton, Wisconsin 54913
414/735-5692

SERVICES OFFERED

- English as a second language
- basic skills education
- GED preparation
- alternative high school credentialing
  program
- vocational
- job training

Career Development Center [state/local]
North Central Technical Institute
1000 Campus Drive
Wausau, Wisconsin 54401
715/675-3331, ext. 413

SERVICES OFFERED

- English as a second language
- basic skills education
- GED preparation
- career development

WYOMING

Adult and Community Education [state/local]
Wyoming Department of Education
247 Hathaway Building
Cheyenne, Wyoming 82002
307/777-6228

SERVICES OFFERED

- English as a second language
- basic skills education
- GED preparation

Adult Learning Center [postsecondary]
Laramie County Community College
College Drive
Cheyenne, Wyoming 82001
307/634-5853, ext. 292

SERVICES OFFERED

- English as a second language
- basic skills education
- GED preparation

Volunteer Tutor Program [postsecondary]
Sheridan College
Sheridan, Wyoming 82801
307/674-6446, ext. 231

SERVICES OFFERED

- English as a second language
- basic skills education
- GED preparation

CANADA

St. Stephen's Community House [CBO]
91 Bellevue Avenue
Toronto, Ontario, Canada M5T 2N8

SERVICES OFFERED

- English as a second language

INDEX